Parties and Electoral Politics in North East India

Parties and Electoral Politics in North East India

Contention of Ethno-regionalism and Hindu Nationalism

V. Bijukumar

KALPAZ

First Published, 2019

Published by

Kalpaz Publications
C-30, Satyawati Nagar,
Delhi – 110052
Ph.: 011-47034999, 9811692060
www.kalpazpublications.com
E-mail: kalpaz@hotmail.com

Printed at: G. Print Process, Delhi

Cataloging in Publication Data—DK
Courtesy: D.K. Agencies (P) Ltd. <docinfo@dkagencies.com>

Bijukumar, V., author.
Parties and electoral politics in North East India: contention of ethno-regionalism and Hindu nationalism / by V. Bijukumar.
pages cm
ISBN 9789353240363

1. Elections—India, Northeastern. 2. India, Northeastern—Politics and government—21st century. 3. Political parties—India, Northeastern. 4. Bharatiya Janata Party. 5. Hindutva—India, Northeastern. 6. Minorities—Political activity—India, Northeastern. 7. Coalition governments—India, Northeastern. I. Title.

LCC JQ298.8.B55 2019 | DDC 320.9541 23

Dedicated to the loving memories of

Prof. M. Bhaskaran Nair,

former teacher of Political Science, NEHU, Shillong

and University of Kerala, Thiruvananthapuram.

Contents

Acknowledgements

The society, politics and economy of Northeast India have created certain attraction for me as researcher and teacher. Infact, the understanding of Indian politics is incomplete without having an understanding about the politics and society of the Northeast India. However, no concept or theory is adequate to explain the intricacies of politics of the region. As a teacher who taught political science in both Mizoram University, Aizawl and North East Hill University, Shillong, changed my understanding about Northeast India drastically. Though an 'outsider' to the region, the close interaction with students and researchers inside as well as outside the class room enabled me to understand the intricacies of its society and polity in very closer manner. I was also benefited by the interaction of local colleagues of these two universities to engage with the society and communities. The everyday activities of students belonged to different ethnic students organisations often demolished my understanding of Northeast decisively. In writing these articles, I was benefited by the theoretical and analytical rigour imparted by JNU is also commendable. At the personal level, I am thankful to A.K. Thakur, H. Srikanth, Prasenjit Biswas, Roopa Borhogain, D. V. Kumar, L. S. Gassah, R.K. Satpathy for their valuable help and cooperation.

V. Bijukumar

Centre for Political Studies
School of Social Sciences
JNU, New Delhi.

Preface

In the postcolonial India, party politics of Northeast has undergone many drastic changes. After the initial wave of ethno regionalism, the national parties such as the Congress assumed centre stage in many Northeastern states beating the waves of ethno regionalism unleashed by ethno regional parties (ERPs). In Tripura, the Communist Party was able to swim across the wave of ethno-regionalism created by the indigenous ethnic communities and bridge the ERPs both the Bengalis and the Tribals. The national political parties quite often to take on the forced to champion ethno regional issues and thereby reorient their ideology and strategies at the states level. The national parties like Congress which has its mass base and dynamic leadership often driven by the forces of ethno-regionalism. The competitive ethno-regionalism practiced by both the ERPs and the national parties influence the nature and behavior of electoral politics in the Northeast.

The contemporary Northeast is witnessing another great transformation as it has moved from ethno-regionalism to Hindu nationalism.The BJP, which champions the cause of Hindu Nationalism, a new entrant in the politics of Northeast, also pickup ethno-regional issues to strengthen its mass base. In Assam, for instance, illegal migration constituted a burning issue became the political agenda of the Asom Gana Parishad (AGP) when it transformed from All Assam Student Union (AASU). In the recent past, the BJP hijacked the AGP agenda and used for communal mobilization in the state. However, the BJP diluted the early demand by amending the citizenship act by making provision for the migration of the Hindus from neibhouring states. The BJP by hijacking the ethno-regional agenda of the ethno-regional parties and strategically using the communal polarization in various states was able to make inroads into the political constituencies of the regional parties. It also able to attract prominent leaders from other parties encouraging defections and political inducement. The political defection encouraged by the BJP is a cause of worry for the Congress as many of its state level leaders and legislators defected and joined the BJP. Though BJP is a new political force in the region, inspite of RSS intensive work in the region, the BJP does not have popular face to contest election forcing them to encourage political migration from other parties.

The ascendancy of BJP is not only a cause for worry for the ERPs but also for the Congress party in the region. The second wave of regionalism with communal polarization championed by the BJP not only erodes the mass base of the Congress in many states but also the regional political parties, states as many communities shifted their loyalty to the BJP. Some of the ERPs eager to align with BJP even they have reservation about its Hindutva agenda and the sensitive issues such as beef, assault on Christian minorities, etc. Such an alliance with the BJP often seen as to counteract the Congress in their state. The BJP at the state level even prepared to be junior partner in the alliance and the coalition government, to show its influence in the state. For instance, in Meghalaya the BJP won only two seats in the Assembly elections held in 2018 was able to a junior partner in the National Peoples Party (NPP) led government. Sometimes, it split the regional parties promoting a leadership conflicts at the regional level. In Nagaland, the BJP could able to split its long allies the Naga People's Front (NPF) and facilitated the formation of the NDPP and thereby formed a government without NPF.

The onward journey of BJP in the Northeast leading towards the stead and virtual erosion of the Congress party. In other words, when the BJP aggrandize its political power in the region, the casuality is the prospects of the grand old party, the Congress. In the recent past, many communities and social groups already left the Congress and extended their loyalty to the BJP leading Northeast to a 'Congress-free zone'. The elite and the dominant communities in the regions embraced the BJP inspite of its antagonistic ideology and programme. The BJP, on the other hand, keeping aside its pretty issues such as conversion, beef consumption was able to woo a section of the social elite to the party. The smaller parties who consider the Congress as a threat to their existence, have not reluctant to align with the Hindu nationalist politics. The BJP's attraction to the region is often seen beyond the electoral arithmetic strength of the region but its strategic location and the religious milieu.

The articles in this book highlight the changing nature of part systems and electoral politics in Northeast India in the wake of the political ascendance of the Hindu national forces. In addition to this, the nature and role of ethnic organisations in the fastly changing politics of the region also reflected in various chapters. It would be a great leap forward to understand the electoral politics in the region in particular and politics in general.

Part – I
Setting of Electoral Politics

Chapter - 1

Ethno-Regional Parties and Electoral Politics in Northeast India

In the contemporary India, regional politics has emerged as a political reality as many national political parties and administrative set up recognize its significance in contrast to the once prevailed fallacy that regional politics and political parties were posing a threat to national unity and integration. In the era of coalition politics, major national political parties are looking for regional parties as alliance partners at the centre. This political reality reinforces that regional parties are essential for federal system of the country. Regional political parties, however, do not emerge from a vacuum and they are influenced by cultural diversity, social, ethnic, caste, community and religious cleavages. They are defined as an excessive attachment for a particular regional identity based on culture, language, etc. By championing regional culture, history and language, regional parties protect the regional pride and regional identity. As the social cleavages theory argues that cleavages in a society lead to the formation of political parties, the regional cleavages lead to the formation of regional parties. In other words, regional political parties are the important manifestation of regional cleavages which are not recognized by the national parties and national politics.

The emergence of regional political parties in India can be seen in the context of the emergence of small regional bourgeoisie at the state level. As a national political party, the Congress always protected the interest of the big national bourgeoisie and seldom protected the interest of the emerging regional bourgeoisie. The Congress though always claims to be a party of mobilizing all regions, communities and groups under one platform, it for a long time considered regional parties as a threat to national unity. The Congress even was not ready to accept the concrete reality that the regional forces to grow in the state politics of India. The regional bourgeoisie, on the other hand, find regional political parties as the protector of their interest and wanted to strengthen regional politics in states.

There are mainly two dominant views about regional politics. Firstly, regional politics advocated by regional parties are the threat to national unity and integration and this view was dominant in the 1950s. Since regional parties are working in a limited space and social constituencies, it would stall the national development policies. Regionalism in its ethno-regional manifestation increases governmental instability and encourage ethnic conflict and secessionism. This negative regional politics is based on the narrow interpretation of regional politics – politics related to a region – geographical identity – often it reflects certain specificities like religion, culture, language and ethnicity. The negative view validates the construction of dominant narrative that only a national party can bring a national unity. On the other hand, the positive view of regional politics is that a regional party is mobilizing cross sections of the people and stabilises institutional mechanisms and strengthens the democratic process. Moreover, the excluded and marginalized communities and social groups find some political space in the political system due to the mobilization of regional politics. Regional parties posing a counterweight to centralizing tendencies and thereby strengthening federalism. Most regional parties demand autonomy, political decentralization and financial devolution of resources. Further, regional parties ensure the diversity by preventing homogenizing tendencies in the federal system and improves the quality of democracy as it represents all sections of the society. Regionalism has two aspects- positive regionalism and negative regionalism. The positive regionalism is considered to be essential for democracy and negative regionalism often faces to the national unity. In the positive dimension, though regional politics is counterpoising the centralized tendencies of the dominant party, accommodating the interest of minority communities, and marginalized nationalities by the regional parties lead to ease the pressure on the nation-state. Negative regionalism leads to separation and secessionism and considered to be a threat to national unity and integrity. Positive regionalism through its demand for autonomy widens democracy; strengthen national unity through accommodation of various groups and interests at the regional levels. Since 1996, regional parties have emerged as the important element in the formation of government at the national level. The participation of regional forces in national government gives a new dimension to both national and regional politics.

The rise of regionalism in India has a direct bearing on the faulty project of modernization inaugurated after independence. Faulty Modernization generated regional consciousness and regional mobilization as modernity created some kind of discontent among certain groups. The emergence of ethno-regional parties in North East India (NEI) fall into this category. The western democracies are the result of a historical transition from agrarian to industrial economy. In India, modernization took place in the form of industrialization and this bourgeois modernization was conducive to the strengthening of national parties. In the Indian context such modernization did not took place and in fact, state provided all facilities to the development of capitalism. The emergence of state capitalism was benefited by the big bourgeoisie who supported the national political parties. However, the regional parties were supported by the regional bourgeoisie (Baru, 2000). In short, the capitalist modernity created cleavages and that facilitated regionalism.

The causes for the growth of regionalism vary from party to party and region to region. In Tamil Nadu, the anti-Hindi agitation - centre's decision to introduce Hindi as a national language – triggered the ethnic regional politics. The Dravidian parties considered this as an intrusion of Aryan culture to the Dravidian culture. In Andhra Pradesh, the Telegu Desam Party (TDP) emerged as a regional force in protest against the centralized tendencies of the Congress Party. In 1983 election, a year after its formation, the TDP under N.T. Ramarao raised the issue of Telugu nationalism and self-respect. The social base of TDP was the backward class community of Kammas which had rivalry with the upper caste Reddy community which always favoured with the Congress Party. The regional bourgeoisies which mainly invested in industry, cinema, hotel and liquor business mainly belonged to the Kammas community preferred TDP over Congress in the state. In Punjab, the Sikh religious identity gave a direction to the emergence of Akali politics. The agrarian capitalism which developed in Punjab too favoured regional forces over the Congress Party. The Dravida Munnetra Kazhagam (DMK) was formed as a particular ideology of Dravidianism and anti-Brahmanism and later broadened its social base by adopting social security measures. DMK developed an industrial and regional bourgeoisie class. Both DMK and TDP became a part of the Central government due to the pressure from the regional bourgeoisie. In fact, the pressure from these regional business force DMK and TDP to join hands with centre and extended supported for liberalization policies. Both DMK and TDP benefited from the neo-liberal policies in the second generation reforms as they could woo foreign direct

Regional parties often champions ethno-regionalism as it protects the interest of certain ethnic communities in a particular region. It means that all regional political parties are not ERPs and some regional political parties are based on ethnic identities as its political agenda is confined only to particular ethnic community in a particular region. Since an ethnic party champions the interests of one ethnic group or set of groups to the exclusion of another or others, their ideology and mobilization strategy is based on exclusion. The ERPs emerged as the result of ethno-regional movement and uphold ethno-regionalism as its ideology and mobilization strategy. The territorial space occupied by a specific dominant community prefer to ethnic-regional parties rather than national parties. ERPs are the manifestation of the ethno-cultural assertion. Ethno-regionalism is based on the claims of regional identity and of ethnic distinction. It creates a sense of 'otherness' and distinctiveness from others. Ethno-regional parties emerge as critique of civic nationalism, centralization and assimilation of the nation-state. Ethno-regional parties are critique of centralized power structures and its institutions. The demands of a ethno-regional party vary: protection of specific cultural community, ending discriminatory policies of the national state, cultural specificities and preservation of cultural identity, recognition of regional language, medium in education and government services.

Ethno-Regionalism in North-East India

Though regionalism and regional political parties are not a new development in Indian politics, but in Northeast it assumes different connotation as it moves to the direction of ethno regionalism. Ethno-regional parties emerged as the result of ethno-regional movement and uphold ethno-regionalism as its ideology and mobilization strategy. The ERPs emerge as critique of civic nationalism, centralization and assimilation of the nation-state. They are critique of centralized power structures and its institutions. The demands of a ERP varies: protection of specific cultural community, ending discriminatory policies of the national state, cherishing its distinct cultural specificities and preservation of cultural identity, recognition of regional language, medium in education and government services. Ideally, ethno-regional assertions are considered as a response to the homogenizing tendencies of mainstream nationalism and the centralizing attitude of dominant national political party. Ethno-regionalism is the articulation of the relative deprivation of a community within a geographical units or region.

In the NEI regional politics assumed a different dimension as it relates to ethnicity. In other words, ethnic identity and its political mobilization give a new direction to regional politics in this region. As a result we have been witnessing the emergence of ERPs in the region. These parties demand autonomy of the regional and protection of linguistic and cultural identity of the region. The inhabitance of particular community in a particular territory enables regional political parties for mobilizing for electoral politics. In NEI, regional politics assumed ethnic connotations as ethnic identity is mixed with regional identity. Regional parties are based on regional self-determination and regional pride. The factors that contributed to the growth of regional politics include social, ethnic, cultural and geographic. In North-East India, the emergence of regional consciousness and regional mobilization are motivated by ethnic identity and consciousness. In other words, ethnic identity was one of the precipitating factors for the demand for regionalism in North-East. Often certain ethnic groups such as the Mizos, the Nagas, the Khasis, etc. were identified within a region as these regions dominated by different ethnic groups. For stance, Jaintias in Jaintia Hills, Garos in Garo Hills, Khasis in Khasi Hills, Bodos in Bodoland identified their geographical location as their original inhabitance. Sometimes, ethnic identity extends over one region to another giving a different interpretation of ethno-regionalism. For instance, the demand for Greater Nagaland by the Nagas unifying the Naga dominated regions of Manipur, Assam, Arunachal Pradesh and some portions of Myanmar extend beyond the territorial location set up by the state. The assertion ofsuch ethno-regionalism often turns towards chauvinism as it denies space to other minor ethnic communities within the region or from outside. The ERPs often proclaim that they are the true custodian of ethno-regional identity from what they called the social and cultural intrusion by 'others' and thereby preventing larger mobilization by the national political parties. The ERPs mobilize ethnic communities on ethno regional issues such as illegal migration and citizenship rights and special legislative protection such as the Inner Line Permit to protect their distinctive culture from the onslaught of outsiders to their states. The making and maintenance of ethnic boundaries manifest in the political mobilization of these parties and in setting agenda of the parties and to certain extent the governmental policies.

The NEI is the hotspot of different kinds of ethnic regional movements. The existence of regional political parties and active ethnic student and youth organizations are giving a further boost to this ethno-regional upsurge. Most of the regional movements and regionalist parties have an ethnic character in this region. Perhaps, the first movement in the region after independence was the Naga movement which asserted the Naga identity under the leadership of A.Z. Phizo in the 1950s. The class formation among the tribal communities has also a bearing on ethnic regionalism. Though, ideally, the tribal communities, are 'egalitarian' in nature compared to others, class formation began in course of time due to various factors such as capitalist forces, market economy, settled agriculture, changes in the ownership of private property, education and employment, etc. Often the dominant classes assert their ethno-regional identity to secure political power and procure greater share in national cake. In Meghalaya, the formation of the All Party Hill Leaders Conference articulated the regional interest against the imposition of Assamese language as the official State Language of United Assam, in which Meghalaya was a part (Gupta, 2013: 87).

Ethno-Regionalism and Electoral Politics

The electoral politics and political parties in NEI, in contrast to the mainland India, assumes a distinctiveness due to the nature of the social milieu, ethnic composition, cultural mosaic and political infirmities existed in the region. An ethnically diverse society with an outside manifestation of homogeneity and deep rooted internal heterogeneity often reflect in the nature of political system and electoral politics. The ethnic consciousness and identity assertion in the region prefer ERPs and formation of governments led by such political parties. The nature of electoral politics and electoral behavior decisively influence the ethno-regional consciousness and mobilization. The ERPs frequently raise the issues related to ethno-regionalism to obtain legitimacy from the ethnic groups. It also makes use of various ethnic organisations such students, youths, elders and women organisations to perpetuate ethnic consciousness among the ethnic communities. Often such ethno-regional organisations develop better collective bargain with the government and even hijack the governmental administration. Such a situation, the ultimate beneficiary is the ethno-regional parties which can consolidate its position in the state politics.

However, after the initial wave of ethno regionalism, the national parties such as the Congress assumed centre stage in many Northeastern states beating the waves of ethno regionalism unleashed by ERPs. In Tripura, the Communist Party was able to swim across the wave of ethno-regionalism created by the indigenous ethnic communities and bridge the both the Bengalis and the Tribals. The national political parties quite often to take on the ERPs forced to champion ethno regional issues and thereby reorient their ideology and strategies at the states level. In such a situation the electoral behavior and electoral politics also assumes a ethno-regional connotation. The national partieslike Congress which has its mass base and dynamic leadership often driven by the forces of ethno-regionalism. The competitive ethno-regionalism practiced by both the ERPs and the national parties influence the nature and behavior of electoral politics in the Northeast.

Ethno-Regionalism and Hindu Nationalism

The BJP, which champions the cause of Hindu Nationalism, a new entrant in the politics of Northeast, also pickup ethno-regional issues to strengthen its mass base. In Assam, for instance, illegal migration constituted a burning issue became the political agenda of the Asom Gana Parishad (AGP) when it transformed from All Assam Student Union (AASU). In the recent past, the BJP hijacked the AGP agenda and used for communal mobilization in the state. However, the BJP diluted the early demand by amending the citizenship act by making provision for the migration of the Hindus from neibhouring states. The BJP by hijacking the ethno-regional agenda of the ethno-regional parties and strategically using the communal polarization in various states was able to make inroads into the political constituencies of the regional parties. It also able to attract prominent leaders from other parties encouraging defections and political inducement. The political defection encouraged by the BJP is a cause of worry for the Congress as many of its state level leaders and legislators defected and joined the BJP. Though BJP is a new political force in the region, inspite of RSS intensive work in the region, the BJP does not have popular face to contest election forcing them to encourage political migration from other parties.

The ascendancy of BJP is not only a cause for worry for the ERPs but also for the Congress party in the region. The second wave of regionalism with communal polarization championed by the BJP not only erodes the mass base of the Congress in many states but also the regional political parties, states as many communities shifted their loyalty to the BJP. Some of the ERPs eager to align with BJP even they have reservation about its Hindutva agenda and the sensitive issues such as beef, assault on Christian minorities, etc.Such an alliance with the BJP often seen as to counteract the Congress in their state. The BJP at the state level even prepared to be junior partner in the alliance and the coalition government, to show its influence in the state. For instance, in Meghalaya the BJP won only two seats in the Assembly elections held in 2018 was able to a junior partner in the National Peoples Party (NPP) led government. Sometimes, it split the regional parties promoting a leadership conflicts at the regional level. In Nagaland, the BJP could able to split its long allies the Naga People's Front and facilitated the formation of the NDPP and thereby formed a government without NPF.

The ERPs who align with the BJP for fulfilling its political ambitions, gradually swallowed by the BJP as it uses the alliance as means for reaching out to the political constituencies of the regional parties and thereby shrinking its mass base. In other words, in the alliance building process, the regional parties are worst affected and the beneficiaries is always the BJP. The BJP is also uses the boggy of development as a mobilization strategy in the development deficit states of Northeast. The developmental initiatives of the NDA government such as the much fancied Act East Policy and North East corridor project were used for its mobilization strategy.

Unlike other regional parties in India such as the Dravidian and Akali Parties and the TDP in Andhra Pradesh, ERPs in Northeast couldnot build a regional bourgeoisie which often back the regional political parties for their economic pursuits. On the other hand, these parties only emerged their strength out of ethnic communities championing ethnic cause and mobilization which was easily hijacked by the national party like BJP. The BJP also reached one step forward not only in alliance building but also appropriating local icons and creating counter narratives in various states. The cultural symbols and local morality it one way could attract the minor ethnic communities.

The NEI is affected by a new wave of regionalism practiced by the BJP and its alliance partners in the state. In addition to ethno-regionalism, the bogey of national security is used by the Hindu nationalist forces for their mobilization. The BJP uses the bogey of national security threat in the Northeast as a mobilization strategy in the region as they are the border states. In Arunachal Pradesh, BJP raise the Chinese claim on the state as political mobilization strategy to strengthen its position. The vulnerability of the border states can be tackled by strong government committed to nationalist values. In this context, migration is stopped to protect the integrity of the nation.

Of the all eight northeastern states, the BJP reins political power in Arunachal Pradesh, Assam, Manipur and Tripura. The party is also share power with its alliance partners in Nagaland and Meghalaya. In Nagaland, the BJP extended its support to Nationalist Democratic Progressive Party, led by former Chief Minister, Neiphiu Rio after dumping its longtime ally the NPE. In Meghalaya the two member BJP in the Assembly was able to strike a deal with NPF and formed the government surpassing the Congress which emerged as the single largest party in the Assembly. While the regional party SDF controls political power in the Himalayan state of Sikkim, the Congress confined only to Meghalaya. It is obvious that in some states the ride of ethno-regionalism and Hindu nationalism go hand in hand, while in other states, Hindu nationalism hijacked the agenda of ethno-regionalism of ERPs to expand its mass base and strengthen its electoral constituency.

North East Regional Political Front: An Effort to Collective Bargaining

The NEI, in the recent past, witnessed the conglomeration of ERPs to bargain effectively with the centre and to counteract the influence of the Congress. On 20th October, 2013 major regional political parties in the NEI held a convention in Guwhati and formed the North East Regional Political Front (NERPF) aimed at creating a common platform to pursue the issues concerning the region and 'make the voice of the region heard' at the national level. It was claimed that the objective behind the NERPF was to lend a collective voice to the people of the region as their individual voices were unheard at most times. The convention was attended by the leaders of various regional parties of the North East such as the Asom Gana Parishad (AGP), Naga People's Front (NPF), United Democratic Party (UDP), Mizo National Front (MNF), Sikkim Democratic Front (SDF), People's Party of Arunachal Pradesh (PPA), Manipur People's Party (MPP) and the Indigenous People's Front of Tripura (IPFT). The convention elected the Nagaland Chief Minister Neiphuri Rio of NPF as the convener and former Assam Chief Minister Prafulla Kumar Mahanta of AGP as the chief advisor of the Front. The move to form a common Front came in the context of predictions of most of the surveys that neither United Progressive Alliance nor National Democratic Alliance is going to get absolute majority in the 2014 election as its own present strength. Keeping this situation in mind both national political formations are tried to woo parties into their fold to secure comfortable majority in 2014. Perhaps, the Front was thoroughly aware of the current situation and felt that forging a Front is better than individual alliance to any of these two national political formations. However, the political agenda of the NERPF was set by Paul Lyndoh, leader of the UDP, the main opposition regional party in Meghalaya, who observed that "the main objective behind the formation of the Front is to minimize the political fight among the regional parties so as to consolidate their political base to take on the Congress Party" especially in the upcoming 2014 Lok Sabha elections.

The Convention unanimously adopted 17 resolutions which aimed at safeguarding the territorial, cultural, social, economic and political rights of the people of the Northeast in the national context. A Resolution adopted in the Convention further states that security of North-Eastern students and women in other parts of the country, eighty per cent reservation of jobs in all private and public sectors in the region; and re-look centre-state relations and constitutional safeguard for the indigenous people of the region. It further demanded the scrapping of the draconian laws such as Armed Forces Special Powers Act, and steps to check infiltration and cancellation of the land swap deal with Bangladesh arising out of the concern over the construction of Dams on the Chinese side.

Northeast Democratic Alliance: Building Alliance for Expansion

Another significant development in the party politics of Northeast is the formation of Northeast Democratic Alliance (NEDA), a conglomeration of regional parties led by the BJP. The formation of such an alliance with Himanta Biswa Sarma as its convenor not only counter the influence of the Congress in various states in Northeast, but also went a step forward to hijack the ethno-regional agenda of the regional parties. Being allied with regional parties and often a junior player to them, the BJP in some of the states was able to share the political power and to approach divergent social groups. The BJP also went ahead of the Congress in the alliance building activity as it was able to form a conglomeration of regional parties such as NEDA similar to that of the NDA at the centre. The Congress which has mass presence in various states of the region failed to attract them to UPA fold. The class formation takes place in various communities contributed for the craze for assessing political power for which they thought that the Congress is not accommodative to their political ambition due to its strong political presence, which is facilitated by the BJP. The elite in different ethnic communities were attracted by the political perks offered by the BJP and shared political power with it inspite of its hostile ideology and programmes in the region. The smaller parties, which were eagerly waiting for an opportunity to exercise political power in the state, not hesitant to extend support to the Alliance led the BJP. Through NEDA, the BJP was able to expand its mass base by reaching out to various communities and groups, inspite of its Hindu nationalist agenda.

The electoral politics in the region set certain trends in NEI. Firstly, the prominent ERPs in the region is the result of the transformation of ethno-regional movements. As the movement-turned political parties, their ideological mobilization and electoral strategy often tilted towards generating ethnic consciousness and ethnic boundary making. Secondly, in NEI, women active in agitation politics and seldom find a place in electoral politics. Often traditional values and customs prevent their entry into electoral politics. Both national political parties and ERPs reluctant to champion the cause of women in electoral politics. As a result, there is a skewed representation of women in legislature, inspite of many tribal communities practice matrilineal system. Ethno regional sentiments often leads to strengthening patriarchal values in the society, leads to male domination and representation in politics. Electoral politics is a political action involved by various individual and groups as the stakeholders in representative democracy. Conventional wisdom regarding democracy is that the existence of deep rooted ethnic cleavages would hamper the process of deepening of democracy. However, the ethno-regional parties used the primordial identities for electoral mobilization and support. Various ethnic communities, though initially reluctant to the mainstream politics, come to the electoral politics adding a more inclusive character to democratic process. Such political parties also accepted the superiority of the constitutions and the representational norms set by the Constitution. Thirdly, the electoral politics is influenced by non- governmental organizations and institutions. Ethnic organisations such as students and youths decisively influence the electoral politics, adding a new dimension to party politics in various states. Fourthly, the Congress which was a major player in the electoral politics of the states which enjoyed political power with its own in many states, is diminishing its preeminence. Except Mizoram, the party is losing to either BJP or the regional parties. Finally, the BJP by building alliance with the small regional parties, and championing ethno-regionalism expanding its base in the region adding a new dimension to regional politics.

Conclusion

Electoral politics in Northeast is influenced by cleavages like ethnicity, religion, regionalism and tribal divisions. Primordial loyalties, ethnic organisations such as students and youths, traditional institutions such as village dorbor and religious institutions such as church play crucial role in the electoral politics and shaping the electoral behavior. Most of the regional political parties in NEI are ERPs based on ethnic identities. The political agenda of such parties is confined only to particular ethnic community in aspecific region. Ethno-regionalism, however, is based on the claims of regional identity and of ethnic distinction creates a sense of 'otherness' and exclusion to others.When an ERP champions the interests of one ethnic group or set of groups, itleads to the exclusion of another or others. In other words, ethnic identity and its political mobilization give a new direction to regional politics in this region. As a result, we have been witnessing the emergence of ERPs in NEI. Regional politics assumed ethnic connotations as ethnic identity is mixed with regional identity. Regional parties are based on regional self-determination and regional pride when they demand autonomy of the region and protection of its linguistic and cultural identity. The inhabitance of particular community in a particular territory enables regional political parties for mobilizing for electoral politics. Though, most of the regional parties claim that they represent the interest of the people of the respective states but the fact is quite contrary to the reality. In most cases they failed to protect the interest of all communities in the state and become the voice of the dominant ethnic groups and often leading to inter-community and intra-community animosity and conflicts. For instance, the growing assertion of smaller communities such as the Bodos and Karbis in Assam and Hmars in Mizoram can be seen in the context of the failure of the mainstream regional political parties to address their grievances.

The ethno-regional politics of ERPs. Though initially contributed to its expansion in the region in its first wave, during the second wave, such politics enabled the Hindu nationalist politics to take roots in NEI. By hijacking the ethno-regional politics, the BJP not only surpassed the ERPs but also battered the mass base of other national parties such as the Congress and the CPI (M). For instance, in Assam, the drive against illegal migrants was first raised by the Assam movement and subsequently by became the agenda of the AGP and later nicked by the BJP, adding with more religious colour, enable to strengthen its political base. In fact, the fertile ground for the Hindu nationalist forces in NEI in general and Assam in particular was prepared by the ethno-regionalism advocated by the ERPs. In other words, the BJP's ambitious project of a 'Congress-mukht (Congress-free) Northeast materialized out of ethno-regional politics practiced by the ERPs.

References

Baru, Sanjaya (2000), "Economic Policy and the Development of Capitalism in India: The Role of Regional Capitalists and Political Parties", in Francine R. Frankel, Zoya Hasan, Rajeev Bhargava and Balveer Arora (eds.), *Transforming India: Social and Political Dynamics of Democracy*, New Delhi: Oxford University Press, pp. 207-230.

Gupta, Susmita Sen (2013), "Social Forces and Politics of Regionalism in Meghalaya" Apurba K. Baruah and Susmita Sen Gupta (eds.), *Social Forces and Politics in North East India*, Guwahati: DVS Publishers, pp. 80-95.

Chapter - 2

Ecclesiastical Authority and Political Action: Church and Electioneering in Mizoram

The conventional wisdom regarding political action is that it always relates to state and its institutions and are often legitimised and assumed predominance as it is based on reason and public good. However, apart from state, other institutions also plunged into political action, especially in democracy. For instance, religious institutions recourse to political action and thereby facilitate or undermine democratic process. Religious institutions recourse to political action through Ecclesiastical Authority (EA) applying values involved in the religion. The religious mission of the church motivates political activity infusing ecclesial ethics or Christian values and morality in the political action. In other words, religious cultures,values and privileges also influence political action of the church. Since people are extending their obligation to EA and the religious principles, religion smoothens political action. Political action in this context is based on morality which includes principles of action personal ethics. When state recourse to political action, political morality is considered to be the basis of a political action. Aristotle the hallmark of human action including politics is the pursuit of moral virtue which ultimately ensures common happiness for the individual and society at large.

The role of religious values and institutionsin liberal democracy was recognised by many scholars. Max Weber, for instance, recognised the role of Protestant ethics in flourishing democracy in Europe. It is often argued that evangelism often promote moralism and associational life conducive to democratization. Fukuyama also establishes a link between religion and democratization highlighting religious institutions and religious values. Religion's relevance in political life is recognised by Tocqueville who argues that religion as a unifying social force to maintain democratic life. According to him, Christianity is responsible for rise of political freedom in America and a free society necessarily requires religious foundation. Religion is the most important source of common beliefs for citizens and as the preservation of a decent political order. He also recognised contribution of religion to sustain public morality and religion can bring morality in public life. Moral convictions rooted in religious belief can be used to solve the malaise of politics. According to him, almost all human actions "arise from a very general idea men have conceived of God, or his relations with the human race, of the nature of their souls, and of their duties towards those like them" (Tocqueville, 1969: 12). Democratic citizens need a shared understanding of religion. He uses Christian morality for political action in a democracy. Democracy can be saved from authoritarianism invoking religious morality, sensitising and teaching the people.

The conventional wisdom regarding the state and church relationship is that when church interferes in politics it denigrates governmental autonomy. When state interferes in religion it would erode religious authority. Secular reason is the basis of a political action. It is argued that "a secular reason for an action (or a belief) is roughly one whose status as a justifier of action (or belief) does not evidently depend on (but also does not deny) the existence of God; nor does it depend on theological considerations, or on the pronouncement of a person or institution as a religious authority" (Audi, 2011: 67).Secular reason is based on governmental neutrality in religious matters. Secular reason may not be put in watertight compartment as it sometimes involves religious matter for the common cause.

In a secular democracy, churches have a prima face obligation to abstain from supporting candidates for public office overtly. Such obligation of neutrality would be good as it confines to its commitment to its own religious mission. It is argued that "political involvement is often highly preoccupying, and competent political action requires time and energy that could instead be devoted to the internal needs of the church and its members" (Audi, 2011: 5). Church is not only an institutional character but also a way of life setting certain values as its identity and faith premised in Christ. Moltmann sees the identity of the church primarily as a missionary identity and while spreading the gospel, it creates certain consciousness among the believers.

Rationalisation and modernization of the world do not dither the spirit of church in society (Moltmann, 1965).

In EA, legitimacy is derived from religion obligation of individual. In most cases, religious legitimacy surpasses political legitimacy enjoyed by the state and thereby undermines its political action. Religion organises people for political action by involving its religious obligation and legitimacy. In other words, the political action of the church can distort the state authority and power. The legitimacy enjoyed by the church in society influences political action. However, the political action of religion raised the question of the political neutrality of the religion. Religious citizens should be guided by religious morality not political morality. However, others argue that since liberal democracy is morally guided, the absence of political morality leads other forms of morality, including religious morality.

Advent of Ecclesiastical Political Action

The genesis of political action of EA traced back to the advent of the Christianity in Mizoram. The EA established with the arrival of Christian missionaries in the Lushai Hills for proseletarization work. The pioneer Missionaries Rev. J. H. Lorrain and Rev. F.W. Savidge arrived in Mizoram on 11th January, 1894. The church missionaries promoted evangelicalism through education, health, etc. and the tribals embraced evangelical Christianity and thereby influenced by evangelical ethics. In Mizoram, one of the largely Christian inhabited states in North East India, church plays vital role not only in social and religious life but also in political life of the people. Church exercises social control and go beyond the boundaries of sacred space. The social and political life revolves around the Church making the inseparability of religion and politics difficult. Church is not merely a religious institution but also a social institution where lot of social activities are coordinated and performed. Its contribution to the social development of the state, especially in the areas of literacy, education and health, and making people awareness of social issues such as drug abuse and alcoholism is well known. Church is attached to web of institutions such as schools, hospitals, training centres, associations, etc. link with youth organisations and thereby exercise its social control and public legitimacy. In many occasions, Church recourses political action that aimed at influencing the everyday life of the people in state. Church mission is not confined only to propagate Gospel in Mizo society and to focus on philanthropic responsibilities but also to engage political activities too.

The church was instrumental in enacting the Mizoram Liquor Total Prohibition and Control Act and as result prohibition was imposed in 1997. The MNF's defeat in the Assembly election in 1989, among other things, considered as the consequence of Church's political action due to government's reluctant to impose a ban on liquor sale in the state. In fact, the Church complied with the demand of YMA on prohibition. In July 2014 prohibition was lifted in spite of the stiff opposition by the Presbyterian Church. Confrontation between state and church over lifting a prohibition in the state can be seen as confrontation over two obligations enjoyed by church and state. However, the government adopted a tactical position that the move was to curb illegal spurious liquor and thereby able to reduce the church's grudge against the government's decision. Thus, the government was able to neutralise the political action of the church against lifting ban on liquor in a positive way.

The church not only engages in religious activities but also exercises its ethnic role. Church imposes moral values and norms among the Mizos and at the same creating ethnic consciousness among them. Church beliefs and doctrines deeply rooted in Mizo society and its role is evident in creating identity consciousness and erecting identity boundaries among the Mizos. Rising ethnic conscious and sentiments through its political action was considered to be an effort to indigenise the churches and win back the support of the ethnic communities. Church through its political action initially rise the ethnic conscious of the tribals and fused with the Christian theological consciousness. Often, the ethnic identity of the Mizos submerged with religious values propagated by the church. Even the self-identity of the Mizos is defined in terms of values of Christian religion. It also stands for protecting ethnic identity and culture. The church offers incentives for the ethnic communities to encourage couples to have more babies. The church also imposes dress code on women as they should not wear see-through dresses or clothes that expose the breast and show too much skin. The church in many occasion insists on people to wear tradition Mizo 'puan' - a piece of cloth woman wrap around their waists reading their ankles".

The political action of Church explicated in its role in conflict resolution when it emerged as the broker of peace in the insurgency hit Mizoram. During the insurgency, the Presbyterian Church initiated peace process and dialogue and played a vital role in the signing of the Mizo Accord in 1986. It negotiated peace talks between church and MNF leaders. The Presbyterian church condemned the violent activities of the MNF. Beginning of 1982, peace talks initiated by church against insurgency and gruesome killing.

On 30th July, 1982 twenty-fourrepresentatives of various denominations formed a Committee ZoramKohhranHruaitute Committee (ZKHC), - Christian Peace Committee - Mizoram Churches Leaders Committee to bring peace in the state. The church committees brought the insurgent groups to dialogue with the Government of India. The political action of the church, especially its role in peace negotiations in the late 1960s was criticised by the Mizo National Front which accused the church of interfering politics. In 1966, the conflict between the church leaders and MNF surfaced when the Church leaders condemned the violence unleashed by the Mizo movement. The MNF claimed that church should not interfere in politics. The political action of church was criticised by the insurgents.

Church as an Election Watchdog

The Church in Mizoram normally does not overtly support any political party in polls and never give a call the people to voter for particular party candidates. Unlike other societies, the Church does not anchor on any particular candidates sponsored by any political parties or issue statement to particular party for power. Church is not proposing but pushing for a candidate on the basis of his/her merit and cleanness in public life. However, it sets new morality in political life which enables for ensuring a peaceful, free and fair elections, public and institutional morality and religious duty. Often posters appear in the form of "vote for Christ" manifesting exercising franchise as a religious duty. The electoral politics in Mizoram is centred around state, YMA and Church. Political parties use Sunday mass to connect the electorate. In 1993, state level coordination committee on Election was set up to monitor the process of election in the state. In 2004, the Mizoram Presbyterian Church in its synod agreed to take electoral reforms to clean the electoral system. As Fernandes asserts that the "church does not mention names of particular political candidate but highlights what kind of people are trustworthy and can have a government relationship with church and society. Church in Mizoram therefore gives Mizo citizen a guide to elect responsible leaders" (Fernandes, 2009: 141).

The more overt form of church's political action in Mizoram was the formation of Mizo People's Forum (MPF), a conglomeration of major churches and non-governmental organisations to "cleanse" electoral politics, in June 20, 2006. The major churches include: Presbyterian Church of Mizoram, Catholic Church of Mizoram, Evangelical Free Church of India, Wesleyan Methodist Church, Evangelical Church of Maraland and Lairam Jesus Christ Baptist Church. Apart from major church organisations, the

MPF constitutes the ethnic organisations such YMA, Mizo Hmeichhe Insuihkhawn Pawl (Women's Federation), Mizo Upa Pawl (Elders' Association), Mizo Zirlai Pawl (Students Association) Though MPF involves diverse stakeholders, it is controlled by the Presbyterian Church, the largest church in Mizoram in which 85% Christian belongs and it has local wing in various localities and decentralised units across the state.

The twenty-seven-point Memorandum of Undertaking signed with major political parties in the state, the MPF enforced certain "Dos" and "Donots" to political parties during the electioneering. Accordingly, parties were requested to refrain from organising grand feasting on the eve of election and distribution of money during election, prohibiting parties from dropping the voters to their polling station by means of vehicles, restricting number of flags, posters and banners, allocation of designated places for political speeches and rallies, etc. It also bans door to door campaign ten days prior to the polling day, which feel that it would encourage bribes. It also ensures that no political campaign on Sundays. It also insists that political parties should only make an election manifesto which they can implement. The MPF volunteers distribute pamphlets of political parties to people, distribute voters identification slips to people, monitoring sitting arrangement outside the polling stations for those waiting for casting their votes. It also sensitising people and political parties in respecting the integrity of candidates by each other.

The 'Election Guidelines', often described as 'Moral Code of Conduct' enforced by the MPF, in par with the 'Model Code of Conduct' issued by the Election Commission of India, among other things, stressed the need for ensuring peaceful election by monitoring the selection of party candidates by the parties taking into account of their hard work and integrity. It urges desisting from selecting candidates having corrupt and criminal backgrounds.According to the MoU, if any party violates the Moral Code of Conduct leads to the invalidation of the party. Further, church ensures peaceful election, selection of party candidates, monitors election campaign and sensitises people. It also plays important role in educating the public on political matters and issues guidelines on election campaign. It monitors the spending by parties and candidates, imposes restrictions on use of microphones and littering public places with pamphlets and posters. The campaign should not be a disturbance to public and prohibits any form of use of force. Political parties in the state have to acquire the prior permission of MPF to organise political rallies. The Guidelines often read out at churches to sensitive the believers under its denominational jurisdiction. While the

Church's Moral Code of Contact was abiding by all people, it also warns of "exemplary punishment" for the violation of guidelines both by the parties and voters.

The church's political action as the 'election watch dog' was even appreciated and endorsed by the Election Commission of India. The ECI meets ethnic organisations along with parties in discussing the electoral preparedness. The former Chief Election Commissioner of India, S Y Quraishi appreciated the role of the church in the Seventh Regional Consultation of Electoral Reforms in Guwhati in 2011 stating that "this is wonderful idea. Electoral corruption creeps in from door-to-door campaigning. So banning such campaigns is one of the most effective ways of stopping corruption in poll process".[1]

EA and Ecclesial Citizenship

The church assumes its legitimacy in enforcing 'Moral Code of Conduct' derived from the ecclesial citizenship joyed the EA. The EA, in the footsteps of Jesus, creates a form of ecclesial citizenship where everyone belongs to an ecclesial community. As against political citizenship, where citizens are considered to be members of a political community, membership in ecclesial community is based on theological morality and emotional values attached to religion. In most cases, ecclesial citizenship conflict with values of political citizenship. Since membership in ecclesial community do not accommodate others and thereby denying others political freedom. The moral principles invoked by the EA contradicts the values of other religious communities and thereby leading to systematic exclusion of certain sections in the society. The EC enforced by the Church derive from religious norms. While political citizenship grounded in the principles of equality, believes that self-realisation is possible in the political community, the ecclesial citizenship believes that self -realisation is possible only through its adherence to religious values. EC guarantees a citizen's rights and responsibilities towards Church authority. Political citizenship also recognises the importance of guaranteeing religious freedom to its citizens. State recognises the religious groups and ensure religious freedom, and not guided by any religious values. Political citizenship involves legitimate political action that people have to act the rules set by the state, establishing a legitimacy between the state and citizenship. Ethics of good citizenship has certain moral principles. When democracy moves away from morality, religious morality steps in.

Secondly, obeying the 'Moral Code of Conduct' gains legitimacy from the idea of obligation enjoyed by the EA. The EA establishes a kind of obligation of people which is parallel to the political obligation of the state. Religious citizenship brings rights and duties of individuals to the EA. The political action of the church gets legitimacy through ecclesial citizenship. Religious obligation is not only pious but also physical also. Obeying the EA was equated with obeying God. The ecclesiastical obligation often forces the believer to pay tax to Church. It is to remind that Under Sixth Schedule of the Constitution, tribals in Mizoram are exempted from paying income tax to the Government of India, but they have to contribute one-tenth of their income to the Church in the name of God for the welfare of the people. As William Singh argues that Reverence towards the church remains strong in Mizoram and the church's authority has never been questioned inMizoram since the evangelisation of Mizo society in 1903. Indeed, so revered is its role that the church functions likea state within a state. Not surprisingly, the church, which should remain confined to matters pertaining to religion, often intrudes into Mizoram's institutional and political sphere. So while criticism of the church is absent in Mizoram, the stategovernment is criticised on issues like corruption, price rise, rising in equality between rich and poor, etc. (Singh, 2012: 24).

EA sans Political Authority

The EA often take on the political authority in ransom where the state in most cases unable to exercise its will on the people. Church through its action ensure that no political activity take place in Sundays. Political parties and people also ensure no political encroachment is taking place in the state during the Sunday, a day devoted to sacred purposes, cessation from worldly labourers and employment. During the day, worldly occupations are forbidden. It is based on the obligation to God. Detracting from temporal affairs, it focuses on spiritual concerns. Six days for promotion of temporal interests and seventh day for spiritual life. In October, 2008, the major political parties in Mizoram submitted a memorandum to the CECI asking him to change the date of state Assembly polls as the poll day (November 29) falls on Sabbath (Saturday) a sacred day for some churches and Mizo Jewish community. Sabbath is observed as a holy day by other smaller Church denominations and also by Jewish community in the state who believe that they are the lost tribe of Israel. The Seventh Day Adventist Church even asked the extension of polling time, if change of date is not possible. It appealed the ECI that church members can exercise their franchise after six in the evening on polling day when the sacred day gets over then. In the 2013 State Assembly election, the Mizoram Kobharan Hruaitute Committee, a conglomerate of leaders of thirteen major churches has pressurised the ECI to change the dates of polling (December 4) and counting of votes (December 8) to accommodate the Presbyterian Church's five-day synod. The polling and counting days fell on Sundays which isconfined to prayer. The ECI later preponed the poll day to November 25 and postponed counting toDecember 9 to suit their convenience.

In the exercising its political action, the Church always seek the help of the ethnic organisations such as Young Mizo Association (YMA), a quasi-Church youth organisation which has over 40000 members to promote good Christian life in the state. YMA exercises its social control and political control in the state, in many times exercises act as the arm of the Church. The community life is cemented by the agency of Church. The office bearers of YMA have direct line with the Church. In many occasions such critical dependence perverts the stated goals of its political actions. The YMA terrorise the non-Mizo communities during the electioneering checking their electoral identity cards. In many times, church inability to discipline the YMA as the former is critically depends on the later in its political action. Church for its political action empowers YMA makes it difficult to comply with political authority. Many actions of the YMA in the past contributed to the erosion of community relations between the Mizos and non-Mizos. It weakened even the bridging capital between various communities in the state and fail to create an inter-ethnic networking (Bijukumar, 2008 & 2014).

The church-led MPF's political action in electioneering in the state undermines the autonomy of the political institutions and functioning of democracy though church through its political action makes the state accountable to the people. In other words, the political action of church and ethnic organisation overshadow the institutions of the state. The subservience of political and constitutional institutions to a religious institution, even for a good cause, can dampen the institutional values and its independent functioning. In exercising political action in electioneering the church and other ethnic organisations emerge as the parallel institutions to public institutions. It is argued that "the style of electioneering in Mizoram where the church acts like an authority and supervises the electoral process is simply the manifestion of religious politics in Mizo society which can also be called as "desecularization of politics" (Shyamkishor, 2014: 144).The MPF's demand that only genuine citizens of India should have the right to vote often create political mess in the state. It gives leverage to the ethnic organisations to tease the non-Mizos and small ethnic communities in the state such as the Reagnas.

Putting Religious Morality over Political Morality

The church political action based on religious morality overshadows the principles of political morality. Election in a democracy as a secular activity assumed the image of divine activity. The religious morality employed in the electioneering proves that political morality does not yield much result. Election demeaned as a divine activity infused with religious morality. Invoking religious morality in a secular political action has much repercussions on democracy itself. Often questions raised whether religious moral principles can apply to a political action of the state. Even the political action of the Church in electioneering was legitimised to cleanse politics and to bring new political culture in the state, it has devastating effect on the politics. Church is invoking its morality to cleanse electoral politics in the states.

Religious obligation violates political obligation leading to chaos in the society. Obeying EA is to is part of religious obligation. The active engagement of church in the electoral process of Mizoram turns to be critical of the principles of ecclesiastical political neutrality as it interferes imposing reasonable restriction on candidates during electioneering. It violates the very idea of ecclesiastical political neutrality. Religious institutions such as church should ensure neutrality. Church involvement in political action trigger a debate on the principle of ecclesiastical political neutrality. The ecclesiastical political neutrality is justified on the ground that "political involvement is often highly preoccupying, and competent political action requires time and energy that could instead be devoted to the internal needs of the church and its members" (Audi, 2011: 95). Neutrality ensures the institutional sustainability and the welfare of the church itself. The ecclesiastical political neutrality principle is justified from the point of view of institutional ethics. When it inters in political action, the role of church tends to be compromised by political activity. Opposite view that neutrality will not work when political morality is declining in democracy. So the principle of political neutrality should be modified.

Church "Selective" Political Action

Though church engages in political action which gained wider acceptability in the Mizo society, it was not able to extend its political action in many other areas. While Church pushes for candidates having integrity and hard work, it is always silent on ensuring women representation in the selection of candidates by various political parties. It has to be reminded that in Mizoram, female voters outnumber male voters. And women representation in Assembly. In 2011 the women voters outnumbered their male counterpart by 16,573. The total number of female voters was 3,88,046 and the male were 3,71,473. The representation of women in Assembly is meagre, though outwardly projected as women friendly state where most of the women run shops and markets. Though church was successful in bringing peace in the insurgency hit areas and achieving high social development, it failed to ensure the 'second democratic upsurge' – the representation of women in the government and Assembly. Since 1972, when Mizoram became a Union Terrirory and full-fledged state in 1987, only three women – Thanmawi (1978), K. Thansiami (1979) and Lalhlimpui (1987)- could able to win to state legislature and Lalhlimpui was the only woman minister in 1987 in the MNF government.

Secondly, the church was also silent on giving representation to both smaller tribals communities. For instance, the church took a laccidical attitude towards the problems faced by the Hindu Reangscommonly described as Brus. The Reangs faced ethnic cleansing and displacement in Mizoram from the dominant Mizo community forced to settlein the refugee camps in neibhouring Tripura. Though a tripartite agreement was arrived at by the Government of India and the governments of Mizoram and Tripura on the repatriation of displaced Brus, they declined to back in Mizoram fearing further ethnic cleansing. It has to be reminded that in 1997, the ethnic organisations such as YMA and MZP with the connivance of the church, went on rampant ethnic cleansing in the aftermath of the killing of a Mizo forest guard allegedly by the Brus. The political deprivation of the Brus reached its acumen when their demand for a separate Autonomous District Council (ADC) for the Brus inhabited areas of Mizoram was rejected by the Mizoram government under pressure from ethnic organisations. In a political retaliation, and the pressure from ethnic organisation, around 17000 names of Brus were deleted from voters list. The move was seen as an attempt to reduce the political voice of the minority Brus in the state politics. The church's selective political action also visible when the Election Commission of India, conducted voting in Brus settlement areas in Tripura for the Mizoram Assembly election in 2013 under the direction of the Supreme Court. When the ethnic organisations critical of the government's move to extend right to franchise beyond its state jurisdiction to ensure the political rights of the Brus, the church which is considered as the watch dog in the election and torch bearer of clean politics in the state, remained as a mute spectator.

Conclusion

The political action of church in the name cleansing electoral politics in the state has serious repercussion not only for the democracy but also peace and stability. The church warms exemplary punishment for the violation of Election Guidelines by people and political parties show the political obligation is more physical than moral or ethical. The critiques often see that since the EA promotes an ecclesial citizenship it exhibits certain exclusionary tendencies. The church's critical dependence on ethnic organisation for monitoring electioneering in the state leads further ethnic animosity among other communities in the state. In most cases, the social elite which control church use political action for igniting ethnic polarisation in the state. It has to be reminded that with the class formationin Mizo society,the church augmented its role as ethnic organisation. It fails to control bandhs, blockades and even atrocities against non-tribal communities. Church had no voice in the issue of Myanmar refugees along border especially in Lawngtlai district. Often it became an instrument in the hands of the ethnic organisations to legitimise their actions against other ethnic communities.

The elusive peace achieved by the state often hampered by the activities of the YMA when it unleashes atrocities against the non-Mizos. Sometimes, the government often comes under undue pressure of the ethnic organisations. In many cases, the Church was not successful in cleaning electoral politics in the state. Sometimes, the ethnic based organisation are liability for the church itself. Church's political action in some other level leads to the inciting ethnic identity consciousness. As Fernandes argues that "in some extreme cases, church leaders even play a role in fanning communal tensions and ethnic rivalries by resurrecting age-old myths about tribal difference and the wrongs done to one tribe by another" (Fernandes, 2009: 144).

The invocation of religious identity for political action has implications for democracy. The Christian identity is not only used by the church in its political action but the extremist groups to gain legitimacy for their activities. In the 1960s, the Mizo National Front (MNF) legitimised its action claiming that they are the true defenders of Christianity. The Mizo movement claimed that the impoverishment of Mizos in the Lushai Hills of Assam is of their stigmatised Christianised identity and it was used to legitimise its radical political action. There was a competitive use of Christian identity in political action by both church and extremist organisation to legitimise its action. As Fernandes argues that "insurgency groups, terrorist organisations, and separatist movements taking the idiom of Christianity as a way of defining their political project have at times come up against the church, which tends to be more moderate politically and more conciliatory towards the Indian government and the Indian security forces" (Fernandes, 2009: 144). The National Socialist Council of Nagalim (NSCN) legitimised its demand for *Nagalim* - integration of all Naga inhabited areas – invoking "Nagaland for Christ". In such situations, differentiating a political action of the church for a good or bad cause really cumbersome task as invoking religious morality for the political action for a good cause, such as election watch dog and cleansing electoral politics, can be used for the most virulent forms of ethnic segregation and assertion in democracy.

References

Audi, Robert (2011), *Democratic Authority and the Separation of Church and State*, Oxford: Oxford University Press.

Bijukumar, V. (2008), "Civil Society and Social Capital in Mizoram: Changing Dimensions and Emerging Trends", *Man and Society (A Journal of North-East Studies)*, Vol. V., Spring, 2008, pp. 57-80.

Bijukumar, V. (2014), "Ethnicising Social Capital in Mizoram: The Role of Young Mizo Association", *Eastern Quarterly*, Vol. 10, Nos. 3&4, Autumn & Winter, pp. 111-123.

Fernandes, Sujatha (2009), "Ethnicity, Civil Society, and the Church: The Politics of Evangelical Christianity in Northeast India", in David Halloran Lumsdaine (ed.), *Evangelical Christianity and Democracy in Asia*, Oxford: Oxford University Press, pp. 131-151.

Moltmann, Jurgen (1965), *Theology of Hope: On the Ground and the Implications of a Christian Eschatology*, New York: Harper & Row Publishers.

Shyamkishor, Ayangbam (2014), "Church as Election Watch Dog: The Mizoram Model", *Eastern Quarterly*, Vol 10, Nos. III & IV, Autumn & Winter, pp. 133-146.

Singh, N. William (2012), "Politics of Divine Edict and Reverse Secularism", *Economic and Political Weekly*, Vol. XLVII, No. 52, 29 December, pp. 23-24.

Tocqueville, Alexis de (1969), *Democracy in America*, New York: Doubleday & Company.

Notes

1. "EC pat for Mizo Church ban on door-to-door campaigning", The Mizoram Post, 17 June, 2011.

Part – II
Parties in Action

Chapter - 3

Dwindling Congress: Quandary of Mobilization and Leadership

The Congress Party's worst ever existential crisis in Indian politics is not only visible in the mainland India but also in the peripheral region of the Northeast India. In fact, the grand old party's such crisis is attributed by both internal and external factors. Internally, almost all state units in the Northeast India, the Congress is afflicted with the growing dissident activities and the demand for leadership change where the party in power. Externally, the BJP's strategy of *Congress Mukt Bharat* (Congress Free India) creates more odd situations to the party which the central leadership finds it difficult to counter. Though, the BJP's mass base is not so impressive to come into power on its own and provide an alternative government to the present Congress dispensation in many northeastern states, the party's shrewd strategy to overthrow the Congress governments in the region shrinking the space of the Congress.

India's northeast, for a long time, is considered to be strong political bastion of the Congress party, inspite of highly volatile identity politics, ethnic assertions, extremist activities and strong sense of alienation of some ethnic communities from the national mainstream. Though, number of ethno-regional political parties sprang up at various point to time, the fortunes and the widespread presence of the Congress however has not been seriously challenged. As a 'catch- all party' it could mobilize divergent social groups and categories to its fold and crafted an art of governance as an inclusive mechanism. Even though, in many occasions, the Congress met adverse situations in mainland India, its mass base and electoral fortunes rarely dwindled in the northeast. The party's constructed image of the architect of many accords intended to bring peace and normalcy in the region and the sacrifice of its own governments in the aftermath of the conclusion of such accords always found in the imagination of the people. It has to be reminded that Congress governments at the Centre at various points of time scripted history in the region by signing many accords such as the Shillong Accord (1975), Assam Accord (1985), Mizo Accord (1986), Tripura Accord (1988), Darjeeling Accord (1988), Bodo Accord (1993) by entering peace talks with extremists elements within the constitutional framework. However, there are certain instances that in the aftermath of the Assam Accord and Mizo Accord, the Congress lost power in Assam and Mizoram to the ethno-regional political parties such as the Asom Gana Parishad (AGP) and Mizo National Front (MNF) respectively.

The Beginning of the Congress Diminution

The Congress, though undergoing vulnerability due to its internal scuffles and growing anti-incumbency against its governments for quite some time, the penetration of the BJP in the region further aggravated the situation. It may be reminded that the Bharatiya Janata Party (BJP), for a long time, in the region, was almost a non-entity and has not much legacy to the history and politics of the region, is fastly stepping its footsteps in various states by putting the issues which it talks at the national level in backburner and igniting local and ethno regional issues. For instance, issues of beef andreligious conversion were over shadowed by the issues of the illegal migration of the Bangladeshi Muslims, the plight of the indigenous tribal people, development issues, etc. In the 2014 general election, like the rest of India, the BJP followed an alliance strategy of 'go it alone' wherever it has strength and a forge an alliance with regional forces wherever it was not a decisive force to counter the Congress. For instance, it forged an alliance with Naga Peoples Front (NPF) in Nagaland and in Meghalaya it extended support to National People's Party (NPP) of P.A. Sangma. In Mizoram, BJP formed a coalition of eight state parties under the banner of United Front led by the MNF to fight against the Congress candidate of the lone Parliamentary constituency of the Christian dominated hilly state.

The performance of the BJP in the 2014 general election is not an isolated event and it has to be put in right perspective. Since the general election 1991, the BJP is improving its electoral strength in various northeastern states. Apart from emerging as a major force in Assam and Arunachal Pradesh, the saffron party could intrude in many other states posing a challenge to the Congress, regional parties and the left parties. In some states, the opposition space vacated by the regional parties is filled by the BJP making inroads into its social base thereby posing a challenge to the Congress party. Interestingly, the regional agenda of many regional parties are taken by the Hindu nationalist party and approaching to the new social groups and communities with renewed ethno-regional agenda.

The BJP, in many occasions, destabilized the Congress governments through defection and allurement and thereby prepares for its backdoor entry into some states. In the past, in some other Congress ruled states, the BJP's strategy of communal polarization and social engineering gave more political dividends to the saffron party. Though, the entry of BJP in northeast India is a new phenomenon, especially beginning from the 1990s, the Sangh Parivar organizations are actively engaged their activities in some pocket of tribal areas with a focus on education and social servicing. However, in the electoral politics of these states their role was limited due to the Congress party's and other ethno-regional parties mobilization and aggregation of the interests of various ethnic communities. Recently, the Congress party further went a step ahead to form its own governments in the northeast as the ethno-regionalism practiced by the ethno-regional parties like AGP and MNF are fastily declining. However, the diminishing role of ethno-regional parties gave only a temporary advancement to the Congress party as the vacuum created by the ethno-regional parties and the ethno-regional issues championed by them are taken over by the Hindu nationalist forces to emerge as formidable political force in the region. In fact, the BJP's new found interest in the region cannot be seen as securing electoral support for the formation of a government at the centre as these eight north-eastern states send only 25 members to the lower house of the Parliament. Beyond the arithmetical strength of these states in the Parliament, the BJP was attracted to this region with a predetermined agenda of dislodging the Congress regimes and thereby erasing the image of the Congress from the public imagination. Its alliance with AGP, NPF and NPP in Meghalaya and other smaller parties in the rest of the states can be seen in the context of its ulterior motive of implementing its agenda over electoral predilections. For the realization of its agenda, the BJP adopted different policies and strategies in different Congress rules states.

Arunachal Pradesh, the first political experiment

In the north east region, apart from Assam, the BJP built up its base in Arunachal Pradesh and over the years, the BJP's vote share has increased and made inroads into the electoral base of the Congress. In the border sensitive state of Arunachal Pradesh the BJP often raises the bogey of protecting the territorial integrity of the state. It has to be reminded that China claims Arunachal Pradesh as part of Southern Tibet. Perhaps, the BJP's attempt to destablise the Congress governments in the northeastern states goes back to 2003. In July 2003, during the Vajpayee led National Democratic Alliance (NDA) government,the dissident Congress leader Gegong Apang toppled the Mukut Mithi led Congress government with 34 Congress MLAs and became the Chief Minister of the state under the newly floated United Democratic Front (UDF) which later merged to the BJP. When the United Progressive Alliance (UPA) government came into power at the centre, however, Apang rejoined the Congress Party and contested the next election under the Congress symbol. In 2004 general election the BJP could win all two seats in the state with a vote share of 53.85%. Though, in the subsequent general election in 2009, the party lost all two seats to the Congress and its vote share reduced to 37.17%, in 2014 general election the BJP wrested one seat from the ruling Congress with an vote share of 46.62%. In 2014 general election, the BJP's spectacular victory in one of the two seats added an advantage to the NDA in the region. In the State Assembly election held along with the General Election 2014, the BJP own 11 seats with a vote share of 30.97% in the 60 member Assembly against its performance in 2009 when the BJP could secure only three seats. However, in 2016, the BJP orchestrated defection in the ruling Congress party which saw political instability in the state culminating the resignation of the Nabam Tuki government and the House was under suspended animation. Subsequently, President rule was imposed under Article 356 on the recommendation of Union cabinet with the allegation of the constitutional failure in the state. On 19 February, 2016 the dissident Congress leader Kalikho Pul finally overthrew the Tuki government with the outside support of the BJP which have 11 members. Though the Congress had the support of 47 MLAs in the 60 member house, 21 of them supported the rebel leader Pul which later formed the People Party of Arunachal. By encouraging defection, overthrowing the government and installing a government led by the rebel Congress leader with its outside support, the BJP score over Congress in the border state.

However, in a major setback to the BJP and the Centre, the Supreme Court of India, on July 13, 2016 ordered restoration of the Congress government under Nabam Tuki. Subsequently, the Governor set July 16 as the deadline for proving the government's majority in the Assembly though Tuki sought atleast ten days time. Though he was confident of winning the trust vote by appealing to the dissent party MLAs to support his government in the confidence motion, the central leadership sensed the danger. On the eve of the trust vote, the party decided to change it Chief Minister taking into account of mood of the dissident MLAs. Tuki was subsequently replaced by Pema Khandu, the son of former Congress Chief Minister, Dorjee Khandu. However, after a gap of two months, the state once again witnessed more political drama with the switch over, posing a challenge to the central leadership of the Congress. The state witnessed the mass migration of 43 Congress MLAs, including the Chief Minister, Pema Khandu, to People's Party of Arunachal (PPA), a constituent of a regional front led by the BJP. On 31 December 2016, Pema Khandu joined BJP along with 32 other MLAs from PPA dashing the hope of the Congress as a key player in the state (Bijukumar, 2016). The state of affairs in border state of Arunachal Pradesh reveals the victory of BJP's strategy of organizing defections and allurement in the Congress and the incapacity of the Congress to protect its governments and keep its organizational unity. The Congress party in Arunachal Pradesh became a victim of its own fallacies and misdeeds which paved the way for BJP in accessing political power in an unscrupulous manner.

Assam, Ascending BJP and Dwindling Congress

Assam is the first state in the north-eastern region, the BJP could form its own government with the support of the AGP and Bodoland People's Front (BPF) ending the fifteen consecutive years of Congress government led by Tarun Gogoi. In May 2016, when the election result declared in the 126 seats in the State Assembly the BJP won 60 seats with a vote share of 42%, its alliance partner AGP secured 14 seats with a vote share of 8%. The Congress could secure only 20 seats with the vote share of 31% and the BPF, another partner in the BJP alliance won 12 seats with a vote share of 3.9%. The BPF, former ally of Congress, initially moved towards the BJP for the development of Bodo Territorial Council (BTC). It has to be reminded that the BPF ended its ties with the Congress and had withdrawn its ministers from the Gogoi government instigating Bodo tribals against Bangladeshi Muslim migration raising the bogey of threats from migrants.

The three consecutive term of the Tarun Gogoi government witnessed strong wave of anti-incumbency and charges of corruption. During the tenure of the Gogoi regime witnessed many clashes in the Bodo areas in the State especially between Bodos and Muslims. The growing resentment against containing frequent clashes and the civil administration's failure to rehabilitate the victims of clashes added further blow to the Gogoi administration. When the Assembly election was approaching and the BJP was chalking out its strategy to win the Assembly election in the state, the Congress faced disarray within the party and the government. In the recent past, many Congress legislators joined the BJP. In August, 2015, an embarrassment to the state Congress, former Minister Himanta Biswa Sarma joined the BJP. Himanta who was Tarun Gogoi's trusted aid disillusioned with the Congress due the realization that his political ambition to become the Chief Minister of the state was dashed by the Congress as the Gogoi is promoting his son Gaurav Gogoi. While contesting such argument Assam Congress leader Kishore Bhattacharjee said that "Gaurav's entry into politics has no role in their differences. It started way back when (now Congress MLA) Pijush Hazarika was elected the Assam Pradesh Youth Congress President in June 2008. Then there were speculations in 2012 that Tarun Gogoi would resign as Chief Minister and become the country's Vice-President, Sarma was really hoping to become the Chief Minister".[1]

The ascendancy of the BJP and the diminution of the Congress in Assam was contributed by the former's alliance with the AGP. The AGP which formed in the aftermath the Assam Movement (1979-84) occupied a predominant space in the politics of the state. The ethno-regional sentiment aroused by the Assam Movement over the issue of illegal migration from Bangladesh contributed to the consolidation of the AGP as a regional force in the state. After occupying power in two times (1985 to 1989 and 1996 to 2001), the party's mass base in the state was eroded due to factional feuds and frequent splits. Moreover, over the years, the party diluted its stand on the issue of illegal migration from Bangladesh and its governments took a lukewarm attitude towards the determination and deportation of illegal migrants to Bangladesh according to the provisions of the Illegal Migrants (Determination by Tribunal) Act 1983. While the AGP is losing its electoral base in the state and diluting its stand on the issue of illegal migration, the BJP emerged as a potential political force with the agenda of illegal migration. During the three consecutive terms of the Congress government, the state witnessed further erosion of the AGP and opposition spaced vacated by the AGP was filled by the BJP. The gradual and steady emergence and consolidation of the BJP culminated in the ascendancy of power in 2016 Assembly election replacing the Congress.

Manipur, Social Engineering for Political Gain

The Congress ruled Manipur was another attraction for the BJP in the region due to its ethnic composition and complexities of the issues it confronted over time. The state of Manipur having area of 22, 327 square kilometers is a highly pluralized society with a complex ethnic composition. Manipur has three major ethnic groups such as Meiteis, Kukis and Nagas and the smaller groups like Mizos, Zomi, Chins, Paites, Hmars etc. The Meiteis resides in valley which constitutes only 10% of the state's total area which include four districts such as Imphal East, Imphal West, Thoubal and Bishnupur. According to the 2011 census, 60% of the total population of Manipur resides in the valley region and the remaining 90% constitute the Hill areas which comprised of five districts such as Chandel, Churachandour, Senapati, Tamenglong and Ukhrul where other tribal communities inhabit. The Meiteis cannot buy lands in the hill areas while the tribals can possess land in the valley. Interestingly, as per the constitutional provisions, the outsiders, including the Meiteis needs the permission of the Hill Area Committee (HAC) while those in hill areas can by land in the Meiteis inhabited areas. Over the period of time, the Meiteis control over land is shrinking due to the tribal inhabitance in the valley as well as the migration of the outsiders such as Biharis, Marwaris, and Punjabis for business purpose. The Meiteis often allege that in the district of Bishnupur, the north Indian population outnumbered the indigenous Meiteis. The growing sense of reducing into a minority in the valley forced the Meiteis to demand for Inner Line Permit (ILP) to restrict the entry of the outsiders to the region.

The advent of BJP in the state was marked by the by-elections to the two Assembly constituencies in November, 2015 where the BJP candidates defeated the ruling Congress candidates and thereby opened its account for the first time in the state. In Thangmeiband Assembly constituency Khumukham Joy Kishan Singh and in Thongju Constituency Bishwajit Singh of BJP defeated the Congress candidates adding another feather in the crown of the BJP in the region. It has to be reminded that for some time the BJP is wooing many regional leaders of other parties and prominent figures of the state to the party fold. It has to be reminded that in September, Radhabinod Koijam, the former Manipur Chief Minister, Okran Joy Singh, the former leader of the Manipur People's Party (MPP) and Yumnam Joykumar Singh, the former DGP joined the saffron party. Way back, in his maiden visit on 18th April, 2015 in the Congress ruled state of Manipur, Amit Shah appealed the people to "elect BJP, get benefit" emphasizing the need for BJP governments both in the state and the centre for the better development of the state. In a dig to Congress, the BJP president pleaded for making North East a 'Congress –free Zone' where the people of Manipur has a decisive role. The BJP president said that apart from corruption it was the Congress government that was holding Manipur back from progress and development.[2]

In the civic elections too the BJP is emerging as a potent force in the state. In the January 2016 municipal and nagar panchayat election, the BJP won 62 seats in the 278-member municipal council. In the 27 member Imphal Municipal Corporation held on 2nd June, 2016, the BJP emerged as second largest party winning 10 seats after the Congress which could secure only 12 seats. The emerging trends shows that the BJP is emerging as an alternative to the Congress both in the rural and urban areas keeping its goal of capture political power in the state in the February 2017 Assembly election.

After successfully dislodging the Congress regime and installing a rebel Congress led government with the outside support of the BJP in Arunachal Pradesh and forming its first government in Assam, the BJP subsequently concentrated on Manipur to dislodge the Congress government of Okram Ibobi Singh. Hoping to secure political power in the 2017 Assembly election, the BJP was alluring a section of Congress legislators and preparing a roadmap to topple the Congress government which enjoys the support of 47 members in the 60 member Manipur Assembly. Like Assam, Congress was in power for the last three consecutive terms under the leadership of Ibobi Singh faced a strong anti-incumbency. The BJP was hoping to win on the anti-incumbency wave as well as the internal bickering of the ruling party along with social engineering. In a further boost to the BJP ambition in the state, on 24 May, 2016 the four NPF legislators in the Manipur Assembly joined BJP in the formation of North-East Democratic Alliance (NEDA) in Guwahati in the presence of Amit Shah and Ram Madhav. Himanta Biswa Sarma, the former Congressmen and the current BJP Minister in Assam was elected as the Convener. The objective of the Alliance was to strengthen the BJP's base in the region outwardly it claims that the intension of the NEDA was on the agenda of the overall development of the region. Moreover, the BJP is planning to extend NEDA to all Congress ruled states such as Meghalaya, Mizoram and Manipur with the alliance of the regional parties to out the Congress in the Assembly elections.

In August, 2016 the Ibobi Singh government passed three anti-hill areas Bills triggered widespread protest by the Manipur Tribals Forum (MTF) in the state. The three controversial bills – the Protection of Manipur People Bill, 2015, the Manipur Land Revenue and Land Reforms Bill (Seventh Amendment), 2015 and the Manipur Shops and Establishments (Second

Amendments) Bill, 2015 were allegedly passed by the Assembly in just six minutes. The passing of these Bills created Hill-Valley tussle which was a great concern for the Congress government in the state as the BJP tactically adopted a stand against the Congress. The BJP was monitoring the volatile situations in Manipur without antagonizing Hill and the Valley. In the midst of the recurring tussle between the hill and valley, the BJP created instability in the state.

Though the BJP was trying to woo the Meiteis to its Hinduvta fold without antagonizing the hill tribes, the move is bottlenecked by certain developments in the state. Firstly, the BJP's trusted alliance with the NPF in Nagaland was suspiciously watched by the Meiteis. The Naga Accord concluded between the National Socialist Council of Nagaland (Isak Muivah) (NSCN (IM)) and the government of India in August 2015 created more apprehension among the Meiteis. It may be recalled that the NSCN(IM) was demanding all Naga integrated areas in Manipur, Assam, Arunachal Pradesh though the provisions of the Accord kept secret. Moreover, the entry of the ruling NPF in Nagaland in the Manipur Assembly which has four members was a matter of worry for the Meiteis. Further, the strain in the relationship between the Meiteis and RSS on the issue of controversial AFSPA 1958 is added further concern for the BJP's attempt to woo the Meiteis. It has to be reminded that the Meiteis are against the Act (Irom Sharmila who is in fast for the last 15 years is a Meitei), while the RSS firmly support it. In his maiden visit on 18th April, 2015 in Manipur, Amit Shah even kept silence on the long standing demand for the repeal of the Armed Forces Special Powers Act of 1958, ending the decade old fast of Irom Sharmila, civilian causalities in counter insurgency operations, fake encounters, human rights violations by the Indian army, border issues between various states, etc.

In the 2017 Assembly election, the BJP undertook another masterstroke to the Congress in Manipur. Although emerged as the second-largest party to the incumbent Congress, the BJP could form the government for the first time in the state, with support of smaller parties like the Naga People's Front (NPF), National People's Party (NPP), Lok Janshakti Party (LJP) and independents. It may be reminded that in the 60-member Assembly, the Congress emerged as the single largest party winning 28 seats, followed by the BJP 21, NPF 4, NPP 4, LJP, Trinamol Congress and independent one each. The BJP not only dislodged the incumbent Congress regime's effort to form its government for the fourth consecutive term, but also sharpened its plan to bring a Congress *mukht* Northeast India.The verdict of the Manipur election shows the BJP's political manoeuvre to deal concrete situations with appropriate strategy of mobilising contending social constituencies, which has proved success. The party's strategy of mobilisation of both the Meiteis and the tribal communities on different issues dashed the Congress' electoral chances in the state. The fortunes of the Congress were adversely affected by the resentment aroused of the ILP agitation and movement against the creation of the new districts by the UNC, in addition to the strong anti-incumbency and allegations of fake encounters, corruption and human rights violations.

Meghalaya, Engineering Political Defections

In the hill state of Meghalaya, the BJP for quite some time wasdesperately looking for a change from the Congress led Mukul Sangma government. However, the party's inadequate strength to topple the government forced it to form alliance with smaller parties in the state. In 2014 general election, the BJP trucked an alliance with NPP of P.A. Sangma. It has to be reminded that Sangma who quit Nationalist Congress Party (NCP), a constituent of the UPA government at the Centre few months before the election and formed the NPP and later entered into a tactical electoral understanding with the NDA. The Garo inhabited Tura seat was won by the Garo veteran Sangma by securing 22.84% of votes adding one more seat to the NDA alliance at the centre.

After engineering defection in Arunachal Pradesh and installing its own government by overthrowing the Congress regime in Assam, the BJP posed a challenge to the Congress government in Meghalaya. In a prelude to make state free from the Congress, the BJP showed much interest in the internal squabbles within the state Congress. In fact, though the Congress in the state was vulnerable to factional squabble for a long time, the important one was due to the defeat of the Congress candidate to Conrad K. Sangma of NPP in the Tura Loksabha bi election 2016. The Garo Hills in which the Tura constituency belongs was considered to be the stronghold of the Chief Minister Mukul Sangma who was picked up by the central leadership of the Congress party to counter the influence of the Garo strongman, Purno Sangma. Though in the state assembly election Mukul could erode the base of the Purno, in the 2014 Loksabha election and the 2016 by-election, he was miserably failed to canvass the Garos to the party. Interestingly, Mukul was able to garner support in favour of his wife, Dikkanchi D. Shira, the sitting MLA as the candidate of the bieletion. In the election, the mandate was in favour of Conrad K. Sangma, the younger son of Purno Sangma as the Garo people endorsed the family politics of Purno s once again over that of Mukul. The electoral defeat rekindled the factional politics in the state as D D Lapang, the MPCC president and the former Chief Minister and Vincent Pala, the MP from Shillong constituency demanded leadership change in the state. In his three page letter to party president Sonia Gandhi and the Vice President Rahul Gandhi, Mukul Sangma calaimed that "the BJP is campaigning in Shillong and are in connivance with cabinet ministers and looking to sir trouble for the state government".[3]

Though the BJP had eye on Meghalaya to capture power from the Congress, unlike Assam, the BJP had many hurdles in the largely Christian dominated state. Its Hinduvta agenda often cannot be operated in the hilly state with deep rooted influence of Church and other ethno-regional organisations. This realization was more evident in the reaction to the Amit Shah's visit to the state and the reaffirmation of the BJP central leadership in 2015. It has to be reminded that with great hope of boosting the party organization by wooing Hindu Nepalese and Bengali population in the state, the visit of the BJP President in the Congress ruled state of Meghalaya on 22nd April, 2015 was greeted with bandhs by outlawed extremist organizations such as the Hynniewtrep National Liberation Council (HNLC) and massive protest by Non Governmental Organisations such as Thma U Rangli-Juki (TUR), Hynniewtrep National People's Front (HNPF) and Khasi National Union (KNU). The ethnic organizations organized beef party to protest against the BJP governments move to ban beef which is the favourite food for the tribals in the state. The three regional parties in the State – United Democratic Party (UDP), Hill State People's Democratic Party (HSPDP) and *Khun Hynniewtrep National Awakening Movement* (KHNAM) – voiced their concern on issue of ban on cow slaughter in separate meetings with the BJP national president Amit Shah. Amid growing resentment against the BJP government on the issue of banning beef, Ram Madhav, the BJP general secretary who accompanied Shah stated that "there is no such proposal to ban cow slaughter in the Northeastern states".[4]

Failing to polarize communally, the BJP relied on the bogey of 'development 'in the state to mobilize its support base. The BJP President in his visit to the state on 22nd April, 2015asserted that the BJP government initiated construction of hostels for the welfare of North East students in Bangalore, Delhi University and Jawaharlal Nehru University. Further the BJP leader Nalin Kohli made it clear that BJP is not an anti-Christian Party but a development –oriented party.[5]The Prime Minister Narendra Modi's visit to Shillong in the last week of May 2016 to attend the 65th NEC plenary session meeting can be seen in this context. Though the visit was entirely official, a section of the political class believes that by reiterating the developmental mantra, BJP can woo certain sections of the society and thereby emerge as a potential alternative to the Congress in the state.

In the Assembly election 2018, the Congress faced a setback as it could not form the government, though it emerged as the single largest party. In the 60-member Assembly, the INC emerged first position with 21 seats followed by the NPP which secured 19 seats, UDP 6, PDF 4, BJP 2, NCP 1, KHNAM 1 and independents 3. While the internal bickering of the ruling Congress and the shaky government further gave a boost to the electoral strategy and political mobilization of BJP in Meghalaya. Moreover, the ascendancy of BJP government in neighbouring Assam in 2017, accelerated the BJP's inclination towards the state.During the election campaign congress was able to deploy a contingent of it national leaders and leaders from other states in its bid to retain its government in the hilly state, it could not counter the shifting loyalty of Congress men to the BJP. Further, Hiamanta Biswas Sarma, the convener of NEDA and the BJP turned Congress politician in Assam masterminded defection in the Congress and choked out the electoral strategy for the party. The BJP was able to defect two sitting Congress MLAs to the party. Even the NPP in Meghalaya is a conglomeration of former congress leaders. Moreover, in the run up to the election, the BJP deputed K.J. Alphons Kannanthanam, its Christian face and the Union Minister for State to coordinate its activities even before the election declared in the state. The former bureaucrat who belonged the Syrian Christian community in Kerala was made the party's election-in-charge for Meghalaya hoping dispel its image as anti-Christian. The election verdict and the subsequent government formation shows that though the BJP won only two seats, it could project its victory as a decimation of the Congress in one of the citadels in Northeast India.

The poor state of affairs of the Congress is visible in two other states- Nagaland and Tripura - where assembly election held in 2018, the party virtually outed in the Assembly. In the 2018 Nagaland Assembly election, the Congress could not win a single seat and its vote share plummeted to 2.1% inspite ofhigh spirited campaign led by the Party under Rahul Gandhi.Nagaland is of the other north-eastern states, where the Congress enjoyed much support base, inspite the commanding role of regional party such as the Naga People's Front. In Tripura, the worst ever performance of the Congress was perceptible in the state election where it could not win a single seat and its voting share reduced to 1.8%. It may be recalled that, Tripura witnessed frequent defections in the Congress and subsequent mass migration to the Trinamol Congress.

Mizoram, Difficult but Confident

Perhaps, among the above mentioned state, Mizoram is an exception where the Congress insulated from the politics of dislodge of the BJP. In the Christian majority state, the BJP finds it difficult to take root where the Church has decisive voice in the politics of the state, especially during the election time. Lal Thanhawla, the two consecutive Congress Chief Minister since 2008, however, could consolidate its position over time inspite ofthe belligerent opposition from the MNF. However, the BJP is looking for fertile ground for its expansion by forging alliance with the major opposition party MNF and the smaller regional parties such as the Zoram Nationalist Party (ZNP). In the past three years, it has been reported that the BJP is gaining popularity in some parts of the minority dominated Mizoram. In February, 2015 in the Chakma Autonomous District, the BJP registered its strong presence after the Congress. Of the 81 village councils, the BJP secured five seats which was otherwise the stronghold of the Congress. In January, 2016, in a further move to consolidate its position in the state, John V. Hluna, a university professor, was appointed as the new BJP president. Though the BJP has minimal support base in the state and is not able follow strategy that of Manipur, it may extend its support to MNF to accomplish the goal of Congress *Mukt Bharat*in Mizoram which is going to the polls later in 2018.

Multiple Reasons and No Defense

The current existential crisis of the Congress in the north-eastern state is perhaps the strong anti-incumbency wave against the Congress regimes where its Chief Ministers were in power for the two or three consecutive terms, denying the same opportunity to other leaders of the party. In fact, one of the reasons for the huge electoral adversity of the Congress in the Assam Assembly election is that of the strong anti-incumbency of the three consecutive term of the Chief Minister, Tarun Gogoi. Similarly, in Manipur, too, Okram Ibobi Singh continued to hold power for the three consecutive term generated anti-incumbency wave which was benefited by the BJP. The lone Congress ruled state of Mizoram, the party was in power under the leadership of Lal Thanhawla for the two consecutive terms. Though, in many occasions, the state level Congress leaders expressed their anguish over these consecutive chief ministers, the Congress central leadership took a lackadaisical attitude to the demand leading to aggravation of resentment against these chief ministers.

Secondly, most of the Congress state units in Northeast India, like mainland India, are riddle with factional feud and open fight against leadership which shatters the prospects of the party at the state levels. The High Command, in many cases, either failed to solve the organizational problems or adopted a wait and watch policy leading to its disarray. Thirdly, the emergence of family politics, putting the kith and kin of the leaders both in the electoral fray and party organizational positions often brings adverse impact on the fortunes of the party at the state level in the long run, though it can reap short-term benefits. Such an argument is strengthened by the fact that former Assam Chief Minister Tarun Gogoi even promoted his son Gaurav Gogoi, the sitting Loksabha MP from Assam as his political heir. In fact, Himanta Biswa Sarma, the once trusted aid of Tarun Gogi and the current BJP Minister in the Sarbananda Sonowalgovernment, disillusioned with the Congress due to the realization that his political ambition to become the Chief Minister of the state was dashed by the Congress as the Gogoi is promoting his son Gaurav Gogoi. In Meghalaya, Dikkanchi D. Shira, the wife of the Congress Chief Minister Mukul Sangma, a sitting MLA in the current Assembly, was fielded as the Congress candidate in the Tura Loksabha by-election of May 2016 against the NPP candidate, Conard Sangma, the younger son of the late Pruno Sangma. In fact, the current spurt of factional politics led by D D Lapang, the Meghalaya Pradesh Congress Committee (MPCC) president and the former Chief Minister and Vincent Pala, the Loksabha MP from Shillong constituency and the growing demand for leadership change in the state in the aftermath of the electoral defeat of the Congress can be seen as the adverse impact of family politics promoted by the Congress in the state.

Fourthly, after having lost political power at the Centre in 2014, the Congress party also lost its command over the Chief Ministers and leadership at the state levels. The interesting observation is that these small states always heavily depend on the central government for financial allocation for developmental projects in their states. The ruling party at the centre utilizes this opportunity to hobnobbing with opposition state government by alluring impressive financial allocations and special packages thereby bringing them under its disposal. One can cite many empirical evidences that the BJP government at the centre used its good offices to allure the Congress Chief Ministers by offering perks. In most cases, the factional feuds and the dissident party activities the ruling Congress confront in the north-eastern states have the covert support of the BJP government. The BJP was able to poach number of top and middle levels leaders from the Congress encouraging defection and factionalism.The NEDA convener is also once a heavy weight in the state leadership of Assam who later ditched his loyalty to the BJP. In the run up to the assembly election in Meghalaya and Tripura, number of sitting MLAs defected from the Congress and joined BJP and other regional parties. The assembly election in Tripura and Nagaland proves that the huge share of Congress transferred to the BJP and other regional political parties. After losing power at the Centre in 2014, the central leadership of the party found it difficult to bring the many of the state units in the north east in its fold. Sometimes, there is problem of reconnecting the local leaders with top leaders and it was often alleged by the state leaders that the central leadership declined to meet them and insensitive to the issues related to the state level organization. The NDA government at the centre often uses the developmental projects and programmes for region to augment its political base and thereby causing great destablising problem for the Congress. For the BJP the acquiring power in the northeast region is not only a political objective but to achieve a long term goal of realizing its ideological and geopolitical goal taking into account of its social milieu and strategic occasion with neighouring states like China, Bangladesh, Myanmar, etc…

Fifthly, the BJP was able to champion ethnic and regional issues among certain disgruntled sections of the society and succeeded in channelizing their anger towards the Congress. The BJP also entered into an alliance with smaller ethnic parties and quite often rising ethno regional sentiment for their cause. The BJP was also succeeded in rousing ethnic consciousness and sentiment among some marginalized communities in the region.In building alliance with the regional parties and smaller parties and fighting electoral battle with their support, the BJP went a step forward to the Congress. Since in many northeastern states, it is the dominant party and its strong visible presence forcing the Congress to not have an alliance with the regional parties. Moreover, as a National party with a broader national agenda, the congress often was not ready to comply with the ethno-regional demands of the smaller parties. The BJP though a national party, takes different approach at the state levels and often reoriented its policies and programmes to reap the electoral benefits. For instance, in BJP could a strike deal with the IPFT in Tripura, NPP in Meghalaya and NDDP in Nagaland. However, the Congress was constrained to go for such alliance in the states.

Finally, the changing nature of ethnic composition of the state has an impact on the losing support base of the Congress party in north-eastern states. Often the Congress failed to sustain its umbrella image – attracting and accommodating diverse ethnic groups and social forces – due to the communal polarization and social engineering of the BJP. For instance, the BJP's aggressive campaign against illegal migration of Bangladeshi Muslims and the communal divide created by the BJP between the Bodos and the Muslim minority community in the Bodo areas and its electoral alliance with the Bodo People's Front (BPF), the communal mobilization of Bengali Hindus in Barak valley and the upper caste Assamese Hindus in Brahmaputra valley on the hysteria of illegal migration gave much electoral dividends to the BJP and the rout of the Congress in the recently concluded Assembly election. In the Congress ruled Manipur, the stage set for the communal polarization by the BJP before the Assembly election stated to be held in the early 2017. The BJP is fishing the troubled waters in the ongoing tussle between the Hill and Valley. The BJP is alluring the Hindu Meiteiscommunity who largely dominated in the valley who constitute 40% of the state population without antagonizing the interest of the Nagas, the dominant Hill tribe and other smaller tribal communities such as Kukis, Mizos, etc.

To conclude, while the BJP adopts a multi-prolonged strategy according to the social and political chemistry in various Congress ruled north-eastern states, the Congress is often become less defensive to the onslaught of the BJP's mobilization. The BJP clinching on a strategy of concrete analysis of concrete situation in these states – either creating communal polarization, raising emotional issues, orchestrating defection and factional feuds, or highlighting the bogey of 'development'(wherever it fails to mobilize on the basis of above issues) – the Congress party is at the receiving end due to its own inner contradictions and complexities. No doubt, the crisis of the Congress in north-eastern states like that of the mainland India is disturbing as it has a larger implication for the protection of the ethnic plurality and cultural diversity, social harmony, national security of the north-eastern states of India.

Notes

1. *The Assam Tribune*, 28th August, 2014.
2. "Elect BJP, get benefits, Shah tells Manipur-BJP Chief addresses Imphall rally", *The Telegraph*, 19th April, 2015.
3. "Letter bomb jolts state politics", *The Shillong Times*, 2nd June, 2016.

4. "No Ban on Cow Slaughter in North East", *The Shillong Times*, 23rd April, 2015.
5. "BJP is not an anti-Christian Party: Meghalaya, Nalin S. Kohli", *The Economic Times*, 14th July, 2015.

References

Bijukumar, V. (2016), "Shape-Shifting Parties", The Hindu, 20 September.

Chapter - 4

Ascending BJP: Mobilisation Strategy and Alliance Building

The North-East India (NEI), known for its ethnic diversity, identity politics, demands for autonomy and secessionism, extremist activities, self-determination, political defections, prevalence of draconian laws, human rights violations, is witnessing new developments since 1990s due to the entry of Hindu nationalist forces. For a long time, in the region, the Bharatiya Janata Party (BJP) was almost a non-entity and remained as the strong hold of Congress and regional parties. However, since 1990sthis border region with great ethnic complexity emerged as an attractive destination for the Hindu nationalist forces not only because of its electoral ambition but of its larger agenda ofbringing the tribal communities into the Hindutva fold.The emergence of BJP, whose ideology and programmes are often contradict the ethos of the region, as a potential political force has to be analysed in the larger context of the decline of ethno-regional parties and the crisis of secular and progressive forces. By expanding its mass base in NEI, the BJP wants to shed its image as a North-Indian Hindu Nationalist Party and to projectits image as an all inclusive political entity crosscutting caste, region and religion and trying to occupy the vacuum created by the Congress and other regional parties.

Since the NEI as a region of distinct social and cultural identities, BJP realisedthat a common universal ideology is not applicable and adopted multiple mobilization strategies according to the political and social reality of the states. In other words, the BJP's policies and mobilization strategy in the region differ according to the social, political, geographical and demographic nature of the states. The 'party with difference' is adopting a strategy of concrete analysis of the concrete situation in various states, keeping its hard core Hindutva in its national agenda. Setting aside the core communal issues such as religious conversion, ban on cow slaughter, etc. which the BJP often raised and pushed through at the national level, the issues gained prominence include development, security, corruption, illegal migration, youth empowerment, etc. As Bhattacharjee argues that "given the complexity of the demography of this region that consists of a mélange of races, ethnicities, faiths, customs and cultures, and the multiplicity of issues, it becomes extremely difficult for an ideology riding on religious nationalism to identify common ground that enables it to make a dent in the region" (Bhattacharjee, 2016:80). Further, the mobilization strategy not only confine to political but also cultural – either appropriating cultural personalities or narratives or constructing an alternative cultural narrative in the place of the existing dominant one. For instance, in Assam, the party is appropriating the cultural legacy of Srimanta Sankardev, a medieval saint, and in Nagaland, Rani Gaidinliu, Naga spiritual leader and freedom fighter.

Another reason for the adoption of multiple strategies in NEI is the compulsions of the state level leadership of the party. Taking into account of the socio-cultural specificity of the region, the issues raised at the national level by the BJP often go against its interests as many regional leaders as they find it difficult convince the common masses. For instance, when the belligerent BJP talks about banning of beef, the great realization that it would adversely affect its electoral prospects in the various north eastern states. The BJP thus find it difficult to explain its position on beef ban in North-east India as majority of tribal population consider beef as a staple food. As a result, the protests even emanated from the Ministers and Members of Parliament from the North-east. In response to Mukhtar Abbas Naqvi's remark that those who want to eat beef can go to Pakistan, the BJP leader and Union Minister Kiran Rijju who is currently a Member of Parliament from Arunachal Pradesh even declared that "I eat beef. I am from Arunachal Pradesh. Can somebody stop me? So let us not be touchy about some body's practices"[1]. Dissident voice against Naqvi's remark even came from Sarbananda Sonowal from Assam and Meghalaya BJP president Khlur Singh Lyndoh, and Manipur BJP's general secretary M. Asnikumar Singh.

Though the BJP confronts with the local realities and compulsions, it has not abandoned its larger project in the tribal belt of this region. However, putting the real agenda under backburner, the BJP time and again talks about its "development plank" in this region. For instance, based on its regional specificity, the party is able to prepare a vision documents for each of the north-eastern states. In Manipur, the document stresses on building of arterial roads and in Meghalaya it focuses on areas like skill development. The BJP often cites the previous NDA government's efforts in the development of the region such as the creation of the Ministry of Development of North East Region (DoNER) and the launching of Look East Policy during the Vajpayee regime. The DoNER was formed in September 2001, is responsible for the matters relating to the planning, execution and monitoring of development scheme and projects in the region. In another significant development, on 23rd August, 2013 the BJP launched the North East India Sampark Cell (NEISC) aimed at strengthen its emotional integration with other parts of the country. Among other things, the Cell aims to check the illegal migrants in the region as it challenges development, security and national integration of NEI.

General Election 2014

In the run up to the general election 2014, the region witnessed electrifying campaign by Narendra Modi who promised to overall development of the region. On 8th February, 2014, in an election rally in Manipur, Modi talked about the controversial India-Myanmar border fencing, corruption, unemployment and the failure of the Congress government in Manipur. Reminding the killing of Arunachal student, Nido Tania on 29th January 2014 in New Delhi and assault of two Manipuri girls in New Delhi as a "national shame" Modi demanded justice for the North East victims. In another election rally on 22nd February 2014 Modi asserted that after May (date of the declaration of the election result) illegal immigrants will have to leave India. He asserted that "there is no place of infiltrators from Bangladesh who have come to further votebank politics agenda of others. They should be sent back. At the same time, not Assam alone but all states must accommodate Hindus coming from Bangladesh and offer them a life with dignity".[2]

Before analyzing the electoral performance of various parties in the NEI, it is pertinent to analyse the nature and composition of electoral politics in the region. Of the 545 Parliamentary seats, the eight North-Eastern states altogether send only 25 representatives to the Lower House of the Parliament were not considered as a decisive voice in national politics. Due to the low numerical strength, the political significance of NEI was largely reduced during the one party dominance and one party rule at the Centre. However, in the era of coalition politics at the centre, the electoral politics in the region often find much attention from the national parties and alliances. In the 2014 general election, like the rest of India, the BJP followed an alliance strategy of 'go it alone' wherever it has strength and a forge an alliance with regional forces wherever it was not a decisive force to counter the Congress. For instance, it forged an alliance with Naga Peoples Front (NPF) in Nagaland and in Meghalaya it extended support to National People's Party (NPP) of P.A. Sangma. In Mizoram, BJP formed a coalition of eight state parties under the banner of United Front led by the Mizo National Front (MNF) to fight against the Congress candidate of the lone Parliamentary constituency of the Christian dominated hilly state.

The General Election 2014 brought mixed development in the politics of NEI. Of the 25 seats spreading across the region, the Congress could win only 8 seats while the National Democratic Alliance (NDA) secured 10 seats (BJP-8, NPP -1, NPF -1), Communist Party of India (Marxist) (CPIM) retained 2 seats, All India United Democratic Front (AIUDF) -3, Sikkim Democratic Front (SDF) and Independent one seat each. It has to be reminded that in 2009 election, of the 25 seats in the region, the Congress secured 13 seats, BJP – 4, CPIM – 2, Asom Gana Parishad (AGP) – 1, AIUDF – 1, Bodo People's Front – 1, NPF -1, SDF -1.Nationalist Congress Party (NCP)-1.Apart from winning seats in Assam and Arunachal Pradesh, in other NE states like Manipur, Meghalaya, Sikkim and Tripura, the party's candidates secured 11.98%, 9.16%, 2.39% and 5.77% votes respectively.

The performance of the BJP in the 2014 general election is not an isolated event and it has to be put in right perspective. Since the general election1991, the BJP is improving its electoral strength in various states in NEI. Apart from emerging as a major force in Assam and Arunachal Pradesh, the saffron party could intrude in many other states posing a challenge to the Congress, regional parties and the left parties. In some states, the opposition space vacated by the regional parties is filled by the BJP making inroads into its social base. The regional agenda of many regional parties are taken by the Hindu nationalist party and approaching to the new social groups and communities with renewed regional agenda. In the recent past it could attract leaders from various political parties and make an alliance with the regional players.

Statewise Vote Share of BJP in General Elections in NEI (in %)

General	*Assam Election*	*Arunachal*	*Manipur Pradesh*	*Mizoram*	*Meghalaya*	*Nagaland*	*Sikkim*	*Tripura*
1991	9.60	6.11	8.10	-	6.89	3.00	-	2.99
1996	15.92	17.41	5.25	-	9.13	-	-	6.5
1998	24.47	21.75	12.61	2.94	9.01	-	-	8.19
1999	29.84	16.30	1.02	-	9.45	5.12	-	12.82
2004	22.94	53.85	20.65	-	8.63	-	-	7.82
2009	16.21	37.17	9.49	-	-	-	1.77	3.38
2014	36.86	46.62	11.98	-	9.16	-	2.39	5.77

Source: Data drawn from www. eci.nic.in

The astounding victory of BJP in the 2014 general election under Narendra Modi's leadership gave further boost to the party as it decided to expand its mass base beyondits traditional strong hold of the Hindi heartland. Though the NEI was the main focus of the RSS for a long times due to various reasons, the ascendancy of the BJP government under Modi and the leadership of Amit Shah augmented this further. Modi made number of visits to different states and raised the issue of development and security. In the renewed strategy of the BJP, NEI emerged as focal point of mobilization and further consolidation after the 2014 general election. The BJP President Amit Shah's ten days tour of all eight North-Eastern states during the month of April 2015 to strengthen the party organization in the region can be seen in the larger context of party's strategy to go beyond its traditional strongholds. In fact, this was the first extensive visit of any BJP national president to all the eight north eastern states. In different states, Amit Shah raised certain pertinent issues which he thought that bring the party more closely to the people. In the aftermath of 2014 election, the party desperately entered alliance with smaller regional parties and orchestrated defections in the major regional and national parties and thereby by destabilized the Congress ruled state governments.

Assam, the Gateway to North-East India

Among all the states in the NEI, Assam is considered to be the gate way of BJP to the rest of the states in the region. For quite some time, the BJP is turning its much attention to the political developments in Assam and trying to occupy the opposition space vacated by the Asom Gana Parishad (AGP). It has to be reminded that Assam is a complex society which constitutes Assamese Hindus, Bengalis, migrant Bangladeshis and tribal population considered to be a fertile ground for communal tensions. The Assamese Hindus are dominant in Brahmaputra valley and the Bengalis are dominant in the Barrak valley. Initially, the BJP's traditional stronghold was the Bengali dominated Barrak valley. As Srikanth argues that "although the BJP did not initially get the support of the Assamese Hindus, as early as in 1991, it could make a dent into the Bengali dominated Barak valley region, where it won parliamentary seats from Silchar and Karimganj constituencies (in 1999)" (Srikanth, 1999: 3413). Recently, in the Brahmaputra valley too, the BJP is wooing the Assamese Hindus by raking up the issue of illegal migration of Bengali Muslims and its impact on the Assamese society. It accused the Congress of playing votebank politics of Bengali migrants. In fact, the BJP's promise to check illegal immigration presumably gained its wider acceptability among both Assamese elite of caste Hindus and the Bengali elite of the state.

In a significant move to reach out the Bodos, on 29th December, 2014, Amit Shah constituted a five-member committee headed by its senior leader S S Ahluwalia to visit and review the condition of tribal victim of National Democratic Front of Bodoland -**Songbijit** (NDFB (S)) violence in Assam relief camps. More than seventy tribals were killed in the violence in Assam in attacks by pro Bodo militant groups in December 2014. In fact, few days before the visit of Shah in April, the BJP government was contemplating to delink Assam from the Land Boundary Agreement (LBA) with Bangladesh. The Protocol to the 1974 LBA, signed on 6th September 2011, paves the way for settlement of the outstanding land boundary issues between the two countries. The 2011 Protocol has been prepared with the full support and concurrence of the State governments concerned – Assam, Meghalaya, Tripura and West Bengal. As agreed upon through several rounds of negotiations started during UPA-II, Assam is set to lose around 268.39 acres in the final arrangement with Bangladesh under LBA, but does not get any land in return. West Bengal is supposed to lose 1,957 acres, but get 2,398 acres, while Meghalaya will lose 41 acres and get 250 acres in return from Bangladesh. Assam giving up land is part of settling a disputed 6.1 km stretch that's been with Bangladesh since Partition. For quite some time, this is an emotive issue in Assam's polarised and volatile politics and BJP's Assam unit has always opposed the land loss. The BJP top brass considers Assam, a major Northeastern state that goes to polls next year, a winning prospect and these poll calculations may result in delinking LBA with Bangladesh for now. Due to the growing resentment against the LBA in Assam, the BJP is revising the actual plan and accordingly the Indo-Bangladesh LBA will now involve only West Bengal, Tripura and Meghalaya on the Indian side. The Constitution Amendment Bill to ratify the Indo-Bangladesh Land Boundary Agreement is likely to be introduced in Parliament with a major change by delinking Assam.[3] Prior to 1991, the

BJP was not a significant force in the electoral politics of Assam. In 1991 Assembly elections, however, the BJP won 10 seats out of 48 Assembly seats it contested securing a vote share of 6.4%. In the 1991 general election, the BJP won two seats with a vote share of 9.6 per cent. In the 1996 general election its vote share went up to 15.9% with one seat. However, in the Assembly election in 1996 it could manage 10.4 per cent votes winning 4 seats. In 2001 Assembly election with the alliance of AGP the party bagged 8 seats and 35.8 per cent seats. In 2004 general election the BJP won 2 seats and the 2006 Assembly election won 12 seats with a vote share of 11.98 per cent. Like elsewhere in India, initially, the BJP allied with the regional party, AGP in 2006 assembly election and 2009 general election. Setting aside its national agenda and issues, the BJP was able to rake up regional issues such as illegal migration, detection and deportation of foreigners which were once raised by the AGP. In fact, the BJP hijacked the regional agenda of AGP, especially on the issue of illegal migrants. However, though BJP wakes up the migration issue, it only focuses on the Muslims not the Bengalis Hindus whom it considered as the mass base.

In the 2014 general election by winning 7 seats (of the total 14 seats) and securing a vote share of 36.86% the BJP is now emerging as credible alternative to Congress focusing on 2016 Assembly elections. The Bodo People's Front (BPF), former ally of Congress, showing its inclination to BJP for the development of Bodo Territorial Council (BTC). It has to be reminded that the BPF ended its ties with the Congress and withdrawn its ministers from the Gogoi government instigating Bodo tribals against Bangladeshi Muslim migration raising the bogey of threats from migrants. Moreover, the anti-Muslim sentiment generated in Bodo areas of Assam describing it as anti-Muslim went in favour of the BJP. Moreover, the tea tribes traditionally voted for the Congress moved to BJP, especially Dibrugarh and Jorhat where the BJP put up the candidates belonging to the tea community in the 2014 election. In February 2015 municipal polls the BJP made a clean sweep winning 21 municipal boards and 24 town committees compared to 2009 elections when it won only at 5 municipal boards and 11 town committees.

The BJP's growing influence in the state politics was contributed by multiple factors. Firstly, the strong anti-incumbency and corruption charges against the three consecutive term of the Congress government of Tarun Gogoi. Secondly, during the tenure of the Gogoi regime witnessed many clashes in the Bodo areas in the State especially between Bodos and Muslims. The government's failure to contain the frequent clashes and the civil administration's failure to rehabilitate the victims of clashes added further blow to the Gogoi administration.Thirdly, in the run up to the Assembly election, many Congress legislators joined the BJP which overshadowed its electoral prospects. In August, 2015, an embarrassment to the state Congress, former Minister Himanta Biswa Sarma joined the BJP. Himanta who was Tarun Gogoi's trusted aid disillusioned with the Congress due the realization that his political ambition to become the Chief Minister of the state was dashed by the Congress as the Gogoi is promoting his son Gaurav Gogoi. While contesting such argument Assam Congress leader Kishore Bhattacharjee said that "Gaurav's entry into politics has no role in their differences. It started way back when (now Congress MLA) Pijush Hazarika was elected the Assam Pradesh Youth Congress President in June 2008. Then there were speculations in 2012 that Tarun Gogoi would resign as Chief Minister and become the country's Vice-President, Sarma was really hoping to become the Chief Minister".[4] Further, a section of Congress is questioning chief minister Tarun Gogoi for promoting his son, the Lok Sabha MP from as his political heir in the state. In November, nine Congress MLAs joined BJP.

Further, the erosion of ethno-regional nationalism championed by the AGP in the eighties went into the advantage of the BJP. It is to be reminded that the Assam movement (1979-84) sowed the seeds of ethno-regionalism which witnessed the emergence of AGP making inroads into state politics eroding the Congress mass base. The AGP which came into power with the cause of 'Asomiya Nationality' and the issue of illegal migration, in course of time, diluted its stand on Illegal Migrants Determination by Tribunal IM(DT) Act, 1983 due to compulsions of electoral politics. As a result, there was a growing disillusionment among the Hindus against the AGP, this created a fertile ground for the BJP in Assam. Over a time, the BJP used the issue of illegal migration of Muslims for expanding its mass base in the state. As Srikanth argues that "the politics of regional identity had kept Hindutva at bay in Assam for over two decades. But the AGP government's poor performance and the bogey of Muslim fundamentalism led Bengali and Assamese caste Hindus to the BJP" (Srikanth, 1999: 3412). As a result, the AGP, the prominent regional political force is declining its space in the state. Moreover, AGP's alliance with BJP in the 2006 Assembly and 2009 Loksabha election cost more to the AGP. The BJP could grow at the expense of the decline political space of the AGP. It is argued that the traditional support base of AGP – the Assamese Hindus, the Assamese Muslim and tribals – gradually shifted their allegiance to other political parties (Mahanta, 2014:20). The regional agenda of the AGP, especially detection and deportation of illegal Bangladeshi migrants were hijacked by the BJP. In the recent past, many leaders of the AGP joined the BJP adding further boost to the BJP in the state. In December 2015, the BJP constituted its campaign panel for the Assembly elections 2016 with number of former AASU, AGP leaders.

New Leadership and Renewed Strategy

The appointment of Sarbananda Sonowal, the Union Minister of State for Sports, as the president of the State BJP in 2015 gave further boost to the saffron party. Sonowal, the former leader of the AASU and subsequently MLA of the AGP switched over to the BJP some time back, is a crusader against illegal migration of Bangladeshi in Assam. In 2012, he accused the illegal migrants of deteriorating the life of the indigenous people of Assam. He said that in the last 32 years the indigenous people of Assam have been cornered and pushed to the status of minority due to the huge influx of illegal immigrants from Bangladesh.[5] It has to be reminded that the illegal migration from Bangladesh is a sensitive issue in Assam as it developed far reaching consequences in the political, economic and socio-cultural life of the people. As it stated earlier, the Assam movement which put the demand for the detection and deportation of illegal migrants (often used as 'foreigners') in the state. In its effort to end the movement the Indian government formulated the IM (DT) Act 1983 to protect the interest of Assam. According to the Act, anybody settled in Assam before March 25, 1971 was a legal citizen. However, rest of India, the cut of date for acquiring Indian citizenship is July 9, 1948. Further, the person accused had to do nothing to prove his/her citizenship whereas the compliant had to prove that someone was illegal. The Act also provides special protections against undue harassment to the minorities affected by Assam Agitation. The Act is applicable only to Assam while rest of the states in India is covered by the Foreigners Act, 1946. The Act it was viewed that the provision designed to make it difficult for authorities to identify, leave alone, deport illegal Bangladeshi from Assam.

In a petition filed by Sarbananda Sonowal, who was with AGP contended that the IM(DT) is only encouraging vote bank politics without addressing the problem of illegal migrants. In July 2005, the Supreme Court observed that the Act was the biggest barrier to deportation of the illegal migrants from the state. The Supreme Court in its 114 page judgment stated that "the Act has created the biggest hurdle and is the main impediment or barrier in the identification and deportation of illegal migrants". Further, it observed that, "the presence of such a large number of illegal migrants from Bangladesh, which runs into millions, in fact an aggression on the state of Assam and also contributed significantly in causing serious internal disturbances in the shape of insurgency of alarming propositions".[6]

The invalidation of the IM(DT) Act by the Supreme Court in 2005 further communally polarized the state. When both BJP and AGP welcomed the court verdict, the Muslim communities expressed their anguish. The BJP claimed that 'discriminatory' Act failed to effectively identify and deport illegal migrants in the state and the Supreme Court observation was a setback to the Congress which is using this as a vote bank politics. After the Supreme Court verdict, the BJP took out a rally in Guwhati in July 2005 demanding the deportation of all illegal Bangladeshi nationals from Assam. It has to be reminded that the RSS and the BJP supported the Assam movement to end the illegal migration in the state. Over a time, the Party shared the sentiments of the AGP on the issue of illegal migration and supported this provision in the Assam Accord of 1984 between the AASU and the Rajiv Gandhi government.

The Supreme Court's invalidation of the IM(DT) Act was viewed by the All India United Democratic Front (AIUDF), the Muslim political party as the inability of the Congress to defend the Act. However, foreseeing the possible minority resentment against the Congress which had to face the Assembly election in 2006, the Prime Minister, Manmohan Singh constituted a Group of Ministers to examine the fall out of the repealing of the IM(DT) Act, particularly its impact on minorities. The BJP and the AGP criticized this action and describes as the backdoor entry of the Act.

Even after ten years of the repeal of the IM(DT) Act, the issue continues to haunt the politics of the State. The BJP accused the Congress of following a policy of appeasement which created grave security implications for the country. It says the large scale intrusion of illegal Bangladeshi immigrants has significantly altered the demographic complexion of North-Eastern states and has serious long-term political, social and economic implications.[7]In September 2012, Ram Madhav, the RSS leader once said that, "we need to detect and defranchise the Bangladeshi infiltrators from the country. There is very little done by the central government to deport them, just 1 per cent per 5 days, though the rate of infiltration is about 6, 000 per day"[8]. The BJP's Vision Document released before the General Election 2014 contained a separate section on North East which promised to put an end to infiltration from Bangladesh and vigorously pursue the 3 D – formula – Detect, Delete and Deport (illegal migrants from Assam).[9]

In his visit to Assam on 26th April, 2015 the BJP president asserted that "Bangladeshi infiltrators have taken away everything. They have taken away land of the Assamese people. They have taken away your jobs. They have eaten into the development funds. Yet the Congress government does not have the guts to touch them. It is only the BJP which can free Assam from the clutches of the Bangladeshis,"[10] He also took credit for the process of updating the National Register of Citizens currently going on in the state and said the NDA government had earmarked Rs 140 crore to the state for this purpose. In his opinion, "once the NRC is revised and updated, all the Bangladeshi infiltrators will be exposed". Accusing the Congress of not stopping illegal migration as it is playing vote bank politics, the BJP president promised to stop illegal migration of Bangladeshis into Assam.[11]

The BJP president Amit Shah's visit in fact, sounded the bugle for the electoral campaign for the 2014 Assembly election in the state. Setting the agenda for the campaign for the Election, Shah was categorical that "next elections will be fought on this issue. Assam poll will be for freeing the state of illegal Bangladeshi migrants. Assam polls will also be for development of Assam and North-East".[12] Perhaps, the BJP's communal outburst against Muslims which can influence electoral verdict of about 40 Assembly constituencies spreading over nine parliamentary constituencies in the state can be seen in the context of the initial indication of 2011 census show that Assam records the highest rise in Muslims population in India. It recorded highest decadal rise in the Muslim population from 30.9% in 2001 to 34.2% in 2011.[13] In the Socio Economic and Caste Census 2011 also Assam records the second highest rise in Muslim population (34.2%) in India after Jammu and Kashmir (68.3%). This often finds communal polarization by the BJP. The BJP often depict majority of the Muslims as "illegal Immigrants" from Bangladesh which cause imbalance to the state demography and socio-cultural mosaic of the state.

The BJP while criticizing the illegal migration from Bangladesh, in the recent past took another turn in this issue. The Party now welcoming the migration of Hindus from Bangladesh stating that those Hindus who face religious persecution in that would be accommodated to India and would be given citizenship. Shah in his visit to the state asserted that the BJP would provide all support to Hindus who came to India due to religious persecution and promised that the Hindu refugees from Bangladesh will be given Indian citizenship if the BJP comes to power in Assam in 2016 Assembly election. The communal fervor of the BJP is explicated when it was critic of Muslim migrants, and taking the burden of supporting Hindus who came to India because of the so called harassment and religious discrimination. The saffron party's surprise move, however created certain resentment in the state when organizations such as the AASU and the Assam Jatiyatabadi Yuva Saba Parishad (AJYCP) who alleges that it is in fact diluting its stand on Bangladeshi migration problem. However, some sections of the state BJP felt that this would lead to the alienation of Assamese educated and middle class away from the party and the need of the hour is to take the issue of illegal migration in its true spirit.

Assam Assembly Election 2016

The verdict of Assam Assembly election brought some dramatic developments in the politics of the state. It not only brought down the three consecutive Congress governments led by Tarun Gogoi but also consolidated the electoral base of the BJP in Assam. The BJP could form its first government in the North-East India through election with the alliance of the AGP and Bodoland People's Front (BPF). The BJP, in fact, earlier entered into an alliance with former allies such as the AGP and the Bodo People's Front against its earlier stand of 'going it alone' in the Assembly election in May 2016. The change of strategy to alliance with the regional parties emerged out of its realization from the result of the Bihar Assembly election in the late 2015where the Party miserably failed to capture the political power to the strong Janta Dal (United) (JDU), Rashtriya Janata Dal (RJD) and Congress alliance. Secondly, the realization among the BJP leadership that the combined strength of the three party alliance can combat the Congress in the state by consolidating the anti-Congress votes in favour of the three party alliance.

The BJP's entry into Assam shed its image as a north Indian party and moved towards as an All India party. The Party made its presence across the state, region both in the Brahmaputra Valley and Barrak valley. In the Bengali dominated Barrak valley which comprises of districts such as Cachar, Karimganj and Hailakandi the BJP won 8 out of 15 seats leaving AIUDF four, and the Congress three. The BJP made inroads into the Muslim dominated area as it won 15 seats in 49 Muslim-dominated constituencies in the state. Apart from winning all seats in Guwhati city, the BJP swept all 7 seats in Dibrugarh and all 3 seats in Karbi Anglong. Moreover, the BJP was able to penetrate in the tea belt showing its impressive win. Interestingly, for the first time in the history of Dima Hasao, the BJP candidate B B Hagjer won the 16 Haflong (ST) constituency. In the Barrak valley, the BJP's lone Muslim winner Animul Hague Laskar, a businessman, scripted history by wining from the Sonai constituency.

Assam is the first state in the north-eastern region, the BJP could form its own government with the support of the AGP and Bodoland People's Front (BPF) ending the fifteen consecutive years of Congress government led by Tarun Gogoi. In May 2016, when the election resulted declared in the 126 seats in the State Assembly the BJP won 60 seats with a vote share of 42%, its alliance partner AGP secured 14 seats with a vote share of 8%. The BPF, another partner in the BJP alliance won 12 seats with a vote share of 3.9%. The BPF, former ally of Congress, initially moved towards the BJP for the development of Bodo Territorial Council (BTC). It has to be reminded that the BPF ended its ties with the Congress and withdrawn its ministers from the Gogoi government instigating Bodo tribals against Bangladeshi Muslim migration raising the bogey of threats from migrants. In 2011 election, the BPF won 12 seats and joined the Gogoi government and broken its alliance with Congress in 2014. Moreover, the anti-Muslim sentiment generated in Bodo areas of Assam describing it as anti-Muslim went in favour of the BJP. The three party pre poll alliances thus bagged 86 seats with two-third majority in the Assembly. The incumbent Congress party however could secure only 26 seats by winning 31% vote share. The AIUDF which claimed its base in the Muslim community won 13 seats with the vote share of 13%. It has to be reminded that in the 2011 Assembly election the BJP won only 5 seats against the 78 seats of the ruling Congress party. The AGP won 10 seats, the AIUDF won 18 and the BPF only 12. By aligning with BJP in the Assembly election, the AGP strengthened its position in the state. The AGP president Atul Bora elected to the Assembly in Bokakhat constituency. However, the AIUDF chief Dhubri and present Loksabha MP lost to the Congress candidate Wajed Ali Choudhury from Salmara south constituency.

Electoral Performance (Total Seats: 126)

Party	*Seats Won*	*Vote Percentage*
BJP	60	42%
Congress (I)	26	31%
AGP	14	8%
AIUDF	13	13%
BPF	12	3.9%

The BJP's surge in Assam in the Assembly election can be analysed in the context of its strategic approach in the state. Firstly, the BJP could muster the tacit support of the Bodos, the Tiwas and the Rabhas which enabled the BJP to make inroads to the tribal areas and thereby projected as a tribal friendly party. As Misra argues that Apart from its understanding with the AGP, the BJP leadership made another master move in bringing within the foldof the BJP alliance the Tiwa and Rabha organisations. This gave the party a tribal friendly face and helped its fortunes notonly in Tiwa and Rabha areas but also in the hill constituencies of Karbi Anglong and Dima Hasao. Here it virtually replacedthe Congress that had held power for decades (Misra, 2016: 21).

Moreover, the BJP's projection of Sarbananda Sonowal who belonged to the plain tribal community of Kachari, as the chief ministerial candidate gave more tribal attraction to the Party. Secondly, the election saw a strong Hindu consolidation behind the BJP as both Bengali Hindus and Assamese Hindus supported the BJP. However, the Muslim vote (both Assamese and Bengali Muslims) split into the Congress and AIUDF. Thirdly, the BJP's pre poll alliance with the AGP and the BPF consolidated anti Congress votes in its favour. Initially there were local protests from both the BJP and AGP in certain regions like Bongaigaon, Sivasagar, Sonitpur, Amguri and Tezpur against the alliance. However, the BJP leadership could overcome the dissent voices in forging the alliance. Fourthly, the BJP succeeded in bringing Tarun Gogoi's most trusted Himanta Biswa Sarma served as the minister of Health and Education in Gogoi government to the party, who in fact the mastermind in the BJP's alliance with other two regional parties in the state. The seven of the ten sitting Congress MLAs who left parent party and won on BJP tickets.

Further, inspite of the above factors which went in favour of the BJP's fortunes in the state, the BJP's victory more related to the systematic activities of the RSS in the state which has been quiet systematically working in the tribal belt of the state for years. It has to be reminded that in 1979, the RSS founded its first school, Shishu Shiksha Samiti, in the state and about 500 Ekal Vidyalayas was created by the RSS in the state overtime. Though the BJP is a new entry into the politics of NEI, the RSS and other Sangh Parivar organizations have engaged in deep rooted activities in the region The RSS for a long time spreading its roots in the state by appropriating Assam's medieval saint Srimanta Sankardev for political gains. Sankardev led a reformist neo-vaishnavite movement against Brahmanism (Bhattacharjee, 2016). It also actively supported the anti-infiltration of Bangladeshi movements in the Assam movement of 1979-84 as it believed that illegal infiltration is a threat to national security. The strong presence of RSS in the region is attracting youth over the development plank. In the last decades there is exponential growth of RSS training camps in Assam and in other states focusing on tribal issues. In fact, in the 2014 general election in Assam, the vigorous campaign unleashed by the RSS went to the BJP's kitty.[14]

Arunachal Pradesh

In the north east region, apart from Assam, the BJP built up its strong base in Arunachal Pradesh and over the years, the BJP's vote share has increased and made inroads into the electoral base of the Congress. In 2004 general election the BJP could win all two seats in the state with a vote share of 53.85%. Though, in the subsequent general election in 2009, the party lost all two seats to the Congress and its vote share reduced to 37.17%, in 2014 general election the BJP wrested one seat from the ruling Congress with an vote share of 46.62%. In 2014 general election, the BJP's spectacular victory in one of the two seats added an advantage to the NDA in the region. In the State Assembly election held along with the General Election 2014, the BJP own 11 seats with a vote share of 30.97% in the 60 member Assembly against its performance in 2009 when the BJP could secure only three seats.

In the political strategic front, the Party like elsewhere in the NEI, adopts multiple strategy. For instance, in the border sensitive state of Arunachal Pradesh the BJP often raises the bogey of protecting the territorial integrity of the state. It has to be reminded that China claims Arunachal Pradesh as part of Southern Tibet. Secondly, the more importantly, like elsewhere in the North East India, BJP raises the emotive issues of illegal migrants and the plight of the indigenous population in the state. The party raises the Chakma-Hajong issue and accused the Congress of aggravating the issue. It has to be reminded that the Chakma-Hajong were inhabitants of the Chittagong Hill Tracts of erstwhile East Pakistan (now Bangladesh) who had to flee as their land was submerged by the Kaptai dam in the 1960s. The Chakmas are Buddhist, and Hajongs are Hindus also faced religious persecution in East Pakistan. Between 1964 to 1969 they came to India as refugees and were allowed to be settled in the then North-East Frontier Agency (the present Arunachal Pradesh) administered by the Ministry of External Affairs through the Assam Governor. While they were originally treated as refugees, and subsequently New Delhi decided to grant them citizenship under Section 5(i)(a) of the Citizenship Act following a joint statement by the PMs of India and Bangladesh in 1972.

In 1987 when Arunachal Pradesh became the state in the Indian Union, the All Arunachal Pradesh Students' Union (AAPSU) opposed the settling of the Chakmas and Hajongs inhabitants in the state. The refugee population had, meanwhile, been growing, and the 1996 white paper said their numbers had increased more than 300% from the original 14,888 persons of 2,748 families settled in 1964-69 to over 60,000 in 1995. In 2005, the Election Commission issued general guidelines to include the Chakmas and Hajongs in the state's electoral rolls. The AAPSU contested this by saying that the indigenous communities of the state, pose a threat to their identity and culture. According to AAPSU, the population of the refugees has swollen to approximately 60,000 as against the 57 families originally settled in 1966 in Diyun.

The plight of the most of the Chakmas and Hajongs refugees are worse in the state as they face human rights violations and all sorts of deprivation in the form of lack of employment opportunites, medical facilities and frequent termination of their trade licenses. In the light of the inhuman condition of the Chakmas and Hajongs and the growing demand of granting citizenship rights, in September 2015 the Supreme Court said that the Chakmas and Hajongs had a right to be granted citizenship and they could not be discriminated against in any manner. Subsequently, on 16th October, 2015, the Supreme Court, finally granted citizenship to Chakmas and Hajongs which invited strong protest within the State and Delhi by the AAPSU. According to it, once citizenship is granted, the indigenous tribal community reduced into a minority. The student body staged a march in Delhi holding placards which read, among others: "Is Arunachal dumping ground for foreigners", "If Arunachal is part of India, listen to the voice of Arunachalees" and "Despite China's repeated claim(s), we have shown our patriotism, now where do we go?"[15]

The BJP often blames the ruling Congress for the Chakmas and Hajongs settlement issue. The state BJP spokesman asserted that "Prime Minister Jawaharlal Nehru made a blunder by accepting the Buddhist majority Chittagong Hill Tracts to be part of East Pakistan (now Bangladesh) which was created for Muslims, and this forced the Chakmas and Hajongs to migrate into India and allowed to settle in the area" He even accused the Indira Gandhi regime of entering into an agreement with Sheikh Mujibar Rehman, the then Prime Minister of Bangladesh and decided to grant citizenship to Chakmas and Hajongs under the Section 5 (1) of a Citizenship Act". [16] In short, the citizenship issue emerged as new political strategy of the BJP in the state to woo the Arunachalees and to strengthen its base in the strategically contentious border state of India.

In Arunachal Pradesh, the BJP has a history of adopting a strategy of orchestrating defections in the Congress party, bringing down the Congress regimes, supporting the rebel leaders to form government with its support and later merging with the BJP. Perhaps, the BJP's first ever attempt to destablise the Congress governments in the northeastern states goes back to 2003 with the Arunachal Pradesh experiment. In July 2003, during the Vajpayee led National Democratic Alliance (NDA) government, the dissident Congress leader Gegong Apang toppled the Mukut Mithi led Congress government with 34 Congress MLAs and became the Chief Minister of the state under the newly floated United Democratic Front (UDF) which later merged to the BJP. When the United Progressive Alliance (UPA) government came into power at the centre, however, Apang rejoined the Congress Party and contested the next election under the Congress symbol. In 2016, the BJP orchestrated defection in the ruling Congress party which saw political instability in the state culminating the resignation of the Nabam Tuki government and the House was under suspended animation. Subsequently, President rule was imposed under Article 356 on the recommendation of Union cabinet with the allegation of the constitutional failure in the state. On 19 February, 2016 the dissident Congress leader Kalikho Pul finally overthrew the Tuki government with the outside support of the BJP which have 11 members. Though the Congress had the support of 47 MLAs in the 60 member house, 21 of them supported the rebel leader Pul which later formed the People Party of Arunachal. By encouraging defection, overthrowing the government and installing a government led by the rebel Congress leader with its outside support, the BJP score over Congress in the border state.

Politics in Arunachal Pradesh assumed a new turn in the context of the mass migration of Congress MLAs including its Chief Minister Prema Khandu to the People's Party of Arunachal (PPA), a regional outfit with the support of the BJP. When 43 Congress MLAs joined the regional party, the Congress strength in the Assembly reduced to one as the former Chief Minister Nabam Tuki remains as the lone Congress MLA. In the 60 member state Assembly which has the current strength of 57, as the status of two MLAs, Wanglam Sawin and Gabriel D Wangsu pending with the Speaker for the disqualification issue and the death of Kalikho Pul, the former Chief Minister, emergence of PPA as the single largest party is a political victory for the BJP.

The current course of events in the state can be seen as a logical continuation of the political developments taking place in the border state since the close of the previous year. For quite some time, dissident activities both in the Congress party and government are taking place and the central leadership adopted a lukewarm attitude towards it leading to further aggravation. In December 2014 when Nabam Tuki dropped Kalikho Pul, the Health and Family Welfare Minister in the cabinet reshuffle. Amid growing anti party activities in the state, which posed a challenge to the government, the Congress expelled Pul alleging anti-party activities in April, 2015.

In the beginning of the year, the BJP orchestrated defection in the ruling Congress party which saw political instability in the state culminating in the resignation of the Nabam Tuki government and the House was kept under suspended animation. Subsequently, President Rule was imposed under Article 356 on the recommendation of Union Cabinet citing constitutional failure in the state. On 19 February 2016 the dissident Congress leader Kalikho Pul finally overthrew the Tuki government with the outside support of the BJP. Although the Congress had the support of 47 MLAs in the 60-member house, 21 of them supported the rebel leader Pul who later formed the People's Party of Arunachal (PPA). By encouraging defection, overthrowing the incumbent government and installing a new government led by the rebel Congress leader with its outside support, the BJP scored over the Congress in the border state.

However, in a major setback to the BJP and the Centre government, the Supreme Court on 13 July ordered restoration of the Congress government under Nabam Tuki, saying the "clock should be turned back". It quashed the decision of the Governor Rajkhowa in February this year as the violation of the Constitution. The Supreme Court order had jubilated the Congress as it termed as the victory of democracy in the state and setback for BJP's effort to dislodge the Congress regimes in India. However, the governor set the 16 July as the deadline for proving majority in the Assembly though Tuki sought at least ten days time for proving the government's majority. Though the chief minister Tuki was confident of winning the trust vote by appealing the dissident party MLAs to support his government in the confidence motion, the central leadership smelled the upcoming dangers to the party in the state under the leadership of Tuki. On the eve of the trust vote in the floor of the House, the Congress party decided to change its chief minister taking into account of the mood of the dissident MLAs. The replacement of Tuki by the young Prema Khandu, son of former Chief Minister Dorgee Khandu, not only saved the Congress government which had to face the crucial trust vote but also put hurdles to the BJP orchestrated defection and resolved the political instability for time being.The change of guard in the Congress Legislative Party in Arunachal Pradesh has temporarily solved the political crisis engulfed in the aftermath of the reinstatement of the former Chief Minister, Nabam Tuki. It was viewed that the truce in the Congress in Arunachal Pradesh is considered to be a personal setback for Amit Shah, Himanta Biswa Sarma and Kirren Rijju and their strategy towards the Congress regimes in the region. The reinstatement of Congress government under the change of guard in Arunachal Pradesh may stop the BJP's effort to dislodge the Congress regimes both in Manipur and Meghalaya for time being. However, after a gap of two months the state witnessed yet another political drama of merging the Congress MLAs with the PPA not only a challenge to the central leadership of the Congress party but also a morale booster to the BJP.

In Arunachal Pradesh, the BJP has a history of orchestrating defections in the Congress Party, bringing down the Congress regimes, supporting the rebel leaders to form government with its outside support, and also merging splintered political factions with the BJP. Perhaps, the party's first ever attempt to destablise the Congress governments in the northeastern states goes back to 2003 with the Arunachal Pradesh experiment. In July 2003, during the Vajpayee-led National Democratic Alliance (NDA) government, the dissident Congress leader Gegong Apang toppled the Mukut Mithi-led Congress government with 34 Congress MLAs and became the Chief Minister of the state under the newly floated United Democratic Front (UDF), which later merged with the BJP. However, in 2004, when the United Progressive Alliance (UPA) government came into power at the centre, Apang rejoined the Congress Party and contested the next election under the Congress symbol.

After this failed experiment, the BJP built up its strong base in Arunachal Pradesh, and over the years its vote share has increased by making inroads into the electoral base of the Congress. In 2004 general election, the party could win all the two seats in the state with a vote share of 53.85 per cent. Although in the subsequent general election in 2009, the party lost all two seats to the Congress and its vote share reduced to 37.17 per cent, in 2014 general election it wrested one seat from the ruling Congress with an vote share of 46.62 per cent. In a major jolt to the ruling Congress in the state, **the** Union Minister of State for Home Affairs and the BJP's prominent face in the north-east, wrested the Arunachal West constituency from the Congress This spectacular victory in one of the two seats in the state gave added advantage to the NDA in the region. In the State Assembly election held along with the general election 2014, BJP won 11 seats with a vote share of 30.97 per cent in the 60 member Assembly against its performance in 2009 when it could secure only three seats. The Congress won 42 seats with a vote share of 49.9% and the People's Party of Arunachal won five seats and independents two.

The BJP's current effort to install the PPA led government with its outside support has been seen in the larger context of its politics in the region. Though the BJP's attempt to dislodge the state Congress government began soon after the general election in 2014, it further got accelerated in the aftermath of the Assam Assembly election in which the BJP formed its first ever government in the north-east India. For instance, the recently floated North East Democratic Alliance (NEDA) under the convenorship of Himanta Biswa Sarma was trying to dislodge Congress government in the state by encouraging defections and alluring positions and money to the MLAs to achieve Amit Shah's goal of a 'Congress-Free' North-East. It has to be reminded that in another Congress ruled states like Manipur and Meghalaya the BJP under the NEDA is in the mood of dislodging the governments by encouraging defections.

The political developments in Arunachal Pradesh, has bearing on other Congress ruled states in the Northeast India. Political pundits see that after the enthusiased by the emphatic victory in Assam and the reinstatement of a government with its outside support in Arunachal Pradesh, the BJP's next target is Manipur. It has to be reminded that hoping to secure political power in the 2017 Assembly election in Manipur, the BJP is alluring a section of Congress legislators and preparing a roadmap to topple the Congress government in Manipur led by Okram Ibobi Singh which enjoys the support of 47 members in the 60 member Manipur Assembly. In the two Assembly constituencies where by-elections were held in November 2015, the BJP candidates defeated the ruling Congress candidates and thereby opened its account for the first time in the state. In Thangmeiband Assembly constituency Khumukham Joy Kishan Singh and in Thongju Constituency Bishwajit Singh of BJP defeated the Congress candidates adding another feather in the crown of the BJP in the state. In the civic elections too, the BJP emerged as a potent force in the state. In the January 2016 municipal and nagar panchayat elections, the BJP won 62 seats in the 278-member municipal council. In the elections held on 2 June 2016 to the 27-member Imphal Municipal Corporation, the BJP emerged as second-largest party winning 10 seats after the Congress which could secure only 12 seats. The emerging trends showed that the BJP is emerging as an alternative to the Congress both in the rural and urban areas keeping its goal of capturing political power in the state in the February 2017 Assembly election.

The political development in Arunachal Pradesh my evoke an impact on the politics of Meghalaya too. It has to be reminded that the BJP is desperately looking for a change in the Congress-led Mukul Sangma government. In a prelude to make the state free from the Congress, the BJP is showing much interest in the internal squabbles in the state Congress led by former chief minister D.D. Lapang. There are reports that in the Garo region, the National People's Part of late Purno Sangma is alluring the Congress MLAs to dislodge the Mukul Sangma government.

Nagaland

Nagaland is a state with huge Christian population (87.93% according to the 2011 Census) and Christianity peeped into the socio-cultural and religious life of the people since the British period itself. However, for the Hindutva forces Nagaland emerged a focal point in the recent past. Unlike rest of the states in North East, the ruling Naga People's Front (NPF) is alliance partner in the NDA at the centre and the BJP is an ally of the NPF led Democratic Alliance of Nagaland (DAN) in the state. This political realityoften prevents the national and state leadership of the BJP to refrain from attacking directly to the state government. The BJP President Amit Shah in his visit to the state on17th April, 2015 while highlighting the BJP-led government's initiative to develop the North Eastern region also sent a strong message that the Centre "will not tolerate corruption at any cost". Highlighting the general trends and without directing attacking the state government the BJP president asserted that "NE states including Nagaland does not lack funds and central assistance but corruption at many levels has hampered the developmental projects meant for the grass root level. Developmental policies and funds provided by the Central government for developmental purposes do not reach the people."[17]

In the 2014 general election, the NPF leader and chief minister Neiphiu Rio won the lone Lok Sabha seat with the support of BJP hoping his 'greater role' in the national politics. After Rio elected to Lok Sabha, T R Zeliang took over the helm of affairs of the state. On 27th April, 2015, shortly after the visit of Amit Shah, the Nagaland chief minister T R Zeliang inducted the BJP legislator, Paiwang Konyak as a minister in the state cabinet. In the current state Assembly the opposition presence is virtually blank adding a boost to the NPF and the BJP. All 60 MLAs are part of the DAN led by the NPF. In November, 2015 with eight Congress MLAs joined NPF, virtually no opposition in the current Assembly in Nagaland. It has to be reminded that three NCP MLAs joined the BJP which is already a part of the NPF-led DAN. The migration of Congress MLAs was the culmination of the growing dissidence activities in the Congress for some time. However, the Chief Minister hoped that it would strengthen the Naga peace process and the positive response to the Naga Peace Accord between the Government of India and the National Socialist Council of Nagalim (Issac and Muivah) in August 2015.

Constructing a Counter-Narrative

In the largely Christian populated Nagaland, the BJP constructs a counter narrative to Christianity to strengthen its base. The BJP's attempt to glorify the Naga spiritual leader and freedom fighter 'Rani'Gaidinliu by constructing a memorial museum-cum-library in Kohima can be seen in this direction. Gaidinliu (1915-1993) fought against the British and imprisoned by the British in various jails in North East. She composed over 300 song including hymns, patriotic songs, poems. Gaidinliu who was described by the British as the "Terror of North East" involved in an armed struggle against the British. In fact, Nehru was fond of Gaidinliu and called her 'Rani' because she took anti-Naga stand in Naga self-determination movement. It has to be reminded that the Naga movement was in fact the first movement which India faced after independence and tested Nehru's ability as a nation builder. In fact, Nehru wanted to counter the Naga movement forced him to praise Gaidinliu.

Gaidinliu who belonged to the Zleiangrong community also resisted the conversion of Nagas to Christianity and defended traditional Naga religion of animism called "Heraka". It is estimated that today there are around 20, 000 Heraka followers who are scattered in parts of Nagaland, Manipur and Assam. It has to be reminded that to weaken the protest of Zleiangrong community – the British divided them into three states- Manipur, Assam, Nagaland (then Naga Hills). The Zeliangrong Heraka Association (ZHA) opposes the 'westernisation' of the Naga culture and protecting the indigenous religion, culture and language. It also critical of western hedonism and consumerism and reasserting communitarian values in the place of western values. Gaidinliu wanted to bring indigenous Naga groups such as Rongmei, Zemi and Liangmai tribes and campaigned to bring them into one ZHA to save them from religious conversion to Christianity. In December 2014, Modi visited Nagaland during the famous

Hornbill and which coincided with the conclusion of Gaidinliu's birth centenary celebration (26th January 2014 to 26th January 2015). The Prime Minister in his speech in English and wearing Naga traditional dress emphasized the Naga pride. At the end of his address Modi preferred to use the Naga nationalist slogan "Kuknalim"(Victory to Nagalim/Nagaland) instead of his usual nationalist chant "Jai-Hind"(victory to India). The ZHA submitted a memorandum to the Prime Minister demanding that their leader Gaidinliu must be honoured and recognized. The larger demands include: bringing new coins to commemorate the birth centenary of Gaidinliu; opening of a central university in Nagaland with her name and setting up of a department dedicated to the promulgation of the "eternal religion and eternal culture of Nagas", renaming of Naga Nagaland's only airport as "Rani Gaidinliu Airport"; installing Gaidinliu's portrait in Nagaland Assembly, the official offices of Chief Minister, Governor and other ministers. Subsequently, the Centre released coins of Rs.5 and Rs. 100 denominations with her images on them to commemorate her birth century.

In fact, a strong protest came from the Naga community itself as many Naga tribes see her as anti-Naga as she betrayed the Naga national movement for a sovereign state. The organizations such as the Angami Public Organization (AYO) opposed any move to glorify Gaidinliu.[18]Nagas, on the other hand, never recognize her as a spiritual leader and described Gaidinliu as an outside and a cult leader who had opposed Naga nationalism and the advent of Christianity in the state. The Nagas view Gaidinliu as an outsider and call her the cult leader.[19]

The BJP was trying to gain foothold in the state by glorifying Gaidinliu who opposed conversion to Christianity. Though Gaidinliu fought against both British and Christian missionaries, the BJP is only highlighting her opposition to the Christianity and thereby it is attempting to create communal polarization among the Nagas in the state.[20]The BJP, in fact, want to appropriate Heraka (the indigenous faith based on animism) with Hinduism against Christianity by projecting her as the "spiritual leader"of Nagas against Jesus. The Hinduvta forces are hobnobbing with indigenous religious movement such the Zeliangrong Heraka Association (ZHA) to Hinduise it against the Christian associations. By opposing a challenge to Christianity and rejecting the missionary work ZHA asserts the Heraka identity. It has to be reminded that the Hinduvta forces always stand for Bharatvarsha, the larger Hindu imagination. The Akhil Bharatiya Vanavasi Kalyan Asharam (ABVKA) is supporting the activities of the ZHA. The Sangh Parivar now claims that Heraka as the part of the larger Hindu family. It is argued that "since many of the practices of the Heraka are derive from Hinduism, the Sangh parivar has declared them to be vanavasi (forest-dwellers) and sought to assimilate them into the Hindu fold" (Dangmei, 2013: 27). In appropriating Heraka with Hinduism the Hinduvta forces are countering the dominant Christian narrating by constructing a counter alternative premised on Hindutva.

In the Assembly election 2018, the BJP secured 12 seats and extended support to Nationalist Democratic Progressive Party (NDPP), dumping its long term ally the NPF which emerged as the single largest party in the 60-member Assembly. Its estranged ally, the NPF, though made an attempt to stitch together its alliance with the BJP, the later served its 15 years old ties and opted for NDPP, for sharing power in the state. The BJP's ascendancy in the largely Christian dominated state significant development inspite of the warning of the Nagaland Baptist Churches Council (NBCC) during the electoral campaign. It may be recalled that the Council was critical of BJP's growing presence in the state and the regional parties' decision to ally with it.

Manipur

After the installation of the government led by the rebel Congress leader with the outside support of the BJP and the astounding victory in the Assam Assembly election in 2016, the BJP's next focus shifted to Manipur which is emerging as a political laboratory for the Hindutva forces. It has to be reminded that in the two Assembly constituencies where byelections held in the month of November, 2015 the BJP candidates defeated the ruling Congress candidates and thereby opened its account for the first time in the state. In Thangmeiband Assembly constituency Khumukham Joy Kishan Singh and in Thongju Constituency Bishwajit Singh of BJP defeated the Congress candidates adding another feather in the crown of the BJP in the state. In the civic elections too the BJP is emerging as a potent force in the state. In the January 2016 municipal and nagar panchayat election, the BJP won 62 seats in the 278 member municipal council. In the 27 member Imphal Municipal Corporation held on 2nd June, 2016, the BJP emerged as second largest party winning 10 seats after the Congress which could secure only 12 seats. The emerging trends shows that the BJP is emerging as an alternative to the Congress both in the rural and urban areas keeping its goal of capture political power in the state in the February 2017 Assembly election.

In a morale boost to the party in the state, the BJP could woo many leaders from other parties and prominent figures of the state to the party fold. It has to be reminded that in September, Radhabinod Koijam, the former Manipur Chief Minister, Okran Joy Singh, the former leader of the Manipur People's Party (MPP) and Yumnam Joykumar Singh, the former DGP joined the saffron party. In a further boost to the BJP's ambition in the state, on 24 May, 2016 the four NPF legislators in the Manipur Assembly joined BJP in the formation of North-East Democratic Alliance (NEDA) in Guwahati in the presence of Amit Shah and Ram Madhav. Himanta Biswa Sarma, the former Congressmen and the current BJP Minister in Assam were elected as the Convener. The objective of the Alliance was to strengthen the BJP's base in the region outwardly it claims that the intension of the NEDA was on the agenda of the overall development of the region. Moreover, the BJP is planning to extend NEDA to all Congress ruled states such as Meghalaya, Mizoram and Manipur with the alliance of the regional parties to out the Congress in the Assembly elections.

The BJP is now focusing on Manipur to dislodge the Congress government of Okram Ibobi Singh. Hoping to secure political power in the 2017 Assembly election, the BJP is alluring a section of Congress legislators and preparing a roadmap to topple the Congress government which enjoys the support of 47 members in the 60 member Manipur Assembly. Like Assam, Congress is in power for the last three consecutive terms under the leadership of Ibobi Singh is facing a strong anti-incumbency. The BJP is hoping to win over the anti-incumbency wave as well as the internal bickering of the ruling party along with social engineering. In fact, the intention to regimes change was highlighted by Amit Shah few months ago. Way back, in his maiden visit on 18th April, 2015 in the Congress ruled state of Manipur, Amit Shah appealed the people to "elect BJP, get benefit" emphasizing the need for BJP governments both in the state and the centre for the better development of the state. In a dig to Congress, the BJP president pleaded for making North East a 'Congress –free Zone' where the people of Manipur has a decisive role. The BJP president said that apart from corruption it was the Congress government that was holding Manipur back from progress and development.[21]

The Congress ruled Manipur is another attraction for the BJP in the region due to its ethnic composition and complexities of the issues it confronts over time. The state of Manipur having area of 22, 327 square kilometers is a highly pluralized society with a complex ethnic composition. Manipur has three major ethnic groups such as Meiteis, Kukis and Nagas and the smaller groups like Mizos, Zomi, Chins, Paites, Hmars etc. The Meiteis resides in valley which constitutes only 10% of the state's total area which include four districts such as Imphal East, Imphal West, Thoubal and Bishnupur. According to the 2011 census, 60% of the total population of Manipur resides in the valley region and the remaining 90% constitute the Hill areas which comprised of five districts such as Chandel, Churachandour, Senapati, Tamenglong and Ukhrul where other tribal communities inhabit. The Meiteis cannot buy lands in the hill areas while the tribals can possess land in the valley. Interestingly, as per the constitutional provisions, the outsiders, including the Meiteis needs the permission of the Hill Area Committee (HAC) while those in hill areas can by land in the Meiteis inhabited areas. Over the period of time, the Meiteis control over land is shrinking due to the tribal inhabitance in the valley as well as the migration of the outsiders such as Biharis, Marwaris, and Punjabis for business purpose. The Meiteis often allege that in the district of Bishnupur, the north Indian population outnumbered the indigenous Meiteis. The growing sense of reducing into a minority in the valley forced the Meiteis to demand for Inner Line Permit (ILP) to restrict the entry of the outsiders to the region.

Manipur is often described as a Hindu enclave surrounded by Christian population on all sides. According to Census of India: 2011, the Hindus constitute 41.39% of the total population who are mostly Vaishanavites, having more attachment to the Rashtriya Swayamsevak Sangh (RSS). The Meitei claims descent from Lord Arjuna. Hindu Meitei under the leadership of Maharaja Churachand Singh formed the Nikhil Hindu Manipuri Mahasabha to regulate their religious activities during 1934. In just three decades, the Hindus have declined from 70% to 41.39% of the population. It is alleged that the reason for dwindling Hindu population is the high fertility of Christians compared to the Hindus and conversion to Christianity. An article in the 4 January, 2015 issue of the RSS' mouthpiece, **Organiser,** has offered some statistics in support of this argument. It says, "There was a 5.2 per cent decadal (1991-2001) growth in Hindu population of Manipur. However, at the same time, Christians grew by 36.6 per cent and Muslims by 43.1 per cent." It further adds, "North-eastern states, excluding Assam, recorded 50.6 per cent growth in Christians and 42.4 per cent growth in Muslims (in the same period)."The Sangh Parivar who engages in *ghar wapsi* (homecoming) often raises the issue of reduction in Hindu population in the state. In a resolution adopted in RSS' Akhil Bhariya Karyakari Mandal in Ranchi in October, 2015 claimed that in Manipur, the share of the "religions of Bharatiya origin" was over 80 per cent in 1951, but came down to 50 per cent in 2011".[22]

The hill-valley divide and the recurring conflict between the people of hill and valley, perhaps determine the future course of politics in the state. The hill area tribals also have a sense of deprivation as most of the employment opportunities in the state are monopolized by the Meiteis. The relative deprivation of the hill tribes are more glaring as they lack better schooling, health, and housing facilities in the state. On the other hand, the valley dominated Meiteis demand more protective measures from the state as it loses it land and resources from the outsiders including the tribals from the hill areas. The current sprout of tussle between the hill and valley was begun with the passage of three Bills in the state Assembly. In August, the Ibobi Singh government passed three anti-hill areas Bills triggered widespread protest by the Manipur Tribals Forum (MTF) in the state. The three controversial bills – the Protection of Manipur People Bill, 2015, the Manipur Land Revenue and Land Reforms Bill (Seventh Amendment), 2015 and the Manipur Shops and Establishments (Second Amendments) Bill, 2015 were allegedly passed by the Assembly in just six minutes. The ongoing Hill-Valley tussle is a great concern for the Congress government in the state as the BJP is tactically adopting a stand against the Congress. The BJP is monitoring the volatile situations in Manipur without antagonizing Hill and the Valley. In the midst of the recurring tussle between the hill and valley, the BJP is creating instability in the state.

Though the BJP is trying to woo the Meiteis to its Hinduvta fold without antagonizing the hill tribes, the move is bottlenecked by certain developments in the state. Firstly, the BJP's trusted alliance with the NPF in Nagaland is suspiciously watched by the Meiteis. The Naga Accord concluded between the National Socialist Council of Nagaland (Isak Muivah) (NSCN (IM)) and the government of India in August 2015 created more apprehension among the Meiteis. It has to be remained that the NSCN (IM) is demanding all Naga integrated areas in Manipur, Assam, Arunachal Pradesh though the provisions of the Accord kept secret. Moreover, the entry of the ruling NPF in Nagaland in the Manipur Assembly which has four members is a matter of worry for the Meiteis. Further, the strain in the relationship between the Meiteis and RSS is on the issue of controversial AFSPA 1958 is added further concern for the BJP's attempt to woo the Meiteis. It has to be reminded that the Meiteis are against the Act (Irom Sharmila who is in fast for the last 15 years is a Meitei), while the RSS firmly support it. In his maiden visit on 18th April, 2015 in Manipur, Amit

Shah even kept silence on the long standing demand for the repeal of the Armed Forces Special Powers Act of 1958, ending the decade old fast of Irom Sharmila, civilian causalities in counter insurgency operations, fake encounters, human rights violations by the Indian army, border issues between various states, etc.

In the Assembly election 2017, the BJP secured 21 seats with a vote share of 36.3%. The Bharatiya Janata Party's (BJP) emergence as the second largest political party in the Assembly and its success in installing the first-ever BJP government in Manipur is the result of its strategy of winning the support of the hostile communities both in the Hill and Valley. The Hill-Valley divide was tacitly used as the mobilisation strategy on different reasons and occasions to reach out both the Hindu Meiteis and the Christian tribals. The Meiteis' agitation for Inner Line Permit and United Naga Council's protest against creation of new districts during the Congress-led Ibobi Singh government was aptly capitalised by the BJP to make inroads into the electoral base of the Congress. The party uses the much acclaimed Naga Peace Accord of 2015, though the provisions of the accord were not made public, as a rallying point for its Naga mobilisation. Like the mobilisation of the Nagas, the BJP did not take an antagonistic strategy against the Kukis in the state. The Assembly election 2017 shows that the BJP made strong presence even in the Kuki-dominated areas. The majority of the Kukis were traditionally the support base of the Congress. In this election, there was a division within the Kuki extremist organisation. While the Kuki National Organisation extended its support to the Congress, the United People's Front—a conglomeration of Kuki extremist groups—supported the BJP. As a result, the BJP managed to get three Kuki MLAs. The verdict further proves that the BJP's electoral support extended to all major communities such as Meiteis, Nagas and Kuki, and both in the Hill and Valley. Of the 40 Assembly constituencies in the Valley, the BJP won 16 seats including the lone SC constituency. In the 20 constituencies in the Hill areas, the BJP won four seats—Tamenglong, Thanlon, Henglep and Churachandpur. The lone general constituency (Kangpokpi) was also wrested by the BJP. In the government formation too, the BJP strategically went ahead of the Congress. Although the Congress emerged as the single largest party, the BJP early jumped into the formation of the government. In fact, it was alleged that the state governor Najma Heptulla by acting on behest of the centre invited the BJP, ignoring the Congress, the single largest party, which she felt can provide a stable government in the state. The BJP initiated talks with the smaller parties and the independents, before the

Congress. Moreover, it was able to even defect the Congress legislator Shyam Kumar.

Meghalaya

In another largely Christian populated state of Meghalaya, the BJP is trying to make inroads in the state politics. However, unlike Assam, Arunachal Pradesh and Manipur, the party does not have substantial base and on this realization, it is looking for alliances and social groups for its expansion. In the 2014 general election the BJP entered into an alliance with National Peoples Party (NPP) of Purno A. Sangma. It has to be reminded that Sangma who quit NCP, a constituent of the United Progressive Alliance (UPA) government at the Centre, few months before the election before forming the NPP and later formed a tactical electoral understanding with the NDA. In the 2014 general election, the Garo inhabited Tura seat was won by the Garo veteran Sangma by securing 22.84% of votes with the support of the BJP. In October 2015 in the Garo Hills Autonomous District Council (GHADC) the BJP won one seat in Zikzak constituency in alliance with NPP.

After engineering defection and overthrowing the Congress regime in Arunachal Pradesh Assam, the BJP poses a challenge to the Congress government in Meghalaya. The BJP desperately looking for a change from the Congress led Mukul Sangma government. In a prelude to make state free from thc Congress, the BJP is showing much interest in the internal squabbles with the state Congress. In fact, though the Congress in the state is vulnerable to factional squabble for a long time, the recent one was due to the defeat of the Congress candidate to Conrad K. Sangma of NPP in the Tura Loksabha bi election. The Garo Hills in which the Tura constituency belongs was considered to be the stronghold of the Chief Minister Mukul Sangma who was picked up by the central leadership of the Congress party to counter the influence of the Garo strongman, Purno Sangma. Though in the state assembly election Mukul could erode the base of the Purno, in the 2014 Loksabha election and the 2016 by-election, he was miserably failed to canvass the Garos to the party. Interestingly, Mukul was able to garner support in favour of his wife, Dikkanchi D. Shira, the sitting MLA as the candidate of the bieletion. In the election, the mandate was in favour of Conrad K. Sangma, the younger son of late Purno Sangma as the Garo people endorsed the family politics of Purno s once again over that of Mukul. The electoral defeat rekindled the factional politics in the state as D D Lapang, the MPCC president and the former Chief Minister and Vincent

Pala, the MP from Shillong constituency demanded leadership change in the state. In his three page letter to party president Sonia Gandhi and the Vice President Rahul Gandhi, Mukul Sangma claimed that "the BJP is campaigning in Shillong and are in connivance with cabinet ministers and looking to sir trouble for the state government".[23]

Though the BJP may succeed in destabilizing the Congress government by orchestrating defection within the Congress party and may drift the Congress MLAs in the Garo region to the NPP fold, forming a government of its own is a distant possibility in near future. Unlike other states in NEI, the BJP has many hurdles in Meghalaya. Its Hinduvta agenda often cannot be operated in the hilly state with deep rooted influence of Church and other ethno-regional organisations. This reality is more evident in the reaction to the Amit Shah's visit to the state in 2015 and the reaffirmation of the BJP central leadership in the recent past. It has to be reminded that with great hope of boosting the party organization by wooing Hindu Nepalese and Bengali population in the state, the visit of the BJP President in the Congress ruled state of Meghalaya on 22nd April, 2015 was greeted with bandhs by outlawed extremist organizations such as the Hynniewtrep National Liberation Council (HNLC) and massive protest by Non Governmental Organisations such as Thma U Rangli-Juki (TUR), Hynniewtrep National People's Front (HNPF) and Khasi National Union (KNU). The ethnic organizations even organized beef party to protest against the BJP governments move to ban beef which is the favourite food for the tribals in the state. The three regional parties in the State – United Democratic Party (UDP), Hill State People's Democratic Party (HSPDP) – voiced their concern on issue of ban on cow slaughter in separate meetings with the BJP national president Amit Shah. Amid growing resentment against the BJP government on the issue of banning beef, Ram Madhav, the BJP general secretary who accompanied Shah stated that "there is no such proposal to ban cow slaughter in the Northeastern states".[24]

Failing to polarize communally on emotive issues like elsewhere in the region, the BJP relies on the bogey of 'development 'in the state to mobilize its support base. The BJP President in his maiden visit to the state on 22nd April, 2015 asserted that the BJP government initiated construction of hostels for the welfare of North East students in Bangalore, Delhi University and Jawaharlal Nehru University. Further the BJP leader Nalin Kohli made it clear that BJP is not an anti-Christian Party but a development –oriented party.[25] The Prime Minister Narendra Modi's visit to Shillong in the last week of May 2016 to attend the 65th NEC plenary session meeting can be seen in this context. Though the visit was entirely official, a section of the political class believes that by reiterating the developmental mantra, BJP can woo certain sections of the society and thereby emerge as a potential alternative to the Congress in the state.

In the fractured verdict of Assembly election 2018, the BJP though won only two seats, extended its support to the NPP and became a partner in the coalition government, dashing out the hope of the Congress which emerged as the single largest party with 21 seats in the 60-member Assembly. The BJP claimed that its victory and its decision to part with the NPP led government demystified the image of the BJP as an anti-Christian party. However, a postmortem study of the election verdict shows that it is largely the victory of the NPP and the regional parties. The BJP set aside the issues such as beef ban and conversion and focused on developmental issues and corruption in the state. It could mobilise the smaller regional parties and indulge split in the Congress party as number of sitting and ex-Congress MLAs joined the party posing a threat to the Mukul Sangma government.

Mizoram

In another Christian dominated state of Mizoram, the BJP finds it difficult to take root where the Church has decisive voice in the politics of the state, especially during the election time. On realizing to the ground reality, the BJP clinches on developmental agenda by promising skill development to the young Mizos. Like Meghalaya, in Mizoram too in the BJP President Amit Shah's visit in April 2015 assured the youth that the centre would accord priority to their skill development. The BJP is looking for fertile ground for its expansion by forging alliance with smaller regional parties such as the Zoram Nationalist Party (ZNP). The recent reports from the state that the BJP is gaining popularity in some parts of the minority dominated areas of Mizoram. In February, 2015 in the Chakma Autonomous District, the BJP registered its strong presence after the Congress. Of the 81 village councils, the BJP secured five seats which was otherwise the stronghold of the Congress. Perhaps, among the above mentioned states, Mizoram is an exception where the Congress insulated from the politics of dislodge of the BJP. However, Lal Thanhawla, the two consecutive Congress Chief Minister since 2008 face stiff opposition from the MNF, the main opposition party. The BJP is looking for fertile ground for its expansion by forging alliance with the major opposition party MNF by offering perks in the central government. In January, 2016, in a further move to consolidate its position in the state, John V. Hluna, a university professor, was appointed as the new BJP president. Though the BJP has minimal support base in the state and is not able follow strategy that of Manipur, it may extend its support to MNF to accomplish the goal of Congress *Mukt Bharat* in the hilly state of Mizoram.

Tripura

In the alone left ruled state of Tripura, the BJP invokes multiple strategy to gain strength. It spread its communal propaganda among the indigenous tribal community waking up the issue of migration of Bengalis and the subjugation of the former by the migrant Bengalis. It is to be reminded that over the years the CPIM was able to expand its mass base not only among the Bengali community but also among the indigenous tribal community bringing them under a common platform. However, the BJP along with the communal polarization, the bogey of development finds place in its strategy to counter the left dominance in the state. While concluding his ten days tour to all eight North-Eastern states the BJP president on 27th April, Shah asserted that 'People of the country have remove the Communists from other parts of the country, now the turn has come for the people of Tripura to remove them from the only state of the country', Amit Shah said, "The left front govt. in Tripura has brought no development to the state rather than corruption, scams and deprivation for the common masses." In a dig at the Marxist government in the state, Shah said that "the days are not far when their last boat will sink in the sea. In order to join the mainstream of development process of the country, regime change in Tripura is necessary". Alleging massive corruption in MGNREGA, Shah made a clarion call to the people of Tripura to topple the Left Government in 2018 Assembly election and the BJP can provide good governance and development in Tripura.

Over the years, though the CPIM was the dominant force in the State, the BJP is making inroads in rural areas. For instance, the percentage of votes secured by the BJP in the CPIM ruled state was 7.82% (2004), 2.72% (2009) and 5.7% (2014). Though there is slight decline in the percentage of votes secured by the BJP in the 2014 general election in contrast to 2004 general election, the subsequent trends prove that the BJP has not abandon its electoral ambition in the red bastion of the region. In May 3, 2015, in the Tribal Areas Autonomous District Council election the BJP got 7.87% of votes. In the by elections to two Assembly seats in June 2015, the BJP secured 23.33% votes, though CPM retained both the Scheduled Caste reserved states. Subsequently, in the 15th July, 2014 gram panchayat poll, the BJP won 141 of the 6, 111 seats and won a majority in five gram panchayats for the first time. Interestingly, the CPM often blames the Congress, Trinamol Congress for the rise of BJP in Tripura.

Appropriation of Public Figures

In Tripura, the BJP is engaging in the process of appropriating Maharaja Bir Bikram Kishore Manikya Bahadur (born on 19th August, 1908 and died on 17th May 1947), the last tribal ruler to the Hindu fold. Such argument is strengthened by the recent decision of the Union government to install 184 feet bronze statue of Bir Bikram Kishore, the 184th king of Tripura's Manikya dynasty which ruled Tripura for more than 300 years. In fact, such appropriation comes in the light of the BJP's indictment of both the Congress and left in the state of not giving due recognition to the King's contribution to Tripura's development.

It has to be reminded that Bir Bikram Kishore, who ruled Tripura between 1923 to 1947, merged Tripura with independent India. Commonly described as the architect of modern Tripura, the king initiated land reformed and reserved land for the indigenous Tripuris in the last 1930s, and set up schools, colleges and airport. Adorned at the age of sixteen and died at the age of 39, the King also played critical role in the formation of the present TTAADC. However, the premature death of Bir Bikram Kishore engulfed political uncertainty in Tripura as his son, Kirti Bikrm Kishore Manikya was too young to become the King forcing Kanchanprova Debi, his mother and widow of Bir Bikram Kishore to become the Regent who ruled on behalf of his younger son. In fact, the Regent signed the agreement of accession on 13 August, 1947 and on 15 October, 1949 Tripura merged with the Indian Union.

On 19th September, 2013, on the occasion of the golden jubilee of the Tripura Legislative Assembly, speaking in a seminar in Agartala, the Chief Minister Manik Sarkar revealed that the members of Trupura's Manikya Royal family under Bir Bikram Kishore wanted to merge with then East Pakistan (now Bangladesh). However, sensing the public sentiments, Bir Bikram Kishore before his death expressed his desire to keep Tripura with the Indian Union. He also revealed that Bir Bikram Kishore was also planned its integration with Assam. It has to be reminded that the State Reorganisation Commission constituted in 1953 proposed to merge Tripura with Assam. However, the proposal was finally dropped and Tripura became a Union Territory on 1 November, 1956 and achieved statehood in 1972.

The BJP's appropriation of Bir Bikram Kishore can be seen in the larger context of the social chemistry and politics in Tripura. The state having a total tribal population of around 33 per cent and having a history of recurrent the clashes between indigenous tribals and the Bengalis. It has to be reminded that the Indigenous People's Front of Tripura (IPFT) demanding separate state called Twipra, for the tribal by carving out the TTAADC (Tripura Tribal Area Autonomous District Council) from Tripura. The BJP, in fact, is using the tribal indigeneity to counter the consolidation and domination the Marxist regime in the state. It is also hoping that the appropriation of Bir Bikram Kishore would bring more political dividends in its favour as well as to counter the emergence of Trinamol Congress which is replacing the Congress, the principal opposition in the state.

The Assembly election in 2018 brought many cheers for the BJP as it could secure absolute majority alone and able to overthrow the twenty-five years of the left front. In the 60-member Assembly, the BJP secured 35 seats and its alliance partner IPFT won 8 seats. Striking a balance between two major communities such as the Bengalis and the tribals, the BJP conveniently raised issues such as the marginalization of the tribal community, unemployment, inadequate salary for the state government employees and alleged developmental stagnation of the state. The BJP took away some slice from the CPI(M)'s pie which is manifested when its vote share reduced to 42.6% compared to its tally of 48.11% in 2013. In fact, the BJP could wean away the Congress party's vote share as the latter's vote share plummeted to 1.8% from the 36.5% in the 2013 assembly election.

Sikkim

Unlike other states in the North-east region, the BJP has very poor influence in the Himalayan state of Sikkim. However, the Party is trying hard to get some regional alliance as is evident that the Sikkim Krantikatta Morcha (SKM) is trying to merge with the BJP. Moreover, the state leadership is hobnobbing with the ruling Sikkim Democratic Party (SDF) to alliance in the state. Failure to rake up any communal issue, the mask of development further highlighted as a mobilization strategy. In his visit 21st April, 2015 the BJP president, for instance, highlighted the issue of development in the state and the NEI in particular. He asserted that the BJP would systematically spread its roots in Sikkim and foray into the Northeast and weed out corruption and deliver development in Sikkim and rest of northeast. Though, BJP is relatively a new entrant in the state politics, it is benefited by activities of RSS for a long time.

Though a constituent of NEDA, the SDP has a troubled relationship in the politics of the Himalayan state. The BJP in the state is taking every opportunity to dislodge SDF government which is in power since 1994. Anticipating the 2019 Assembly election, the BJP is enticing the higher caste members of the Nepali community and the traders. It also wooing the Limbu and Tamang communities promising them reservation of seats in the Assembly. It has to be reminded that though the Limbus and Tamangs granted Scheduled Tribe status in 2002, their demand for reservation in Legislative Assembly remain unfulfilled. Like other northeastern states, since the BJP lacks credible leaders, it encourages split in the ruling party and wean away towards its fold. It was able to defect three former SDF ministers towards its fold. To tackle the influence of BJP, the SDF government passed the Sikkim Prevention of Cow Slaughter Bill, 2017, the first ever in any North Eastern states, despite large beef consumption by Bhutias and Lepchas.

Conclusion

The BJP's political mobilization assumed a new dimension in India's North-East. Beyond the electoral calculations, social and political factors decide the BJP's interest in the region. The party adopts multiple strategies to mobilize different ethnic communities and thereby strengthen in mass base. For this purpose, it is dislodging the existing narratives and constructing new narratives and appropriating the great personalities to fulfill its political agenda. While the bogey of development is placed high on its agenda, different issues pertinent to different states raised at various juncture to mobilize and consolidate its social base. In some occasions, the party is competing with the ethno-regional parties to snatch their ethno-regional agenda and thereby emerged as a potential political force. For instance, in Assam the issue of illegal migration of Muslims from Bangladesh constituted the key agenda of the AGP since 1980s, later found in the agenda of BJP which vigorously raised this issue to mobilize the support of Assamese Hindus in the Brahmaputra valley, Hindu Bengalis in the Barrak valley and the tribals in the Bodo areas to consolidate its social and electoral base in the state. On the one hand, the BJP is emerging as the self found custodians of the cultural life of the North-east India, there is growing incidents of racial attacks against people from the NEI ever since the NDA government came to power. In the February 2015 Delhi Assembly election, the BJP's vision document described people from NEI to Delhi as immigrant" though it was rectified due to amidst protest by saying that was a printing mistake. Moreover, the failure of the NDA government to implement the provisions of the Bezbaruah committee report show the insanity of the BJP government towards the cause of the people from North East.[26] Further, the BJP's attempt to denigrate the cultural diversity of NEI by forcing them to assimilate into the Hinduvta cultural fold would endanger the social fabric of the region. This would further lead to alienation of these people from the idea of India as it falls outside their political imagination.

Notes

1. "BJP leaders in northeast support Rijiju over "beef remark", slams Naqvi", *The Hindustan Times*, 28thMay, 2015.
2. *The Assam Tribune*, 23rd February, 2014.
3. *The Economic Times,* 13th April, 2015.
4. *The Assam Tribune*, 28th August, 2014.
5. see *Organiser* 16th September 2012.
6. "IMDT Act is the biggest barrier to deportation, says Supreme Court", *The Hindu*, 14thJuly, 2005.
7. see BJP (2006), "Achievements and Looking Ahead; 1980- 2005", Vol. 9, New Delhi.
8. see *Organiser* 16th September 2012.
9. see BJP (2014), *Vision Document*, 2014.
10. "Amit Shah in Guwahati: Get ready to 'oust Congress' in 2016 Assam assembly polls", *The Indian Express,* 28th April, 2015.
11. "Only BJP can free Assam from illegal immigration, Amit Shah", *The Economic Times*, 27th April, 2015.
12. *Ibid.*
13. "Census 2011: Assam records highest rise in Muslim Population", *The Times of India*, 22nd January, 2015.
14. "RSS worked overtime to take Modi wave to Northeast", *The Economic Times*, 18th May, 2014.
15. "Chakma-Hajong Logjam: Arunachal Students Protest in India", *The Times of India*, 16th October, 2015.
16. "Arunachal Pradesh BJP blames Congress for Chakma-Hajong Settlement Issue", *The Economic Times*, 4th October, 2015.
17. "Hoho hopes BJP will solve political issue", *The Assam Tribune 20thApril, 2015.*
18. "Some Nagas are against memorial to Rani Gaidinliu in Kohima: Why?", *The Indian Express*, 28thSeptember, 2015.
19. "Nagas Divided over Modi's Plan to Glorify Spiritual Leader", *The New Indian Express*, 30th August, 2015.
20. "BJP using Gaidinliu to polarize Nagaland", *The Times of India*, 25thAugust, 2015.

21. "Elect BJP, get benefits, Shah tells Manipur-BJP Chief addresses Imphall rally", *The Telegraph*, 19th April, 2015.
22. see, "Review Policy to Check Muslim, Christian Population: RSS Resolution", *The Indian Express,* 1 November, 2015.
23. "Letter bomb jolts state politics", *The Shillong Times*, 2nd June, 2016.
24. "No Ban on Cow Slaughter in North East", *The Shillong Times*, 23rd April, 2015.
25. "BJP is not an anti-Christian Party: Meghalaya, Nalin S. Kohli", *The Economic Times*, 14th July, 2015.
26. The Bezbaruah committee was set up the UPA government in the wake of the brutal killing of nineteen year old boy from Arunachal Pradesh in Delhi in January 2014. The Committee submitted its report to the BJP government in July 2014 and has not been implemented its recommendations so far.

References

Bhattacharjee, Malini(2016) 'Tracing the Emergence and Consolidation of Hindutva in Assam', *Economic and Political Weekly*, LI (16), 16 April, pp. 80-87.

Dangmei, Soihiamlung, 2013; 'Cultural Positioning of Tribes in North-east India: Mapping the Evolving Heraka Identity', *Economic and Political Weekly*, XLVIII(1), 5 January, pp. 27-30.

Mahanta, Nani Gopal, 2014; 'Loksabha Elections in Assam: Shifting of Traditional Vote Bases to BJP', *Economic and Political Weekly*, XLIX(35), 30 August, pp. 19-22.

Misra, Udayon. 2016; 'Victory for Identity Politics, Not Hindutva in Assam', *Economic and Political Weekly,* LI (22), 28 May, pp. 20-23.

Srikanth, H, 1999; 'Communalising Assam: AGP's Loss Is BJP's Gain', *Economic and Political Weekly,* XXXIV (49), 4 December, pp. 3412-3414.

Chapter - 5

Slanting Asom Gana Parishad: Crisis of Agenda and Leadership

The Asom Gana Parishad (AGP), the largest ethno-regional party in the Northeast India, is a product of the Assam Movement (1979-1985) which raised ethno-regional issues such as the illegal migration of Bangladeshi that it felt as threat to the cultural identity of the state. The AGP which formed on 14 October, 1985 as an amalgam of ethnic organisations such as Purbanchaliya Lok Parishad (PLP), Assam Jatiyatabadi Dal (AJD), All Assam GanaSangramParishad (AAGSP) with Prafulla Kumar Mahanta, who led the Assam Movement, as its president. The ideological commitment of AGP was influenced by the ideological bedrocks of these organizations. As an ethno- regional party, it is defending the interest of a specific community within a specific territorial location, it is trying to protect the identity and culture of Assamiya middle class which according to them was under danger due to the illegal migration of Bengalis. In the initial years of its existence, the party was able to arouse ethno-regional consciousness among the people and continued to hold power subsequently.

The Uneasy Transition

Before the formation of AGP, the All Assam Students Union (AASU), as an independent student movement not affiliated to any political parties, and All Assam Gana Sangram Parishad (AAGSP) initially articulated the ethno-regional interest. The Assam movement originally emerged to protect the distinct socio-cultural, economic and political identity of the Assamese people. The issue of illegal migration occupied the centre stage of the movement which felt that the identity crisis was due to migration from foreign countries such as Nepal and Bangladesh. The grave concern is that illegal migration affected the social fabric of the Assamese society and aggravated the unemployment and insecurity problem in Assam. The AASU took up the issue of migration of foreigners from Nepal and Bangladesh and demanded the deportation of all foreigners living illegally in Assam. The AASU contended that the backwardness and growing unemployment of the Assamese youth was due to "outsiders" that broadly include Bengalis, Nepalis and Bangladeshis. It was widely perceived that the growing expectation of people could not be realized due to the inflow of these "outsiders".

Though the Assam movement and the subsequent emergence of the AGP cemented ethno-regionalism, the genesis of ethno-regionalism in Assam traced back to 1960s. The party often constructed a narrative that the Congress government in 1967 which did not give much importance to the regional issues confronted by the State of Assam. This laxity on the part of the Congress not only resulted in growing discontent towards its government but also sowed the seeds of ethno-regionalism. The preparatory ground for the ethno-regional movement was on the issue of language. It is to be remembered that language issue is one of the pertinent reasons for the emergence of sub-regionalism in many parts of India. This argument validated from the Dravidian movement in Tamil Nadu against the imposition of Hindi as a national language in India in the 1960s. In Assam too, the AASU demanded the Asamiya language as the medium of instruction upto the graduate level in addition to the existing English language. As Hussain argues that "though, the movement was apparently on the issue of medium of instruction, the ruling classes in Assam used the movement to revive the Asamiya-Bengali conflict once again in Assam after 1960" (Hussain, 1993: 105). The language issues generated Assamese discontent towards the Bengalis. It is believed that "the conflict, rooted in the centuries-old love-hate relationship between Assamese and Bengalis, has been fuelled in this century by Assamese apprehension that their language and culture are threatened" (Hardgrave, Jr., 1983: 1173). Not only Bengalis, other linguistic communities of United Assam – Nagas, Mizos, Khasis and others expressed concern over the introduction of Assamese as a medium of learning in educational institutions. Apart from this, other tribal groups like the Bodos, Rabha, Cachari, Koch, Hajong, Karbisetc, voiced their discontent against the Official Language Act. The AASU ethnicised the students for the cause of protecting their distinct identity. The ignited minds of the young students became the graveyard of ethnic chauvinism.The outcome of this phenomenon was that the 'little nationalism' (Assamese Nationalism) turned to be chauvinist' (Guha, 1980).

In 1972 the government accepted the demand of the AASU and introduced Assamese along with English at the graduate level. The subsequent years saw the fizzling out of the ethno-regional movement and was moving towards class issues. In the 1978 elections, a year before the beginning of the Assam Movement, the left parties performed comparatively. The Communist Party of India (Marxist) alone captured 11 out of the 126 seats in the Assam Legislative Assembly making inroads into the ethno-regional senitments. For sustaining the ethno-regional consciousness and mobilization, the AASU took up new issues like the illegal migration of foreign nationals in the state. It demanded the detection and deportation of illegal foreign nationals from Assam and the removal of their name from the electoral rolls leading to the launching of a new movement called the Assam movement in 1979.

The six-year-old movement finally ended after a settlement reached between the Union Government and AASU in New Delhi on 15 August 1985. The Assam Accord resolved that 1966 would be the cut off year for detecting foreigners and 1971 was for deporting the foreigners. All persons who came to Assam, prior to 1st January, 1966, including those amongst them whose names appeared on the electoral rolls used in 1967 elections, shall be regularized. Foreigners who came to Assam after 1st January 1966 and upto 24 March 1971 shall be detected and their names will be deleted from the electoral rolls. Initially, the party promised to protest the distinct socio-cultural and political identity of the Assamese people. It promised to find out solutions to illegal migration of Bengali people from Bangladesh. As Mahanta argues that "after the signing of the Assam Accord in 1985, the regional aspirations of the Assamese people got articulated in the formation of the AGP"(Mahanta, 2014: 20).

After the Assam Accord, signed between AASU and the Government of India in 1984, the Assam Legislative Assembly was dissolved and the Congress Chief Minister Hiteswar Saikia resigned paving the way for fresh elections in the state. In the 1985 election, the first ever election after its formation, the manifesto the party promised to protect the political rights of the Assamese people and the implementation of the Assam Accord.Reiterating its commitment to protect the distinct socio-cultural and political identity of the Assamese people, it promised to find out solutions to illegal migration of Bengali people from Bangladesh. It was in fact, an attempt to woo the Assamese educated middle class towards the party. It also promised to implement the Assam Accord and put an end to separatist tendencies and strengthen national integration and bring about trust and good will amongst the various religious, linguistic and ethnic communities of Assam. Further, it promised the people of Assam to strengthen the federal structure (AGP, 1985). It was infact, an attempt to woo the Assamese educated middle class. The ethno-regional consciousness generated by the Assam movement provided a conducive atmosphere for the emergence of a ethno-regional political formation, the AGP. When the AGP turned into a regional political party after the Assam movement, the United Liberation Front of Assom (ULFA) rejected the democratic path established in the Assam Accord of 1985.

In 1985, in the first state assembly elections after its formation, the AGP won 63 seats out 126 Assembly seats it contested with a voting share of 34.54 percent. The Party was able to muster the support of seven independent candidates and formed the government under the leadership of P. K. Mahanta. The great casualty was the national party, Congress which could not tackle the waves of ethnic regionalism unleashed by AGP. The Congress as a national party was under a difficult situation when the regional mobilization took place because it ultimately affected its electoral prospects adversely. As an umbrella party representing the interest of all sections, it faced the dilemma of accommodating regional issues and ethno-regional consciousness. The party came to power with the legacy of ethno-regionalism generated by Assam movement and played a dominant role in the state politics challenging the long year domination of congress politics in the state. When the party came to power, it adopted a lukewarm attitude towards the issues of illegal migration in the state. It was reported that the government could deport only 6,743 Nepalese in 1987 who reportedly migrated from the state of Meghalaya[1]. However, the government could not complete its five years term as President's Rule was imposed in the State.In the late 1980s, when coalition politics griped at the centre, the AGP became an alliance of the National Front government in 1989. While firming its commitment to the cause of ethno regionalism in the state, the party aligned with a conglomeration of national and regional parties at the centre.

As a regional party, the AGP reiterated its commitment to secure more rights for the state in the federal union, to provide full protection of the interests of local candidates in all matters of employment, respect for the legitimate rights of small nationalities (AGP, 2001). The AGP claimed that the sustenance of regionalism in Assam is the result of colonial regime of

New Delhi. The Central government often took an "attitude that the resources of Asom belong to the nation, but the problems of Asom are not national problems. These are the own problems of the state" (AGP, 2006: 2). At the age of 28 Prafulla Kumar Mahanta, AASU's young vibrant leader, became the Chief Minister of Assam, perhaps the youngest Chief Minister in India. The AGP which controlled political power in two times (1985-90 and 1996-2001) in the state took a lukewarm attitude towards illegal migration issue. Perhaps, one of the reasons for such approach was the fear of losing immigrants vote to the Party. The ascendancy of AGP saw the end of long year domination of Congress politics in the state. Initially the AGP had tactic support from the United Liberation Front of Assam (ULFA) later it turned against AGP when it started crackdown its cadres.

In the 1991 election manifesto, the AGP made more promises like greater autonomy and right to self-determination of the state. Surprisingly the key issues which were taken up during the Assam Movement were put into back burner. In the 1991 elections the party lost power to the Congress as it managed to secure only 19 seats with 18.36 per cent vote. One of the reasons for the decline of AGP and the emergence of Congress party was the feeling of the migrants and 0 parties can accommodate their concerns. In the 1996 elections, the party however won 59 seats with 33.48 per cent votes. The subsequent elections of 2001, 2006, 2011 saw the electoral setback of the AGP and the massive erosion of its support base. An in depth analysis of the election manifestoes of 1996, 2001, 2006 and 2011 shows that the two main issues raised by the Party – illegal migration and the implementation of the Assam Accord – got diluted. In other words, these two regional issues on which the party was formed were slowly erased from its agenda.

The manifesto to the 2006 State Assembly election reiterates that:

> "…before the strong advents of regional political trend in Asom, the legitimate demands of the state were being neglected in the national platform. But as the regionalism flourished in the state, the centre is bound to reduce its indifference towards the state at least to some extent. The rise of regionalism is in the root to draw the national level attention towards the problems of Asom since the Assam agitation. But still it is not the time for self satisfaction for the people of Asom. In coming days, regionalism will be the only effective instrument to make New Delhi agreed to provide legitimate dues of the state regarding the issues like the Gas Cracker Project, the fourth bridge over the Brahmaputra

at Bogibill, modernization of railways, development of road communication and permanent solution to the flood problem etc." (AGP, 2006: 4).

As a regional party, the AGP focused on ethnic identity of the Assamese. It demanded regional autonomy for Asom and the control of the state over the resources through a real federal system. The AGP did not favour secessionism on the contrary reposed its commitment to secularism, democracy and socialism. It always insisted on decentralization of power and the centre government should exercise only minimal items like defence, external affairs, foreign currency, communication, economic cooperation, etc. It shows that though championed the cause of ethno-regionalism initially, the AGP has undergone many political churning in its basic ideologies and programmes over time.The AGP is the prominent ethno-regional political party in NEI which not only played a vital role in the politics of Assam but also in the national politics. The Party was a constituent of the V.P. Singh led National Front government in 1989, Deva Gowda and I.K. Gujaral led United Front governments in 1996-97. For short while, the AGP was also a part of NDA and the BJP and AGP jointly contested the 2009 general election in the state. However, in 2011 Assembly election it parted away with NDA. In 2016 Assembly election it once again entered into an alliance with the BJP led NDA.

Though the Assam movement roused regional consciousness among the people, it could not extend its influence among the tribals of Assam. The larger Asamiya identity and regional consciousness created by the Assam movement did not address the problems of the plain tribal communities of the state leading to their virtual exclusion during and after the movement. As Hussain argues that though, officially, the movement was dominated by the AASU, it was not a student movement. Behind the AASU, stood the weak and small Asamiya bourgeois press, the Assamiya professionals, the bureaucrats, the middle class, contractors (Hussain, 1993). The assertion of the Bodos shows that the ethnic consciousness is rising at different levels even though major regionalism accommodated into the system. As Hussain says that, "needless to say that the high caste Asamiya dominate the society, polity and bureaucracy in post-colonial Assam wherein Bodos have virtually no power even to manage their own internal affairs. Since early sixties particularly, they have been trying to revive their culture and distinct identity on the plank of ethnicity" (Hussain, 2000: 4521).

The electoral performance of AGP in the last three Assembly elections shows its diminishing role in the politics of Assam. The BJP was emerging as alternative opposition force to Congress in the political space vacated by the AGP. However, both the Congress which is more centralizing in nature and the BJP which is communal in nature often find to suit the social fabric of the state. The regional politics of AGP has certain limitations as it was based on ethno-regionalism. The 2014 general election witnessed the virtual rout of the AGP as it was not able to win a single Loksabha seat in the state. The AGP contested 12 seats, however, it could not secure even a single in the Loksabha. The Congress and the BJP assumed upper hand in the election. The Muslim voters who constitute one-third of the electorate in the state which had supported the AGP once, shifted their loyalty to the AIUDF. In 2014, the AIUDF won three seats with 14.8% vote share in contrast to one seat with 16.1% vote in 2009. The people of Brahamaputra valley of Assam, once a stronghold of the AGP also drifted away from the AGP and moving towards the BJP. Many Assamese caste Hindus feel that the AGP deviated from the provisions of the Assam Accord especially related to the detection and deportation of foreigners from Assam. In the 2014 general election, the AGP which contested twelve constituencies in Assam could not win even a single seat. In terms of vote share the party could secure only 3.87% against the 14.61% (with one seat) of the 2009 general election. In Assembly Election 2016, with BJP Alliance Assam is the first state in the north-eastern region, the BJP could form its own government with the support of the AGP and Bodoland People's Front (BPF) ending the fifteen consecutive years of Congress government led by Tarun Gogoi. In May 2016, when the election resulted declared in the 126 seats in the State Assembly the BJP won 60 seats with a vote share of 42%, its alliance partner AGP secured 14 seats with a vote share of 8%. Thirdly, the BJP's pre poll alliance with the AGP and the BPF consolidated anti-Congress votes in its favour. Initially there were local protests from both the BJP and AGP in certain regions like Bongaigaon, Sivasagar, Sonitpur, Amguri and Tezpuragainst the alliance. The growing marginalisation and setback of the party compelled the AGP to align with the BJP as a junior partner.

Erosion of the AGP

After initial much fanfare, the prominent regional political party, the Asom Gana Parishad (AGP) is losing its pre-eminence in the state politics as it has undergone a process of crisis. In March, 1991 the Party underwent a major split with the formation of *Natu Asom GanaParishad* (new AGP) under the leadership of the then general secretary Bhrigu Kumar Phukan, Dinesh Goswami and Pulakesh Barua. The second split in 2000 was under the leadership of Atul Bora. On 3 July, 2005, the expulsion of P.K. Mahanta from the AGP led to the formation of the AGP (Progressive). In the recent past, the AGP faced a number of inner party problems and defections. On 3rd July, 2005 Mahanta was expelled from the AGP and he formed the AGP (Progressive). However, in October 14, 2008, Mahanta's party merged with his parent party. However, the merger did not signal the strong position of the party in the state as it faced with worst form of factionalism. In 2011, AGP leader Atul Bora joined the BJP and in 2013 another senior leader SarbanandSonowal joined the BJP.

The appointment of SarbanandaSonowal, the Union Minister of State for Sports, as the president of the State BJP in 2015 gave further boost to the saffron party. Sonowal, the former leader of the AASU and subsequently MLA of the AGP switched over to the BJP some time back, is a crusader against illegal migration of Bangladeshi in Assam. In 2012, he accused the illegal migrants of deteriorating the life of the indigenous people of Assam. He said that in the last 32 years the indigenous people of Assam have been cornered and pushed to the status of minority due to the huge influx of illegal immigrants from Bangladesh.[2] It has to be reminded that the illegal migration from Bangladesh is a sensitive issue in Assam as it developed far reaching consequences in the political, economic and socio-cultural life of the people. As it stated earlier, the Assam movement which put the demand for the detection and deportation of illegal migrants (often used as 'foreigners') in the state. In its effort to end the movement the Indian government formulated the IM (DT) Act 1983 to protect the interest of Assam. According to the Act, anybody settled in Assam before March 25, 1971 was a legal citizen. However, rest of India, the cut of date for acquiring Indian citizenship is July 9, 1948. Further, the person accused had to do nothing to prove his/her citizenship whereas the compliant had to prove that someone was illegal. The Act also provides special protections against undue harassment to the minorities affected by Assam Agitation. The Act is applicable only to Assam while rest of the states in India is covered by the Foreigners Act, 1946. The Act it was viewed that the provision designed to make it difficult for authorities to identify, leave alone, deport illegal Bangladeshi from Assam.

The Second wave of Ethno-Regionalism

Further, the erosion of ethno-regional nationalism championed by the AGP in the eighties went into the advantage of the BJP. The AGP which came into power with the cause of 'Asomiya Nationality' and the issue of illegal migration, in course of time, diluted its stand on Illegal Migrants

Determination by Tribunal IM(DT) Act, 1983 due to compulsions of electoral politics. As a result, there was a growing disillusionment among the Hindus against the AGP, this created a fertile ground for the BJP in Assam. Over a time, the BJP used the issue of illegal migration of Muslims for expanding its mass base in the state. As Srikanth argues that "the politics of regional identity had kept Hindutva at bay in Assam for over two decades. But the AGP government's poor performance and the bogey of Muslim fundamentalism led Bengali and Assamese caste Hindus to the BJP" (Srikanth, 1999: 3412). As a result, the AGP, the prominent regional political force is declining its space in the state. Moreover, AGP's alliance with BJP in the 2006 Assembly and 2009 Loksabha election cost more to the AGP. The BJP could grow at the expense of the decline political space of the AGP. It is argued that the traditional support base of AGP – the Assamese Hindus, the Assamese Muslim and tribals – gradually shifted their allegiance to other political parties (Mahanta, 2014: 20). The regional agenda of the AGP, especially detection and deportation of illegal Bangladeshi migrants were hijacked by the BJP. In the recent past, many leaders of the AGP joined the BJP adding further boost to the BJP in the state. In December 2015, the BJP constituted its campaign panel for the Assembly elections 2016 with number of former AASU, AGP leaders.

Strain in the Relationship with BJP

Though the AGP struck an alliance with BJP in the Assembly Election in 2016 and became a partner in the BJP government, two issues continued to strain its relationship with the BJP. Unlike the first wave of ethno-regionalism championed by the AGP against the illegal migration in the state, the second wave of ethno-regionalism championed by BJP tilted towards Hindu nationalism. It may be recalled that, during the first wave, the AGP was critical of illegal migration to the state irrespective of the religious identities of the migrants. However, in the second wave of ethno-regionalism, the BJP added a religious colour to the illegal migration issue. The Citizenship (Amendment) Bill, 2016 brought by the BJP led NDA government at the centre categorised illegal minorities into two – Muslims and non-Muslims by changing the definition of the illegal migrants. The Bill, introduced in the Lok Sabha on July 15, 2016, seeks to amend the Citizenship Act, 1955 to provide citizenship to illegal migrants, from Afganistan, Bangladesh, Pakistan, who are Hindu, Sikh, Buddhist, Jain, Parsi or Christian extraction. It is also surprising that the Act does not have a provision for Muslim sects like Shias and Ahmediyas who also face persecution in Pakistan.

The AGP, the BJP's ally described the Bill as "Anit-Assam" as it make Assam a "dumping ground for Hindu Bangladeshis" and it is against the cultural and linguistic identity of state. The AGP event threatened to break alliance with the BJP in the state. On the other hand, the BJP claimed that granting citizenship to Hindus persecuted in the neibouring countries is in consonance with its manifesto and very much part of the election campaign in 2014. In the wake of the strained relationship with its ally, the centre government constituted a sixteen-member Joint Parliamentary Committee headed by the BJP Member of Parliament, Rajendra Agarwal visited many places of Assam to seek different shades of opinion.

Conclusion

To conclude, ethno-regional chauvinism leads only to certain groups and communities and often fulfilling the aspirations of middle class and elite sections.AGP as an ethno-regional party that dominated in the Assam politics symbolizing the pride and self-respect of Assamiya middle class as the social base of AGP was primarily premised on the educated middle class. However, unlike other regional parties such as DMK, TDP and SAD, it failed to reorient its ideology and mobilization strategy. They are mobilizing cross sections of the people in their respective states. These parties after initial phase of ethno-regional mobilization began to adopt populist politics and social security policies which helped them to reach out cross sections of the society. For instance, the DMK though initially raised the issue of ethno-regionalism– Dravidian identity with non-Brahmanism –in course of time mobilized cross sections of people in the Tamil Nadu and thereby emerged as a formidable political force not only in the state politics but also in the national politics. Both DMK and TDP became part of Coalition governments in the Centre and developed a bargain politics for the development of the states.

Moreover, the AGP failed to develop a new regional bourgeoisie unlike that of DMK in Tamil Nadu, TDP in Andhra Pradesh and SAD in Punjab. It neither developed a regional bourgeoisie nor corporate business nor agrarian capitalist in the state. The party relied only on the middle class, educated sections and emotive issues of ethno-regionalism and failed to take any other issues to mobilize people. In 1985, people voted to power AGP with high expectation. However, the Party and its government failed to rise up to the expectations of the people. It failed to orient ethnic regionalism to development and to ensure the material wellbeing of the cross sections of the society. The mobilization on the basis of ethnicity and regionalism may produce short term benefit for a political party. The durable existence of a regional party depends on its mobilization of cross sections of the people and it ability to deliver good governance and distributive politics. In other words, for sustaining in a competitive party system based on liberal democracy, the ethno-regional political parties have to transform into regional parties distributing goods to the people.

As a regional political party AGP failed to address the concerns of smaller communities and groups. Though it championed the cause of ethno-regionalism in the State, it ignored sub regionalism and material wellbeing of smaller communities and groups in the state. Regional politics based on ethno-regionalism is a dangerous condition for democracy. The growing ethno-regional consciousness dilute the emergence of class consciousness in a society and leads to the further ethnic and sub-regional mobilization of more ethnic communities leading to ugly identity politics. Ethno-regional parties increase ethnic conflict and secessionism by reinforcing ethnic and regional identities. The major problem with AGP that it thought that rising ethno-regional issues would strengthen the party. In course of time, the AGP developed intolerant attitude towards smaller communities and groups in the State. Though, during the movement and in the aftermath of its ascendancy to power, the AGP proclaimed its commitment to protect the Assamiya identity, it failed to protect the interest of the Bodos, the largest plain tribes in Assam. The upper caste Hindus and the Assamese middle class who extended their overt support to the Assam movement, turned against the concerns of the plain tribals groups in Assam. In other words, ethnic regionalism as epitomized by the Assam movement did not evoke much positive response from these sections. In the late 1980s, the demand for the formation of a separate Bodo state resurfaced in the north of the Brahmaputra. The Bodo movement (1987-1993) led by the All Bodo Students' Union (ABSU) and the Bodo People's Action Committee (BPAC), among other things, demanded the inclusion of Bodo language in the Eighth Schedule of the Indian Constitution. The movement ended in 1993 with the setting up of Bodo Territorial Council (BTC) (George, 1994: 878-892). The assertion of Bodos proves that the regional consciousness roused by the Assam movement and the AGP did not address the concerns of the largest plain tribes of Assam. The access to political and administrative system was denied leading to their further socio-economic deprivation. Moreover, the emergence of the Bodo movement proves that the big regional movement while projecting the Assamiya identity sidelined the identity differences among other ethnic communities of the state. In other words, the larger regional identity appeared to be oppressive to other smaller identities.

The AGP's alliance with the BJP cost the prospects of the party more. The BJP by rising the ethno-regional issues, could attract sizeable number of Assamiya middle class. Though the first wave of ethno-regionalism championed by the AGP brought short term benefit to the party, the second wave of ethno-regionalism with more religious colour championed by the Hindu nationalist politics enabled to consolidate its mass base in the socially and culturally diverse society in the state. On the issue of illegal migration, the AGP always emphasised that all illegal migrants irrespective of their religious identities should be detected and deported to their respective neigbouring state. However, the BJP added a religious dimension stating that the illegal migration of the Muslims would be prevented and other religious minorities from Afghanistan, Bangladesh, Pakistan, who are Hindu, Sikh, Buddhist, Jain, Parsi or Christian extraction would be welcome to India. Such an approach of BJP emerged out of the anticipation of electoral dividends in the politics of competitive ethno-regional politics in the state. By transforming from a predominant ethno-regional party in the region to a junior partner in the BJP government in Assam, the AGP caused great injury to its own cause.

Notes

1. see *The Sentinel*, 1988.
2. see *Organiser*16th September 2012.

References

AsomGanaParishad (1985), *Election Manifesto of AGP.*

AsomGanaParishad (2006), *Election Manifesto of AsomGanaParishad to the 12th Election to the Assembly of Assam.*

Guha, Amalendu (1980), "Little Nationalism Turned Chauvinist: Assam's Anti-Foreign Upsurge, 1979-1984", *Economic and Political Weekly*, Vol. XV, Nos. 41-43, Special Number, October, pp. 1699-1720.

Hardgrave, Jr., Robert L. (1983), "The Northeast, the Punjab, and the Regionalization of Indian Politics", *Asian Survey*, Vol. 23, No. 11, November, pp. 1171-1181.

Hussain, Monirul (1993), *The Assam Movement: Class, Ideology and Identity*, New Delhi: Manak Publication Private Limited.

Hussain, Monirul (2000), "State, Identity Movements and Internal Displacement in the North-East", *Economic and Political Weekly*, Vol. 35, No. 51, 16 December, pp. 4519-4523.

Mahanta, Nani Gopal (2014), "Loksabha Elections in Assam: Shifting of Traditional Vote Bases to BJP", *Economic and Political Weekly*, Vol. XLIX, No. 35, 30th August, pp. 19- 22.

Srikanth, H, 1999; 'Communalising Assam: AGP's Loss Is BJP's Gain', *Economic and Political Weekly,* XXXIV (49), 4 December, pp. 3412-3414.

Chapter - 6

Struggling Mizo National Front: Recap of Ideological Manuring

The emergence of Mizo National Front (MNF) as the political manifestation of ethno-regionalism, generating the ethnic consciousness and perpetuating ethnic sentiments among the Mizos, is a unique experiment in the politics of Mizoram. Unlike AGP, which was formed only after the Assam movement, the MNF as an ethno- regional political party formed in the turbulent years of the insurgency. On 22 October, 1961, after the famine, the Mizo National Famine Front (MNFF) was transformed into a regional political party, the MNF under the leadership of Laldenga though the Election Commission of India did not recognise as a regional political party. For quite some time, the MNF was outlawed and it engaged in underground activities. Initially, the party's goal was to achieve a sovereign and independent 'Greater Mizoram' integrating all Mizo people living in different independent countries under a unified Government of Mizoram having maximum political freedom and independence, to uplift and develop the Mizo people in all respects; and to safeguard the Christian religion and promoting and safeguarding the good traditions and cultural heritage of the Mizos. The MNF Constitution promised to ensure 'highest sovereignty to the Mizos" and affirms that it stands for "preserving and safeguarding Mizoram, the God given land of our forefathers and its sons of the soil". On 30 October, 1965, the MNF submitted a Memorandum to the Prime Minister demanding grant of freedom to the Mizos. Later, the MNF constituted the Mizo National Army (MNA) to free Mizoram from the Indian government. On 1 March 1966, the MNF declared the independence of the Mizo people from India. As Lianzela argues that "the dilemma of the Mizo people in the event of the British withdrawal from India, the impact of 'mautam' famine, the Assamese Language Bill of 1960, the poor economy, cultural differences, etc had been responsible for creating a strong regional consciousness among the Mizo people adding to the advantage of the newly formed MNF" (Lianzela, 2007: 431). Reflecting the same view Baral, argues that "economic backwardness coupled with the apathy of the Assam Government to the problems of the Mizos prepared the ground for the MNF's autonomy movement" (Baral, 1994: 47).

The MNF initially adopted anti-central government stand as a mobilization strategy. During the insurgency and counter insurgency, the Lushai Hills in Assam witnessed atrocities against women and children and the wide spread human rights violation by the security forces. The armed forces engaged in regrouping of Mizos to counter the spread of insurgency. As an ethno-regional party, the MNF aroused the regional sentiment during the drive out activities of non-Mizos out of Mizoram. On 31 December, 1974, the MNF issued a 'Quit Mizoram' notice to non-Mizos to protect its distinct cultural identities from the onslaught of migration of outsiders in the state. The party was successfully able to mobilise large sections of Mizo youths to generate ethno-regional conscious among the Mizos. It is argued that

The MNF-led armed struggle was long in the making. Prior to its declaration of independence on the midnight of 28 February 1966, it was engaged in a hefty mobilisation of volunteers. This mobilisation took place across state borders covering present-day Mizoram, and the Mizo-inhabited areas of Manipur and Tripura. The success of the MNF was reflected in its ability to induct early Mizo educated youth into its organizational fold. (Roluahpuia, 2018: 40).

The Mizo ethnic regional movement was a reaction to the Assam Official Language Act 1960 as well as the failure of the central government to provide assistance to poverty stricken Mizo tribal population of the Lushai Hills district of Assam. In 1959, the Bamboo flowering and the explosion of rat population brought the*mautam*(famine) which resulted in violent ethnic politics in the State. The famine contributed to starvation deaths in Mizo huts. It was argued that even during earlier famines during the British time (1861-62, 1911-12) the Mizos did not face such hunger and humiliation as they were facing in the hands of the Indian state. During the famine, the Mizo Cultural Society (MCS) under the leadership of Laldenga was formed to supervise relief works. Later the MCS itself transformed into the Mizo National Famine Front (MNFF). The poverty and material deprivation was utilized by the MNFF for asserting their ethnic regional identity. During the famine, the resentment against Assam Government was mobilized by the MNFF to rouse regional consciousness among the Mizos. Unlike the Assam movement, the Mizo movement demanded for secessionism to protect their cultural identity – a separate sovereign state for the Mizos from the Indian Union. The governments of Assam and India, on the other hand, treated the identity assertion of the Mizos as a law and order problem and tried to combat it with security forces. On 2 March, 1966, the then Government of Assam declared Mizoram as a 'disturbed area'.

From Ethnic Movement to Regional Party

In the course of insurgency and peace negotiations, the Congress won the 1984 election as it secured 20 seats in the 30 member State Legislative Assembly. The Congress (I) government led by Lalthanhawla came to power and was committed to bring peace and harmony in the Hill state. The Congress governments both at the State and Centre took effective steps in peace negotiations. On 30 June 1986, the Mizo Accord was signed between the MNF and the Government of India ending the twentyyears (1966-86) of insurgent activities. The MNF was represented by Laldenga and the Government of India was represented by R. D. Pradhan, the Union Home Secretary. Under the provisions of the Memorandum of Settlement, Mizoram became the 23rd state of Indian Union on 20 February, 1987. The Accord, among other things, made the provision for Inner Line Regulation to protect the distinct identity of the Mizos. After the accord, the MNF adopted parliamentary democracy and agreed to work "within the framework of the Constitution of India". According to the provisions of the Accord the Congress Ministry under Lal Thanhawla was dissolved paving the way for the formation of the first MNF government under the chiefministership of Laldena on 21 August, 1986.

In the 1987 election manifesto, the MNF did not make any demand for 'greater Mizoram' which was one of its major issues initially. As the editorial of Economic and Political Weekly writes that "clearly, while dropping the issue from the election manifesto might have been dictated by political calculations, the MNF has not changed its stand on the demand for a greater Mizoram – a single administrative unit comprising all the contiguous areas inhabited by Mizos in Assam and Tripura. The Congress (I), on the other hand, perhaps in an attempt to counter the MNF propaganda that it is a *vai* (outsiders) party incorporated the demand of 'greater Mizoram', in its manifesto, as had the People's Conference" (EPW, 1987: 347).

In the 1987 election to the State Legislative Assembly, the MNF won 24 seats out of 40 and formed the ministry on 20th February, 1987. The Party was able to secure 36.5% votes against the 33.5% of the Congress Party which won only 13 seats and People's Conference with 26.6% votes having 2 seats. However, the MNF government could not complete its full five year term due to dissidence in the Party. On 30 August 1988, the MNF split and was reduced to a minority in the State Legislative Assembly. Subsequently, the State came under President's rule which was followed by mid-term election in January 1989. In the 1989 Assembly election, the Congress government with 23 seats formed the government under the chiefministership of Lal Thanhawla. In the 1993 elections, the MNF won only 14 seats and the Congress 16 seats. The Congress formed a government along with its ally Mizo Janata Dal which won 8 seats in the State Assembly.However, the 1998 elections witnessed the reemergence of MNF which won 21 seats against Congress party's 6 seats. In 2003 election to the MNF continued with its tally of 21 seats against the Congress's 12 seats. Moreover, the 2008 Assembly election saw the virtual rout of the MNF as the party won only 4 seats in the 40 member Assembly. The Congress party which won 32 seats formed the Government.

In the 1993 elections, the MNF won only 14 seats and the Congress 16 seats. The Congress formed a government along with its ally Mizo Janata Dal which won 8 seats in the State Assembly. However, the 1998 elections witnessed the reemergence of MNF which won 21 seats against Congress party's 6 seats. In 2003 election too the MNF continued with its tally of 21 seats against the Congress's 12 seats. It is argued that the political journey of MNF from insurgency to electoral democracy is due to the "accommodative politics, combined with political incentives, helped pave the way for the Mizo National Front to turn into a mainstream political party"(Sirnateand Verma, 2013). In the 2008 Assembly election saw the virtual rout of the MNF as the party won only 4 seats in the 40 member Assembly. The Congress party which won 32 seats formed the Government. The ascendancy of the Congress party and the electoral rout of MNF shows the declining trend of ethno-regionalism in the state. Harping on ethno-regionalism, failure to address the grievances of smaller communities such as Hmars, animosity against non-tribals turned against the prospects of the MNF.

The Assembly election 2013 witnessed a three cornered contest – Congress, Mizoram Democratic Alliance (MDA) and Zoram Nationalist Party (ZNP). The Mizo National Front (MNF) which formed a prepoll alliance – MDA -with two other regional parties such as Mizoram People's Conference (MPC) and the Maraland Democratic Front (MDF) was the key player in the opposition camp. The MDF put up candidates in all 40 constituencies with the MNF contested 31 seats, the MPC eight and the MDF one. In the electoral outcome, however, the ruling Congress could win 34 seats and the opposition MNFled MDA won only six seats (MNF 5, MPC 1, MDF 0) in the 40 number State Assembly. The Zoram Nationalist Party (ZNP) which had two seats in the outgoing Assembly, contested in 38 seats drew blank and secured only 17.4% of votes. Though the BJP contested 17 seats could not open its account and it secured just about 0.4% of votes in the tribal state of Mizoram.

The two consecutive term of the Congress government put the MNF in quandary. The consolidation of Congress shows the diminishing influence of ethno-regionalism championed by the MNF. The Congress, on the other hand, was able make inroads into the mass base of the MNF by initiating welfare and people centered public policies. For instance, the election victory of Congress in 2013 was considered as the public endorsement of Congress government's flagship programme New Land Use Policy (NLUP). The NLUP aimed at preserving and regenerating natural resources particularly forests and biodiversity. Among other things, the core objectives include: Firstly, to aim at keeping 60% of Mizoram total land area under rain forest. Secondly, to wean away farmers from destructive jhum practices and assist the workforce higher to engaged in jhuming to be employed in sustainable economic venture to create productive assets in each family. Thirdly, to improve income for both urban and rural poor through sustainable farming, non-farming, micro enterprises including promotion and modernization of small scale and cottage industries. The objective is to put an end to wasteful shifting cultivation designed to transform the state economy focusing on inclusive growth and poverty alleviation.

Being out of power for two consecutive terms, the MNF moved to closer to the BJP at the to counter the Congress. The BJP also found a new constituent in its North East Democratic Alliance (NEDA) to outside the lone Congress ruled state in the Northeast for the realization of a Congress *Mukht* (Free) Northeast. However, smelling the penetration of BJP and its effort to emerge as an opposition party to the Congress, the MNF cautiously keeping distance from the Hindu nationalist party. Though a constituent of NEDA, the MNF recently made it clear that it will contest the upcoming assembly polls in 2018 on its own is clear dumping the BJP. The BJP, is however, hobnobbing with the MNF, for alliance to uproot the lone Congress ruled state in Northeast. The public reluctance of MNF to forge an alliance with the BJP cited was the later's alliance with the Congress in the Chakma Autonomous District Council (CADC) dumping MNF. It has to be remembered that in the 10th CADC election held on 20 April 2018, no political party secured absolute majority. In the 20-member Council, the BJP has five members, congress seven and the MNF with eight (one seat withheld by the Gauhati High Court Aizawl Bench). The BJP extended its support to the Congress to form the Council dumping MNF.

Conclusion

The ethno-regional movements and ethno-regional political parties in NEI stand for protecting their distinct ethno-cultural identities. The spirit of ethno-regionalism and consciousness are the motivating force for their political mobilization and ascendancy to political power. The emergence and ascendancy of MNF as the prominent ethno-regional political party proves that ethnicity and regionalism play an important role in the politics of Mizoram. However, in course of time, one can also see the gradual erosion of its mass support and preeminence of the Congress. In other words, it is obvious that regional consciousness and ethnic mobilization bring short term benefits to an ethno-regional party and in the long run, these issues would be insignificant over development and performance. In other words, the prominence and the subsequent erosion of MNF is sending a clear message that regional and ethnic issues would not be the prime issues for long term mobilization for a ethno-regional political party. From the sagaof MNF it is obvious that the social constituencies of the regional political parties may switch over to other political parties when its delivery mechanism fails to satisfy them.

Moreover,the ethno-regional consciousness roused by the MNFF during the famine concealed the internal exploitation by the village chiefs, political and bureaucratic elite who indulged in massive corruption and diverted resources for poverty alleviation which too contributed to deprivation of the poor Mizos. In fact, under the carpet of ethno-regionalism, the Mizo ruling classes succeeded to a certain extent to cover up their misdeeds on their own society. There was a religious dimension in the demand for ethno-regionalism of MNF. The majority Mizos who are Christians felt that their religious identity would be threatened in the majority Hindu society. The MNF, even at a point of time championed a Christian state for the Mizos. Further, like the Bodos in Assam movement, the ethno-regionalism championed by the Mizo movement, did not benefit the Brus, minor tribal community, in Mizoram. The Brus have been fighting for autonomy from the state of Mizoram. In many occasions, the MNF used many ethnic organizations for its political motive.The ethnic organizations such as the Young Mizo Association (YMA), Mizo Zirlai Pawl (MZA) and the Mizo Students Union who often raise the bogey of 'outsider' problem to the stability of the State. While the 'perpetual peace' attained in the aftermath of the Mizo Accord was often romanticized by the ruling elite, it was, in fact, a cover up to the atrocities committed against the non-Mizos in the State. In other words, ethno-regionalism propagated by the MNF for political dividends constructed a social divide based on 'us' and 'them'. Such a parochial construction of social identity and mobilization, in course of time, contributed to the mass erosion of the party in Mizoram.

References

Baral, K. C. (1994), "Ideology and Ethnic Politics: A Study of Autonomy Movement in Mizoram", in R. N. Prasad (ed.), *Autonomy Movements in Mizoram*, New Delhi: Vikas Publishing House Private Limited, pp. 44-61.

Economic and Political Weekly (1987), "Editorial", Vol. 22, No. 9, February 28, p. 347.

Lianzela (2007), "Insurgency, Peace Accord and its Implementation with Special Reference to Mizoram", in Anuradha Dutta and Ratna Bhuyan (eds.), *Genesis of Conflict and Peace: Understanding Northeast India: Views and Reviews*, Vol. II, New Delhi: Akansha Publishing House, pp. 428-432.

Roluahpuia (2018), "Memories and Memorials of the Mizo National Front Movement: Problems and Politics of Momorialisation", Economic and Political Weekly, Vol. LIII, No.25, 23 June, pp.38-45.

Sirnate, Vasundhara and Rahul Verma. 2013. "From Insurgency to Electoral Democracy", *The Hindu*, November 30.

Part – III
Elections in Stroke

Chapter - 7

Mizoram Assembly Election 2013: Invigorated Congress and Dwindled MNF

The verdict of Mizoram Assembly Elections held on 25th November 2013 gave a much respite for the Congress Party as it retained political power in the second consecutive term. Unlike other states such as Rajasthan, Chhattisgarh, Madhya Pradesh and Delhi which witnessed the rout of the Congress Party in the Assembly elections held during this time, the verdict in Mizoram gave some solace to the central leadership of the party. The 2013 election witnessed a three cornered contest – Congress, Mizoram Democratic Alliance (MDA) and Zoram Nationalist Party (ZNP). The Mizo National Front (MNF) which formed a prepoll alliance – MDA - with two other regional parties such as Mizoram People's Conference (MPC) and the Maraland Democratic Front (MDF) was the key player in the opposition camp. The MDF put up candidates in all 40 constituencies with the MNF contested 31 seats, the MPC eight and the MDF one. In the electoral outcome, however, the ruling Congress could win 34 seats and the opposition Mizo National Front (MNF) led MDA won only six seats (MNF 5, MPC 1, MDF 0) in the 40 number State Assembly. The Zoram Nationalist Party (ZNP) which had two seats in the outgoing Assembly, contested in 38 seats drew blank and secured only 17.4% of votes. Though the BJP contested 17 seats could not open its account and it secured just about 0.4% of votes in the tribal state of Mizoram.

Mizoram is the second most literate state (91.58%) in India after Kerala (93.91%) having the female literacy of 89.41% and male literacy of 93.72%. Of the total population of 10.91 lakhs, 87 per cent population is Christians. Of the total of 6,86,305 voters, female voters constitute 3,49,506 and male voters of 3, 36, 799. In the election of the 40 assembly seats the total votes polled was 6, 90, 860 that is a record of 81.3% which is one percentage point higher than the previous assembly elections. The chief minister Lal Thanhawla won from two constituencies – Serchip and Hrangturzo and became the Chief Minister in his fifth term. In Serchip, he defeated his nearest MNF rival C. Lalramzaua by a margin of 734 votes and in Hrangturzo he defeated his nearest rival Lalthansanga by a margin of 1,528 votes.

The election to the State Assembly also witnessed the elections in six Bru relief camps in North Tripura district such as Asapara, Naisingpara, Hazacherra, Kakau, Khakchangpara and Hamsapara with combining strength of an electorate of 11,612. The much enthusiasm shown by the refuges in the election reflected in the high voter turnout of 74.34%. Brus are the internally displaced groups sheltered in Tripura relief camps in Tripura's north district for the last 16 years. The Brus refused to return to the state despite several pleas from the Centre, state government and civil societies. The Delhi High Court Order in 1999 allowed the Brus in the relief camps in Tripura to cast its vote in Mizoram election. The Mizo Zirlai Pawl (MZP), the powerful students body of the state opposed the Election Commission's move to establishing poll booth in Tripura to exercise vote for Brus. Other organizations such as Mizo Students Union (MSU) and the Young Mizo Association (YMA) also expressed their resentment over the voting rights of the Brus outside the state. The MSU in its memorandum submitted to the CEC, V.S. Sampath, protested against giving more rights to Brus (The Times of India, 2013a).

The highly spirited election campaign saw the strong presence of national leaders including the Prime Minister, Manmohan Singh, UPA chairperson, Sonia Gandhi and Congress Vice-President, Rahul Gandhi. The Congress Vice President promised to create more jobs if the Congress was voted back to power in the State. While the Congress party highlighted the achievements of its Government in the state under the leadership of Lal Thanhawla, among the regional parties, the star campaigner was the former Chief Minister and MNF leader Zoramthanga who focused on the failures of Congress governments in many areas. The MDA election manifest promised the reunification of Mizo-inhabited the areas into one administrative unit with higher political status as per the UN Declaration on the Rights of Indigenous People 2007.

Summary of Results – Seats Contested, Won and Votes Secured by Major Parties in Mizoram Assembly Elections 2013, Compared to the Assembly Elections 2008

Political Parties	*Seats Contested*	*Seats Won*	*Vote Share of Seats since 2008*	*Gain/Loss (%)*	*Vote %Per Seats Contested (% Points)*	*Vote Swing since 2008*
INC	40	34	+2	44.61	44.61	+5.72
BJP	17	0	0	0.37	0.84	-0.07
NCP	2	0	0	0.84	14.08	+0.73
MNF	31	5	+2	28.66	36.65	-1.99
MPC	8	1	-1	6.15	31.44	-4.23
MDF	1	0	-1	0.95	42.60	+0.11
ZNP	38	0	-2	17.43	18.52	+7.21
Independents	4	0	0	0.31	-	-7.38
Other Parties	1	0	0	0.02	-	-0.76
NOTA (None of the Above)	-	-	-	0.66	-	+0.66
Total	142	40		100		

Source: CSDS Data Unit. Published in Economic and Political Weekly, Vol. XLIX, No.6, February 8, 2014, p. 89.

Electoral History

The electoral history of Mizoram is quite interesting to the political analysts. In Mizoram, ethno-regional politics is championed by the MNF which was formed during the insurgency. On 22 October, 1961, after the famine, the Mizo National Famine Front , which undertook relief activities during the famine, was transformed into a regional political party, the MNF under the leadership of Laldenga though the Election Commission of India initially did not recognise as a regional political party. For quite some time, the MNF was outlawed and it engaged in underground activities. Initially, the party's goal was to achieve a sovereign and independent 'Greater Mizoram' integrating all Mizo peoples living in different independent countries under a unified Government of Mizoram having maximum political freedom and independence, to uplift and develop the Mizo people in all respects; and to safeguard the Christian religion. The MNF Constitution promised to ensure 'highest sovereignty to the Mizos". On 30 October, 1965, the MNF submitted a Memorandum to the Prime Minister demanding grant of freedom to the Mizos. The MNF then constituted the Mizo National Army (MNA) to free Mizoram from the Indian government. On 1 March 1966, the MNF declared the independence of the Mizo people from India.

The MNF initially adopted anti-central government strategy as a mobilization strategy. During the insurgency and counter insurgency, the Lushai Hills (earlier name of Mizoram when it was the part of the larger Assam) witnessed atrocities against women and children and the wide spread human rights violation by the security forces. The armed forces engaged in regrouping of Mizo villages to counter the spread of insurgency. During this time the MNF aroused the ethno-regional sentiment to drive out non-Mizos in Mizoram. For instance, on 31 December, 1974, the MNF issued a 'Quit Mizoram' notice to non-Mizos.

In the course of insurgency and peace negotiations, the Congress won the 1984 election as it secured 20 seats in the 30 member State Legislative Assembly. The Congress (I) government led by Lalthanhawla came to power and was committed to bring peace and harmony in the Hill state. Subsequently, the Congress governments both at the State and Centre took effective steps in peace negotiations. On 30 June 1986, the Mizo Accord was signed between the MNF and the Government of India ending the twenty years (1966-86) of insurgent activities. The MNF was represented by Laldenga and the Government of India was represented by R. D. Pradhan, the Union Home Secretary. Under the provisions of the Memorandum of Settlement, Mizoram became the 23rd state of Indian Union on 20 February, 1987. The Accord, among other things, made the provision for Inner Line Regulation to protect the distinct identity of the Mizos. After the accord, the MNF adopted parliamentary democracy and agreed to work "within the framework of the Constitution of India". According to the provisions of the Accord the Congress Ministry under Lal Thanhawla was dissolved paving the way for the formation of the first MNF government under the chiefministership of Laldena on 21 August, 1986. In 1986, according to the Mizoram Peace Accord between Union government under Rajiv Gandhi and MNF leader the Congress Chief Minister Lathanhawla had to step down and gave way to Laldenga of the MNF. After the peace Accord, the MNF won the Assembly elections in 1987. However, Laldenga's government survived for barely two years. Nine of the twenty four MNF MLAs defected to the Congress and President's rule was imposed in the State in September 1988.

In the 1987 election manifesto, the MNF did not make any demand for 'greater Mizoram' which was one of its major demands initially. As the editorial of Economic and Political Weekly writes that "clearly, while dropping the issue from the election manifesto might have been dictated by political calculations, the MNF has not changed its stand on the demand for a greater Mizoram – a single administrative unit comprising all the contiguous areas inhabited by Mizos in Assam and Tripura. The Congress (I), on the other hand, perhaps in an attempt to counter the MNF propaganda that it is a *vai* (outsiders) party incorporated the demand of 'greater Mizoram', in its manifesto, as had the People's Conference" (EPW, 1987: 347).

In the 1987 election to the State Legislative Assembly, the MNF won 24 seats out of 40 and formed the ministry on 20th February, 1987. The Party was able to secure 36.5% votes against the 33.5% of the Congress Party which won only 13 seats and People's Conference with 26.6% votes having 2 seats. However, the MNF government could not complete its full five year term due to dissidence in the Party. On 30 August 1988, the MNF split and was reduced to a minority in the State Legislative Assembly. Subsequently, the State came under President's rule which was followed by mid-term election in January 1989. In the 1989 Assembly election, the Congress government with 23 seats formed the government under the chiefministership of Lal Thanhawla. The Congress under Lalthanhawla returned to power after the 1989 polls, In 1993, the Congress gain formed government with the alliance of Mizoram Janata Dal (MJD).

In the 1993 elections, the MNF won only 14 seats and the Congress 16 seats. The Congress formed a government along with its ally Mizo Janata Dal which won 8 seats in the State Assembly. However, the 1998 elections witnessed the reemergence of MNF which won 21 seats against Congress party's 6 seats. In 2003 election too the MNF continued with its tally of 21 seats against the Congress's 12 seats. It is argued that the political journey of MNF from insurgency to electoral democracy is due to the "accommodative politics, combined with political incentives, helped pave the way for the Mizo National Front to turn into a mainstream political party" (Sirnate and Verma, 2013). In the 2008 Assembly election saw the virtual rout of the MNF as the party won only 4 seats in the 40 member Assembly. The Congress party which won 32 seats formed the Government. The ascendancy of the Congress party and the electoral rout of MNF shows the declining trend of ethno-regionalism in the state. Harping on ethno-regionalism, failure to address the grievances of smaller communities such as Hmars, animosity against non-tribals turned against the prospects of the MNF.

The New Land Use Policy

The election verdict in 2013 was considered as the public endorsement of Congress government's flagship programme NLUP. The NLUP aimed at preserving and regenerating natural resources particularly forests and biodiversity. Among other things, the core objectives include: Firstly, to aim at keeping 60% of Mizoram total land area under rain forest. Secondly, to wean away farmers from destructive jhum practices and assist the workforce higher to engaged in jhuming to be employed in sustainable economic venture to create productive assets in each family. Thirdly, to improve income for both urban and rural poor through sustainable farming, non farming, micro enterprises including promotion and modernization of small scale and cottage industries. The objective is to put an end to wasteful shifting cultivation designed to transform the state economy focusing on inclusive growth and poverty alleviation. The Planning Commission on 25 October 2012 released a sum of Rs. 370 crore grant from the plan out lay of 2012-13 as ACA for taking up activities of the "Comprehensive and Integrated Socio-Economic Development Project under the NLUP". The State Finance Minister Liansailova in his Budget Speech 2013-14 drew road map of the New Land Use Policy. The Finance Minister claimed that "foundation stone for the institution of modern farming techniques and agricultural practices in the rural areas has been laid through implementation of New Land Use Policy" (Government of Meghalaya, 2013: p.1).

In fact, the first NLUP in Mizoram was launched in 1985 but was confined to four development blocks. From 1985 to 1991-91, the total funds released for NLUP was Rs. 21.16 crore. The MNF government led by Zoramthanga discontinued the NLUP and replaced it with Mizoram Intodelhna Programme (MIP) in 2002. The overall objectives of the present NLUP were to improve the livelihood of vulnerable groups mainly jhumi families in a sustainable manner through improved management of their resource base in a way that contributes to protecting and restoring environment. The economic life of the Mizo has always been centered around jhum or shifting cultivation. The crops grown in the jhum are mixed. The Prime Minister, Manmohan Singh, in an election rally promised to improve the NLUP. The background for the NLUP is that the jhum cultivation does not satisfy the growth of Mizoram and as a result, the state witnessed increased food insecurity and poverty. As government claimed that "owning to intervention of various central schemes as well as our flagship programme, New Land use Policy, rice cultivation area under shifting practices has decreased significantly from 25,826 Ha during 2011-

12 to 23,150 Ha during 2012-13 which is 10.36 per cent reduction over the preceding year" (Government of Meghalaya, 2013: 9).

Tribals in Meghalaya for quite some time, practicing the jhum or shifting cultivation constituted the major form of livelihood for Mizo farming community. In the 1960s, the Bamboo flowering witnessed political castrophie in the state in the form of famine which affected 1,30, 621 families in 769 villages in Mizoram. The rodents and insects feeding on the bamboo damaged 16,132 hectares of wet rice cultivation and 1,25, 345 hectares of jhum paddy cultivation in the state. However, in 2008, the *mautam* could be easily handled by the Congress government in preventing another castrophie in the state. On the occasion of *mautam* the Congress wooed voters with promise of implementing the NLUP. During the election campaign, the Congress claimed on the NLUP and its impact on rural economy and its achievement to the people of the state. The NLUP was launched on January 14, 2011 with Rs. 2873.13 crore is targeted to benefit 1,20,000 families over a period of five years.

Positive Role of Church

In the largely Christian dominated state, church is an integral part of both political and civil society. It is to be reminded that church as religious and civil society organization involved in the peace process during the insurgency. Like in the past, the church played an important role in the election process. Churches have been involved in creating mass awareness to all eligible voters to exercise their franchise. The church outlines the dos and do nots for the political parties during election. It also appealed political parties to curb on lavish campaigning. A conglomeration of 14 major churches in the State appealed to all political parties and outfits not to use insurgents and armed groups in influencing voters in the elections. It appealed that voters should be allowed to exercise their free will and choice in the polls and political parties should refrain from intimation, cheating and distribution of money by armed groups (The Times of India, 2013b). The Presbyterian Church controlled Mizoram People's Forum prohibited any kind of political campaign in the state on Sundays. The Mizoram Kohhran Hruaitute Committee (MKHC), leaders of a conglomerate of 14 churches appealed the people to maintain decorum in the election campaign and decency. Mizoram People's Forum, a Church-sponsored watchdog formed in 2006, has signed a 27 point MoU, with major political parties including the ruling Congress and BJP to ensure a free and fair election.

Low Representation of Women

The Mizo society is outwardly described as gender egalitarian society in contrast to its mainstream Indian society which is based on patriarchy and exploitation. Though Christianity brought some elements of modernity in Mizoram it failed to address women representation both in symbolic and substantial terms in public spheres such as legislative bodies. As result, the verdict is disappointing as far as women are concerned. Though Mizoram is the only state where women voters outnumber men and the turnout of women was once again higher than that of men with a gap of 2 percentage points between the two, not single woman candidates found place in the Assembly in the recent election. All the six female candidates contested in the elections lost. In 2008 Assembly Election only 9 women contested and none elected to State Legislative Assembly. The first woman legislator of Mizoram, K. Thansiami was elected to the Assembly in 1984 on a Mizoram Peoples Congress. The Last woman legislator, Lalhlimpui was elected to MLA in 1987 and was made minister of state in the Laldenga's ministry. Mizo Hmeichhe Insuihkhawm Pawl (MHIP), the state's biggest women's body was demanding quite some time the representation of women in Assembly and government. However, most political parties denied ticket to women stating that lack of qualified and efficient women contenders.

Blow to NERPE

The Assembly election verdict was significant in the sense that the formation of North East Regional Political Front (NERPE) has not made any impact on the electoral prospect of the MNF. It is to be reminded that on 20th October major regional political parties in the North-East held a convention in Guwhati and formed the NERPF aimed at creating a common platform to pursue the issues concerning the region and 'make the voice of the region heard' at the national level. It was claimed that the objective behind the NERPF was to lend a collective voice to the people of the region as their individual voices were unheard at most times. The convention was attended by the leaders of various regional parties of the North East such as the Asom Gana Parishad (AGP), Naga People's Front (NPF), United Democratic Party (UDP), Mizo National Front (MNF), Sikkim Democratic Front (SDF), People's Party of Arunachal Pradesh (PPA), Manipur People's Party (MPP) and the Indigenous People's Front of Tripura (IPFT). The convention elected the Nagaland Chief Minister Neiphuri Rio of NPF as the convener and former Assam Chief Minister Prafulla Kumar Mahanta of AGP as the chief advisor of the Front. The move to form a common

Front came in the context of predictions of most of the surveys that neither United Progressive Alliance nor National Democratic Alliance wass going to get absolute majority in the 2014 election as its own present strength. Keeping this situation in mind both national political formations were trying to woo parties into their fold to secure comfortable majority in 2014. Perhaps, the Front was thoroughly aware of the current situation and felt that forging a Front is better than individual alliance to any of these two national political formations. However, the political agenda of the NERPF was set by Paul Lyndoh, leader of the UDP, the main opposition regional party in Meghalaya, who observed that "the main objective behind the formation of the Front is to minimize the political fight among the regional parties so as to consolidate their political base to take on the Congress Party" especially in the upcoming 2014 Lok Sabha elections.

The convention unanimously adopted 17 resolutions which aimed at safeguarding the territorial, cultural, social, economic and political rights of the people of the Northeast in the national context. A Resolution adopted in the Convention further states that security of North-Eastern students and women in other parts of the country, eighty per cent reservation of jobs in all private and public sectors in the region; and re-look centre-state relations and constitutional safeguard for the indigenous people of the region. It further demanded the scrapping of the draconian laws such as Armed Forces Special Powers Act, and steps to check infiltration and cancellation of the land swap deal with Bangladesh arising out of the concern over the construction of Dams on the Chinese side.

It is to be reminded that among the eight North-Eastern states national parties are in power in six states. While the Congress party is holding power in Assam, Meghalaya, Mizoram, Arunachal Pradesh and Manipur, the Communist Party of India (Marxist) is controlling power in Tripura for the last three consecutive terms. The regional parties, however, are holding political power only in Nagaland and Sikkim. The Front is thus as an 'oppositional political forum' which is trying to capture power in their respective states from the national parties. It is to be seen that for quite some time, the regional political parties in the North-East India (NEI) are losing their significance in their respective states against the national political parties. It is a recognized fact that these parties once mobilized people on the basis of ethno-regional agenda and subsequently failed to reorient its ideology and mobilization strategy into a more inclusive manner. Moreover, since its numerical strength in Lok Sabha is minimal, their capacity to bargain with any of the national political formations as against its counterpart in the mainland India such as Dravidian parties in Tamil Nadu, Telegu Desam Party, and Trinamol Congress is very meager in national politics. In rest of India, regional politics assumed a new dimension in the era of liberalization. Since 1991, many regional parties led governments at the state levels adopted economic reforms and were competing for wooing foreign capital and investment in their respective states. This, in fact, contributed to forging alliance with national parties at the centre. However, such developments did not happen in NEI. Further, when Congress is the ruling party in most of the North Eastern states, the boundary disputes and other inter-state problems are solved within the party forums rather than between two governments. On the contrary, when two regional parties are holding political power in two states, there are more chances of further igniting ethnic and communal conflicts between states leading to strained inter-state relations. In other words, when two regional parties are in power in neibhouring states it can generate inter-state conflicts on various issues such as boundary disputes, sharing of water resources and even the migration of people from one state to other for education and employment. The role of national parties, in this context, is justified for peace and development, strategic location and inter-community amenity. In the recent past, the elite and youth are more enthusiastic about national parties which are leading to the crisis of regional political parties in the region.

As stated earlier, most of the regional political parties in NEI are ethno-regional political parties based on ethnic identities. The political agenda of such parties is confined only to particular ethnic community and particular region. Ethno-regionalism is based on the claims of regional identity and of ethnic distinction. It creates a sense of 'otherness' and distinctiveness from others. An ethno-regional party champions the interests of one ethnic group or set of groups leading to the exclusion of another or others. The ideology and mobilization strategy of ethno-regional parties is thus based on exclusion. Ethno-regional parties emerged as the result of ethno-regional movement and uphold ethno-regionalism as its ideology and mobilization strategy. Ethno-regional parties emerge as critique of civic nationalism, centralization and assimilation of the nation-state. Ethno-regional parties are critique of centralized power structures and its institutions. The demands of a ethno-regional party varies: protection of specific cultural community, ending discriminatory policies of the national state, cultural specificities and preservation of cultural identity, recognition of regional language, medium in education and government services.

Ideally, ethno-regional assertions are considered as a response to the homogenizing tendencies of mainstream nationalism and the centralizing attitude of dominant national political party. Ethno-regionalism is the articulation of the relative deprivation of a community within a geographical units or region. In the NEI regional politics assumed a different dimension as it relates to ethnicity. In other words, ethnic identity and its political mobilization give a new direction to regional politics in this region. As a result we have been witnessing the emergence of ethno-regional parties in NEI. Regional politics assumed ethnic connotations as ethnic identity is mixed with regional identity. Regional parties are based on regional self-determination and regional pride when they demand autonomy of the region and protection of its linguistic and cultural identity. The inhabitance of particular community in a particular territory enables regional political parties for mobilizing for electoral politics. Though, most of the regional parties claim that they represent the interest of the people of the respective states but the fact is quite contrary to the reality. In most cases they failed to protect the interest of all communities in the state and become the voice of the dominant ethnic groups and often leading to inter-community and intra-community animosity and conflicts. For instance, the growing assertion of smaller communities such as the Bodos and Karbis in Assam and Hmars in Mizoram can be seen in the context of the failure of the mainstream regional political parties to address their grievances. Ethno-regional politics thus increases governmental instability and encourages ethnic conflict and secessionism. However, the argument of MNF on 2013 assembly election debacle was quite surprising. After the defeat, in his speech before the party members at the MNF party office on 10 December, 2013, Zoramthanga said that "we accept our defeat, but Mizo Nationalism remained undefeated" (The Mizoram Post, 11 December 2013). While accepting the defeat, he asserted that Mizo nationalism on the other hand remained invincible.

Conclusion

The important lesson of the election verdict was that when development is the major issue, ethno-regionalism and identity politics is showing declining trend. The mobilization on the basis of ethnicity and regionalism may produce short term benefit for a regional political party. However, the durable existence of a regional party depends on its mobilization of cross sections of the people and its ability to deliver good governance and distributive politics. In NEI, the ethno-regional political parties have to transform into regional parties focusing on a positive development agenda and distributing goods to the people. Promoting regional politics based on ethno-regionalism produces dangerous condition for democracy in the region. The growing ethno-regional consciousness dilute the emergence of class consciousness in a society and leads to the further ethnic and sub regional mobilization of more ethnic communities contributing to ugly identity politics. In this situation, ethno-regional parties increase ethnic conflict and secessionism by reinforcing ethnic and regional identities. The NERPF should concentrate more on development agenda and inclusive politics rather than raising ethno-regional sentiment among the people.

References

Economic and Political Weekly.1987. "Editorial", Vol. 22, No. 9, February 28.

Government of Mizoram. 2013. *Budget Speech of Pu. H. Liansailova for 2013-14*, Government of Mizoram.

Sirnate,Vasundhara and Rahul Verma. 2013. "From Insurgency to Electoral Democracy", *The Hindu*, November 30.

The Times of India. 2013a. "Stop Postal Ballots for Brus Refugees: Mizo Students to EC", October 23.

The Times of India. 2013b. "Political parties urged not to use insurgents in Mizoram Polls", October 16.

The Mizoram Post. 2013. December 11.

Chapter - 8

North East and General Election 2014: Emerging Trends and Politics

The North-East India (NEI), the region, consists of eight states such as Assam, Manipur, Mizoram, Meghalaya, Arunachal Pradesh, Tripura, Nagaland and Sikkim, known for all wrong reasons – ethnic conflicts, border disputes, refugee infiltration, drug trafficking, insurgency and counter insurgency– in the recent past transformed into an important electoral battleground due to the compulsions of coalition politics at the centre. Of the eight states in the region, the Congress Party controls political power in Assam, Meghalaya, Mizoram, Arunachal Pradesh and Manipur, the Naga People's Front (NPF) in Nagaland, the Sikkim Democratic Front (SDF) in Sikkim and the Communist Party of India (Marxist) (CPIM) in Tripura. For a long time NEI is considered to be the stronghold for the Congress Party where over 220 ethnic groups inhabited in eight states. The Congress Party is credited with the formation of many states in the region for fulfilling the aspirations of smaller ethnic communities mainly from the united Assam. For instance, in 1963 the Congress government under Nehru formed Nagaland, the Indira Gandhi regime formed the state of Manipur in 1971 and Meghalaya in 1972 and Rajiv Gandhi government formed Mizoram in 1985 and Arunachal Pradesh in 1987. Moreover, the Congress government at the centre orchestrated many peace accords such as Assam Accord of 1984, Mizo Accord of 1987, etc .to bring peace in the trouble torn region. For bringing peace in the region the Congress claimed that it sacrificed its own regimes and made way for ethno-regional parties as part of the Accords. For instance, in Nagaland, Meghalaya and Mizoram, governments formed by the Naga Nationalist Organization, All Party Hill Leaders' Conference and Mizo National Front respectively with the sacrifies of the Congress.

Of the 545 Parliamentary seats, the eight North-Eastern states send only 25 representatives to the Lower House of the Parliament were not considered as a decisive voice in national politics. Due to low numerical strength, the political significance of NEI was largely reduced during the one party dominance and one party rule at the Centre. The major political formations and national leaders, as a result, looked down the region electorally, though it assumes a significant role in strategically as it is bordering with number of neibhouring countries such as Bangladesh, Myanmar, Bhutan, China and Nepal. In the diplomatic map of India, the region emerged as a potential route to cross border trade and commerce in the Look East Policy of the Government of India. In trade and commerce, in the recent past, it emerged as the economic hub between India and South East Asian Countries. However, in the political imagination of national life, the region is not adequately figured and represented in the institutional democracy. As a result, there exists a long time perception that the idea of India is distanced from the political realities of NEI. The growing atrocities of people from North-East across India due to racial discrimination strengthen the above argument that how far rest of India sees the sons and daughters of this culturally diverse region.

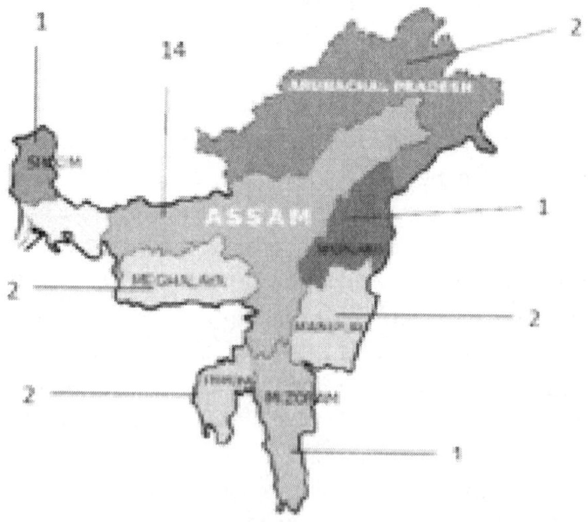

Distribution of Lok Sabha Seats in North-East India

In the recent past, the region witnessed a relative peace which to certain extent, enabled the successful functioning of electoral politics. Though number of minor regional outfits are rousing the ethno-regional sentiments in various North East states, development issues and governance occupy a centre stage in the electoral politics. The new generation of both urban and rural youth is showing much enthusiasm in electoral politics moving towards the idea of India. The high voter turnout in the region is a clear indication that ballot succeeds over bullet as people are shedding extremist activities and moving towards mainstream politics. Instead of taking a confrontationist approach towards the centre, the regional parties ruled states are adopting a more cooperative approach eyeing on developmental schemes, assistance and projects from the Centre. Moreover, the growing competitions among the regional parties to align with national political formations add a new dimension to the party politics in the region.

General Election 2014 – Mixed Trends

The General Election 2014 brought mixed development in the politics of NEI. Of the 25 seats spreading across the region, the Congress could win only 8 seats while the National Democratic Alliance (NDA) secured 10 seats (Bharatiya Janata Party (BJP)-8, National People's Party (NPP) - 1, Naga Peoples Front (NPF) -1), CPIM retained 2 seats, All India United Democratic Front (AIUDF) -3, Sikkim Democratic Front and Independent one seat each. It has to be reminded that in 2009 election, of the 25 seats in the region, the Congress secured 13 seats, BJP – 4, CPIM – 2, Asom Gana Parishad (AGP) – 1, AIUDF – 1, Bodo People's Front – 1, Naga People's Front -1, SDF -1. Nationalist Congress Party (NCP)-1.

Table 1: Party wise seats and vote share in North-East India 2014.

Assam (Total Seats – 14; Voter Turnout – 80.12%)		
Party	***No. of Seats Won***	***Voteshare (in%)***
Bharatiya Janata Party	7	36.86
Indian National Congress (I)	3	29.90
All India United Democratic Front	3	14.8
Independent	1	9.62
Meghalaya (Total Seats – 2; Voter Turnout – 68.80%)		
Indian National Congress (I)	1	39.02
National Peoples Party	1	22.84
Manipur (Total Seats – 2; Voter Turnout – 79.75%)		

(Contd...)

Indian National Congress (I)	2	41.91
Arunachal Pradesh (Total Seats – 2; Voter Turnout – 79.12%)		
Indian National Congress (I)	1	41.60
Bharatiya Janata Party	1	46.20
Tripura (Total Seats – 2; Voter Turnout – 84.92%)		
Communist Party of India (Marxist)	2	64.77
Mizoram (Total Seats – 1; Voter Turnout – 61.95%)		
Indian National Congress (I)	1	49.33
Nagaland (Total Seats – 1; Voter Turnout – 87.91%)		
Naga People's Front	1	68.84
Sikkim (Total Seats – 1; Voter Turnout – 83.64%)		
Sikkim Democratic Front	1	53.74

Source: Data drawn from www.eci.nic.in

In Assam, the BJP won seven Loksabha seats for the first time inroading into the bastion of both the Congress and the AGP. The strength of the Congress which is in power in the state for the last three consecutive terms reduced to three seats. The pro Muslim party the AIUDF won three seats and the independent one. In Meghalaya, both the Congress and the NPP shared one seats each. The Congress retained Shillong constituency while the Garo inhabited Tura seat was won by the veteran Garo politician, P.A. Sangma by securing 22.84% of votes. It has to be reminded that Sangma who quit NCP, a constituent of the United Progressive Alliance (UPA) government at the Centre, few months before the election before forming the NPP. The NPP had a tactical electoral understanding with the NDA. In Mizoram, the lone seat was retained by the Congress by securing 49.33% of vote share. Though the opponent candidate put up by the United Front of opposition parties was defeated, it could secure 47.89% of votes share in the Christian dominated hilly state.

In Nagaland, the chief minister Neiphiu Rio of NPF himself entered into the election fry with the support of the NDA and won the seat by securing 68.84% votes. Though, the Congress put up a strong fight against the ruling party candidate in the state its vote shared reduced to 30.2%. In the Himalayan state of Sikkim the verdict was in favour of the ruling SDF which own the lone parliamentary seat with an vote share of 53.74%. Though both the Congress and the BJP put up their candidates, they could secure only 2.36% and 2.39% of votes respectively. In Manipur, both constituencies - Inner Manipur and Outer Manipur – were won by the Congress securing 41.91% of vote share in the state. The opposition parties such as the BJP and Communist Party of India (CPI) secured only 11.98% and 14.05% of votes in Manipur. In Arunachal Pradesh, the Congress and the BJP shared one seats each. The BJP could wrest one seat from the ruling Congress with a vote share of 46.62%. Although the Congress retains power winning 42 seats, the BJP won 11 seats in 60 members Assembly for which elections were held simultaneously with the General election.

In Tripura both seats – Tripura East (ST) and Tripura West were won by the ruling CPIM. In the Tripura East constituency, which was reserved for Scheduled Tribe, the CPIM candidate, Jitendra Chaudhury won by securing 65.47% of votes. In Tripura West, Sankar Prasad Datta defeated the Congress candidate by securing 62.43% votes.

Election Campaign – Putting Burning Issues under Backburner

In the run up to the general election 2014, the region witnessed electrifying campaigns by flurry of national leaders such as Manmohan Singh, Narendra Modi, Rahul Gandhi and Sonia Gandhi. These national leaders of various parties stressed developmental issues, peace and security in the region. While the Congress pledged to improve the economic and business climate in the region, especially in tourism, horticulture and hydro-power sectors, Modi promised to overall development of the region. On 8th February, 2014, in an election rally in Manipur, Modi talked about the controversial India-Myanmar border fencing, corruption, unemployment and the failure of the Congress government in Manipur.[1] Reminding the killing of Arunachal student, Nido Tania on 29th January 2014 in New Delhi and assault of two Manipuri girls in New Delhi as a "national shame" Modi demanded justice for the North East victims. In another election rally on 22nd February 2014 Modi asserted that after May 16 illegal immigrants will have to leave India. He asserted that "there is no place of infiltrators from Bangladesh who have come to further votebank politics agenda of others. They should be sent back. At the same time, not Assam alone but all states must accommodate Hindus coming from Bangladesh and offer them a life with dignity".[2]

On 18th March, 2014, in an election rally in Arunachal Pradesh Rahul Gandhi claimed that the Congress believed in uniting the country's people irrespective of caste, creed and religion and not in divisive policies like the BJP. The Congress Vice-President asserted that "the opposition wants to divide people on political and religious line, but we want to work for peace, progress and prospects, irrespective of religious affiliations".[3] He asserted that BJP's religion based ideology would ruin the secular fabric of the country and increase incidents of racial discrimination against people from the North-East. According to him, the Congress was committed to root out racial discrimination and all north-eastern states did not deserve to feel neglected in other parts of the country. Though Narendra Modi and Rahul Gandhi unleashed an aggressive campaign in this region, they kept silence on the long standing demand for the repeal of the Armed Forces Special Powers Act of 1958, civilian causalities in counter insurgency operations, fake encounters, human rights violations by the Indian army, border issues between various states, etc.

Blow to North East Regional Political Front

The general election verdict was significant in the sense that the formation of North East Regional Political Front (NERPF) did not evoke any impact on the electoral prospect of regional parties and it failed to forge a united regional front against both the Congress and the BJP. It is to be reminded that on 20th October, 2013 major regional political parties in the North-East held a convention in Guwhati and formed the NERPF aimed at creating a common platform to pursue the issues concerning the region and 'make the voice of the region heard' at the national level. It was claimed that the objective behind the NERPF was to lend a collective voice to the people of the region as their individual voices were unheard at most times. The convention was attended by the leaders of various regional parties of the North East such as the AGP, NPF, United Democratic Party (UDP), Mizo National Front (MNF), SDF, People's Party of Arunachal Pradesh (PPA), Manipur People's Party (MPP) and the Indigenous People's Front of Tripura (IPFT). The convention elected the Nagaland Chief Minister Neiphuri Rio of NPF as the convener and former Assam Chief Minister Prafulla Kumar Mahanta of AGP as the chief advisor to the Front. The move to form a common Front came in the context of predictions of most of the surveys that neither UPA nor NDA was going to get absolute majority in the 2014 general election at its own present strength. Keeping this situation in mind both national political formations were trying to woo parties into their fold to secure comfortable majority in 2014. Perhaps, the Front was thoroughly aware of the emerging situation and felt that forging a Front is better than individual alliance to any of these two national political formations. However, the political agenda of the NERPF was set by Paul Lyndoh, leader of the UDP, the main opposition regional party in Meghalaya, who observed that "the main objective behind the formation of the Front is to minimize the political fight among the regional parties so as to consolidate their political base to take on the Congress Party" especially in the upcoming 2014 Lok Sabha elections.

The convention unanimously adopted 17 resolutions which aimed at safeguarding the territorial, cultural, social, economic and political rights of the people of the Northeast in the national context. A Resolution adopted in the Convention further states that security of North-Eastern students and women in other parts of the country, eighty per cent reservation of jobs in all private and public sectors in the region; and re-look centre-state relations and constitutional safeguard for the indigenous people of the region. It further demanded the scrapping of the draconian laws such as Armed Forces Special Powers Act, and steps to check infiltration and cancellation of the land swap deal with Bangladesh arising out of the concern over the construction of Dams on the Chinese side.

Contrary to the affirmation by the NERPF, in the run up to the general election, various regional parties in NEI either switched over their loyalty to the NDA or went it alone in their respective states. While the AGP fought on its own strength in Assam, the NPP and the NPF got support from the NDA. The solidarity between various regional parties shattered and the beneficiaries are either the Congress or the BJP. The convener of NERPF, Neiphu Rio, the Nagaland Chief Minister, contested the alone Lok Sabha seat with the support of the BJP hoping his decisive role in New Delhi, if the NDA is voted to power. He even claimed that the BJP-led NDA government in the past officially acknowledged the 'unique history and situation of the Nagas' and also conceded to the Naga demand for extension of the ceasefire agreement 'without territorial limits' in June 2001 and accused the Congress government of betraying the Naga demands.

Though the formation of NERPF was initially viewed as the consolidation of regional forces in the NEI, its support to NDA added a dimension to the changing role of regional parties in the national politics. Like rest of the states in India, regional parties are willing to support national government either for material benefit for their respective states or for fulfilling personal political aspirations of its leaders rather than adopting an anti-centre or 'anti-India' approach as in the past. Further, since many of the regional parties aligning with NDA or accepting tactical support of the BJP in their state, the NERPF proved to be an "anti-Congress Front". In other words, since these parties have to fight against the Congress in their respective states, the Front has more option for NDA rather the Congress-led UPA at the centre. Moreover, the Congress which has the larger presence in most of the states in NEI, has to fight against regional parties and to strengthen its mass base and to increase its electoral prospects in these states does not eager to align with such fronts or extending its support to the regional party candidates. In such a situation the growing perception among the regional parties is that accepting the support of the BJP and extending support to NDA as a natural choice for influencing national politics.

Congress Defeated, Not Vanished

At the national level, though the Congress wiped out in many states and its performance was all time low since independence, the Party's performance in NEI gave some solace to the leadership of the grand old party. Though the number of seats won by the Congress reduced in contrast to the 2009 general election, the party's vote share has not heavily reduced across the states of NEI. In Assam, the Congress secured 29.9% vote share, Arunachal Pradesh (41.6%), Manipur (41.9%), Mizoram (49.33%), Meghalaya (39.02%),

Nagaland (30.22%), Tripura (15.38%). Although, the BJP is making inroads into the North-East region the Congress remain as a decisive force in the electoral politics. In Manipur, Mizoram and Meghalaya, the party's electoral performance was impressive in contrast to its political opponents.

The Congress has strong presence in the region and it put up its own candidates in all eight states in NEI. The Congress mobilized cross-sections of the people and adopts an inclusive agenda for the development of the region. The Party has a distinction of combating the ethno-national ideology of the regional parties and bringing back the development agenda in the forefront of politics. In the past, though in various north-eastern states, the Congress faced setback due to the spread of ethno-regionalism, it could bounce back after some point of time. For instance, in Assam, during the Assam Movement and the aftermath, the Party faced sever existential crisis due to the spread of ethno-regionalism and subsequently emerged as a potential political force in the state. In the subsequent years after the formation of AGP government, the Congress regained its faith in the cross sections of the Assamese people and formed government in the states for three consecutive terms. In Mizoram, the Congress could tackle ethno-regionalism of the MNF which came to power in Mizoram after the Mizo Accord of 1987. In the recent past, Mizoram witnessed the erosion of Mizo ethno-regionalism of MNF and the regaining strength of the Congress. In Manipur, in spite of virulent form of ethnic mobilization and identity politics by various ethnic communities, the Congress was able to establish its political preeminence both in the Assembly and Loksabha elections.

Table 2: State Wise Vote Share of Congress in General Elections in NEI (in %)

General Election	*Assam*	*Arunachal Pradesh*	*Manipur*	*Mizoram*	*Meghalaya*	*Nagaland*	*Sikkim*	*Tripura*
1991	28.49	68.92	38.38	38.08	56.62	44.34	-	82.83
1996	31.64	28.83	40.17	42.50	53.64	62.31	-	34.13
1998	38.97	23.90	18.60	34.86	47.62	86.70	33.11	42.12
1999	38.42	56.92	25.29	-	32.75	71.18	4.76	13.88
2004	35.07	9.96	14.88	-	45.55	25.78	27.43	14.28
2009	34.89	51.11	42.96	65.58	44.84	29.36	29.59	30.75
2014	29.90	41.60	41.91	49.33	39.02	30.22	2.36	15.38

Source: Data drawn from www. eci.nic.in

Consolidation of Red Bastion

Though general election 2014 witnessed the massive erosion of communist and other left parties at the national level, the landslide victory of the CPIM in a tiny state of Tripura give some solace to the Party. Since 1996 general election, the CPIM is winning all two constituencies in the state. In spite of Narendra Modi's accusation of the state government in ignoring the interest of the indigenous tribal community who constitute 33% of the tribals in the 24 lakh voters, the CPIM secured 64.77% of the votes against 15.38% vote of the opposition Congress party. The mandate proves that over the years, the CPIM consolidated its political base among the various communities in the state.

Table 3 Electoral Performance of CPIM in General Elections in Tripura

GeneralElection	*Voter Turnout(in %)*	*SeatsContested*	*SeatsWon*	*Vote Share(in%)*
1991	67.28	2	0	6.54
1996	79.09	2	2	52.41
1998	80.86	2	2	48.80
1999	68.14	2	2	56.24
2004	67.08	2	2	68.80
2009	83.91	2	2	61.69
2014	84.92	2	2	64.77

Source: Data drawn from www. eci.nic.in

Emergence of the BJP

For a long time, in the region, BJP was almost a non-entity and remained as the strong hold of Congress and regional parties. In the recent past, however, the BJP emerged as a potential political force in the ethnically sensitive region especially in Assam and Arunachal Pradesh. The emergence of BJP, whose ideology and programmes are often contradict the ethos of the region, as a potential political force in the region has to be analysed in the larger context of the decline of ethno-regional parties and secular and progressive forces. While the ethno-regional mobilization by prominent regional parties is fastly declining, the Hindu nationalist forces are spreading its wings in the region. By expanding its mass base in NEI, the BJP wants to shed its image as a North-Indian Hindu Nationalist Party and emerging as a natural alternative to the Congress in every states and region. Moreover, it has been projecting its image as an all inclusive political entity crosscutting caste, region and religion.

The BJP and other Hindu fringe organizations have a larger project in the tribal belt of this region. However, putting the real agenda under backburner, the BJP time and again talks about its "development plank" in this region. For instance, based on its regional specificity the party is able to prepare a vision documents for each of the north-eastern states. In Manipur, the document stresses on building of arterial roads and in Meghalaya it focuses on areas like skill development. The BJP often cites the previous NDA government's efforts in the development of the region such as the creation of the Ministry of Development of North East Region (DoNER) and the launching of Look East Policy. The DoNER was formed in September 2001, is responsible for the matters relating to the planning, execution and monitoring of development scheme and projects in the region. In another significant development, on 23rd August, 2013 the BJP launched the North East India Sampark Cell (NEISC) aimed at strengthen its emotional integration with other parts of the country. Among other things, the Cell aims to check the illegal migrants in the region as it challenges development, security and national integration of NEI.

Under the developmental plank, the Hindu mobilization is taking place in NEI. The strong presence of RSS in the region is attracting youth over the development plank. In the last decades there is exponential growth of RSS training camps in Assam and in other states focusing on tribal issues. In fact, in the Assam election, the vigorous campaign unleashed by the RSS went to the BJP's kitty.[4] The BJP's effort to focus on North-East is not basically winning seats in the region, but to implement its larger agenda in the region – bringing back the tribals to the larger Hindu fold. In other words, rather than electoral arithmetic, BJP's saffronisation of the region occupies real motive behind in the love for the region.

In the 2014 general election, like the rest of India, the BJP followed an alliance strategy of 'go it alone' wherever it has strength and a forge an alliance with regional forces wherever it was not a decisive force to counter the Congress. For instance, it forged an alliance with NPF in Nagaland and in Meghalaya it extended support to NPP of P.A. Sangma. In Mizoram, BJP formed a coalition of eight state parties under the banner of United Front led by the Mizo National Front to fight against the Congress candidate of the lone Parliamentary constituency of the Christian dominated hilly state.

The state of Assam is considered to be the BJP's political laboratory and gateway to NEI. Assam is a complex society which constitutes Assamese Hindu elites, Bengalis, migrant Bangladeshis and tribal population considered to be a fertile ground for communal tensions. The Assamese Hindus are dominant in Brahmaputra valley and Bengalis are dominant in the Barrak valley. Initially, the BJP's traditional stronghold is the Bengali dominated Barrak valley. As Srikanth argues that "although the BJP did not initially get the support of the Assamese Hindus, as early as in 1991, it could make a dent into the Bengali dominated Barak valley region, where it won parliamentary seats from Silchar and Karimganj constituencies (in 1999)[5]". In the Brahmaputra valley, the BJP is wooing the Assamese Hindus by raking up the issue of illegal migration of Bengali Muslims and its impact on the Assamese society. It accused the Congress of playing votebank politics of Bengali migrants. The recent trends show that both Assamese elite of caste Hindus and the Bengali elite are showing allegiance to the BJP. The BJP's promise to check illegal immigration presumably gained wider acceptability among the Assamese elite. For quite some time, the BJP is expanding its mass base across the state and increasing its vote share over the years.

Like elsewhere in India, initially, the BJP allied with the regional party, AGP in 2006 assembly election and 2009 general election. Setting aside its national agenda and issues, the BJP was able to raise regional issues such as illegal migration, detection and deportation of foreigners which were once raised by the AGP. In fact, the BJP hijacked the regional agenda of AGP, especially on the issue of illegal migrants. However, though BJP wakes up the migration issue, it only focuses on the Muslims not the Bengalis Hindus whom it considered as the mass base.

In the 2014 general election, by winning 7 seats and securing a vote share of 36.86% the BJP made its strong presence in the gateway of NEI. After winning half of the seats in the Loksabha the BJP is now emerging as credible alternative to Congress focusing on 2016 Assembly elections. The BJP won the upper Assam seats like Dibrugarh, Tinsukia and Lakhimpur which were considered as the bastion of Congress for long time. The Bodo People's Front (BPF), former ally of Congress, showing its inclination to BJP for the development of Bodo Territorial Council (BTC). The BPF ended its ties with the Congress and withdrawn its ministers from the Gogoi government instigating Bodo tribals against Bangladeshi Muslim migration raising the bogey of threats from migrants. The tea tribes traditionally voted for the Congress moved to BJP, especially Dibrugarh and Jorhat where the BJP put up the candidates belonging to the tea community. Moreover, the anti-Muslim sentiment generated in Bodo areas of Assam describing it as anti-Muslim went in favour of the BJP.

In Arunachal Pradesh, the BJP's spectacular victory in one of the two seats added an advantage to the NDA in the region. Over the years, the BJP's vote share has increased and made inroads into the electoral base of the Congress. In 2004 general election the BJP could win all two seats in the state with a vote share of 53.85%. Though, in the subsequent general election in 2009, the party lost all two seats to the Congress and its vote share reduced to 37.17%, in 2014 general election the BJP wrested one seat from the ruling Congress with an vote share of 46.62%.

Table 4: Electoral Performance of BJP in General Elections in Arunachal Pradesh

General Election	*Voter Turnout(in %)*	*SeatsContested*	*SeatsWon*	*Vote Share(in %)*
1991	51.28	2	0	6.11
1996	55.04	2	0	17.41
1998	59.17	2	0	21.75
1999	72.15	1	0	16.30
2004	56.35	2	2	53.85
2009	72.40	2	0	37.17
2014	79.12	2	1	46.62

Source: Data drawn from www. eci.nic.in

Apart from winning seats in Assam and Arunachal Pradesh, in other NE states like Manipur, Meghalaya, Sikkim and Tripura, the party's candidates secured 11.98%, 9.16%, 2.39% and 5.77% votes respectively. In Tripura, the BJP spread communal propaganda among the indigenous tribal community waking up the issue of migration of Bengalis and the subjugation of the former by the migrant Bengalis. It is to be reminded that over the years the CPIM was able to expand its mass base not only among the Bengali community but also among the indigenous tribal community bringing them under a common platform. Over the years, though the CPIM won all two seats, the BJP is making inroads in rural areas. The percentage of votes secured by the BJP in the CPIM ruled state was 7.82% (2004), 2.72% (2009) and 5.7% (2014). Though there is slight decline in the percentage of votes secured by the BJP in the 2014 general election in contrast to 2004 general election, the subsequent trends prove that the BJP has not abandon its electoral ambition in the red bastion of the region. It has to be reminded that subsequently in the 15th July, 2014 gram panchayat poll, the BJP won 141 of the 6, 111 seats and won a majority in five gram panchayats for the first time. In Manipur, though the Congress managed to retain all the two seats the BJP is making inroads into the Congress strongholds. Though in the Christian dominated state of Mizoram, the BJP has many hurdles to spread its mass base, it is desperately looking for alliance and forging alliance with smaller regional parties.

Table 5: Statewise Vote Share of BJP in General Elections in NEI (in %)

General Election	*Assam*	*Arunachal Pradesh*	*Manipur*	*Mizoram*	*Meghalaya*	*Nagaland*	*Sikkim*	*Tripura*
1991	9.60	6.11	8.10	-	6.89	3.00	-	2.99
1996	15.92	17.41	5.25	-	9.13	-	-	6.5
1998	24.47	21.75	12.61	2.94	9.01	-	-	8.19
1999	29.84	16.30	1.02	-	9.45	5.12	-	12.82
2004	22.94	53.85	20.65	-	8.63	-	-	7.82
2009	16.21	37.17	9.49	-	-	-	1.77	3.38
2014	36.86	46.62	11.98	-	9.16	-	2.39	5.77

Source: Data drawn from www. eci.nic.in

Erosion of Asom Gana Parishad

The AGP is the prominent ethno-regional political party in NEI which not only played a vital role in the politics of Assam but also in the national politics. The Party was a constituent of the V.P. Singh led National Front government in 1989, Deva Gowda and I.K. Gujaral led United Front governments in 1996-97. For short while, the AGP was also a part of NDA and the BJP and AGP jointly contested the 2009 general election in the state. However, in 2011 Assembly election it parted away with NDA. The AGP as an ethno-regional political party emerged in the context of the Assam movement (1979-85) which was in fact, seen as an ethno-regional movement trying to protect the identity and culture of Assamiya middle class which according to it was under danger due to the illegal migration of Bengalis. The Assam movements sowed the seeds of ethno regionalism and got wider legitimacy in the Assam Accord of 1985. The AGP which formed on 14th October, 1985 as an amalgam of Purbanchaliya Lok Parishad (PLP), Assam Jatiyatabadi Dal (AJD), All Assam Gana Sangram Parishad (AAGSP), and the ex-members of All Assam Students Union (AASU). The ideological commitment of AGP was influenced by the ideology of these organizations. As Mahanta argues that "after the signing of the Assam Accord in 1985, the regional aspirations of the Assamese people got articulated in the formation of the AGP".[6]

In the 1985 Assembly election manifesto the party promised to protect the political rights of the Assamese people and the implementation of the Assam Accord. The party promised to protect the distinct socio-cultural and political identity of the Assamese people. It promised to find out solutions to illegal migration of Bengali people from Bangladesh. It was in fact, an attempt to woo the Assamese educated middle class towards the party. At the age of 28 Prafulla Kumar Mahanta, AASU's young vibrant leader, became the Chief Minister of Assam, perhaps the youngest Chief Minister in India. The AGP which controlled political power in two times (1985-90 and 1996-2001) in the state took a lukewarm attitude towards illegal migration issue. Perhaps, one of the reasons for such approach was the fear of losing immigrants vote to the Party. The ascendancy of AGP saw the end of long year domination of Congress politics in the state. Initially the AGP had tactic support from the United Liberation Front of Assam (ULFA) later it turned against AGP when it started crackdown its cadres.

In the recent past, the AGP faced a number of inner party problems and defections. On 3rd July, 2005 Mahanta was expelled from the AGP and he formed the AGP (Progressive). However, in October 14, 2008, Mahanta's party merged with his parent party. However, the merger did not signal the strong position of the party in the state as it faced with worst form of factionalism. In 2011, AGP leader Atul Bora joined the BJP and in 2013 another senior leader Sarbanand Sonowal joined the BJP. The 2014 general election witnessed the virtual rout of the AGP as it was not able to win a single Loksabha seat in the state. The Muslim voters who constitute one-third of the electorate in the state which had supported the AGP once, shifted their loyalty to the AIUDF. In 2014, the AIUDF won three seats with 14.8% vote share in contrast to one seat with 16.1% vote in 2009. The people of Brahamaputra valley of Assam, once a stronghold of the AGP also drifted away from the AGP and moving towards the BJP. Many Assamese caste Hindus feel that the AGP deviated from the provisions of the Assam Accord especially related to the detection and deportation of foreigners from Assam.

In the 2014 general election, the AGP which contested twelve constituencies in Assam could not win even a single seat. In terms of vote share the party could secure only 3.87% against the 14.61% (with one seat) of the 2009 general election.

Table 6: Electoral Performance of Major Parties in Assam.

General Election	*Voter Turnout (in %)*	*Parties*	*Seats Contested*	*Seats Won*	*Vote Share (in%)*
1991	75.30	Congress	14	8	28.49
		AGP	14	1	17.62\
		BJP	8	2	9.6
1996	78.50	Congress	14	5	31.64
		AGP	11	5	32.64
		BJP	14	1	15.92
1998	61.10	Congress	13	10	38.97
		AGP	10	0	17.74
		BJP	14	1	24.47
1999	71.30	Congress	14	10	38.42
		AGP	8	0	20.38
		BJP	12	2	29.84
2004	69.08	Congress	14	9	35.07
		AGP	12	2	23.53
		BJP	12	2	22.94
2009	69.52	Congress	14	7	33.91
		AGP	6	1	14.61
		BJP	8	4	16.21
2014	80.13	Congress	14	3	29.90
		AGP	12	0	3.87
		BJP	13	7	36.86

Source: Data drawn from www. eci.nic.in

The state of Assam is passing through a critical phase in the field of party politics. The prominent regional political party, the AGP is losing its preeminence in the state politics. On the other hand, the Congress Party which is in power for the last three consecutive terms is moving towards more centralization of power and authority is facing with anti-incumbency. The state in which former Prime Minister Manmohan Singh represents in the Rajya Sabha for 23 years, the BJP is emerging as alternative opposition force to the Congress in the political space vacated by the AGP. The AGP is undergoing a process of existential crisis. The electoral performance of AGP in the last three Assembly and the general elections shows its diminishing role in the politics of Assam. As it stated earlier, the AGP as an ethno-regional party that dominated in the Assam politics symbolizing the price and self-respect of Assamiya middle class. The AGP thought that rising ethno-regional issues would strengthen the party. However, in course of time, the AGP developed intolerant attitude towards smaller communities and groups in the State. In other words, ethno regionalism in most cases leads to the emergence of ethnic chauvinism leading only to animosity and hatred between different groups and communities[7]. Further, the AGP failed to develop a new regional bourgeoisie unlike that of Dravida Munneta Kazhakam (DMK) in Tamil Nadu, Telugu Desam Party (TDP) in Andhra Pradesh and Shiromani Akali Dal (SAD) in Punjab. It neither developed a regional bourgeoisie nor corporate business nor agrarian capitalist in the state. It only relied on the middle class, education sections and emotive issues of ethno-regionalism and failed to take any other issues to mobilize people. In 1985, people voted to power AGP with high expectation. However, the Party and its government failed to rise up to the expectations of all people of the state. It failed to orient ethnic regionalism to development and an alternative to the agenda of the national parties.

In the context of the crisis, the ethno-regional politics in Assam has to be reshaped with more participatory and inclusive regional politics. Unlike other regional parties such as DMK, TDP and SAD, it failed to reorient its ideology and mobilization strategy. These parties after initial phase of ethno-regional mobilization began to adopt populist politics, social security politics which helped them to mobilize cross sections of the society. The DMK initially raised the regional ethnicity – Dravidian identity with non-Brahmanism – is mobilizing cross sections of people in the Tamil Nadu. Both DMK and TDP became part of Coalition governments in the Centre and developed a bargain politics for the development of the states.

Conclusion

The emerging trend in the North-East in the aftermath of 2014 general election is quite disturbing. On the one hand, the secular and progressive forces are weakening and, on the other, divisive forces are taking root in the politically volatile region. The emergence of communal forces like BJP is dangerous to the ethnically polarized NEI. The intrusion of Hinduvata forces would further vitiate the situation and bearing on the social amenity and peace in the state. It would further polarize the communities and spread communal distress in the region. In Assam, BJP is making a polarization between the Muslims (from East Bengal origin described as foreigner) and the Assamese caste Hindus. The BJP's propaganda on the detection and deportation of illegal migrants got wider acceptability among the caste Hindus and indigenous tribal communities who often see the illegal immigration of foreigners lead to Tripura like situation where the immigrants outnumbered the indigenous tribal community who reduced to minority. Like the majority Hindu communalism, the minority religious mobilization is posing a threat to the social and political stability of the region. For instance, in Assam, the consolidation of Muslim votes in favour of the AIUDF can be seen with great concern. Perhaps Modi's campaign generated more apprehensions and insecurity among the Muslim population who constitute 31% of the population. The AIUDF was able to capitalize this situation by winning the Muslim majority constituencies of Dhubri, Barpeta and Karimganj (SC) in Assam.

To sum up, the general election trend shows that the 'first wave' of ethno-regionalism propagated by the ethno-regional parties such as the AGP and MNF is waning and the 'second wave' of ethno-regionalism is spreading by the national parties like BJP. In other words, the first wave of ethno-regionalism propagated by ethno-regional parties is hijacked by the national parties like BJP and uses as a second wave to political mobilization of various ethnic communities. Like the first wave, the second wave of ethno-regionalism is divisive and would further widen the gap between various ethnic communities.

Notes

1. "Modi promised overall development in Northeast", *The Times of India*, 9 February 2014.
2. *The Assam Tribune*, 23rd February, 2014.
3. "India has a lot to learn from the northeast, says Rahul", *The Times of India*, 19th March 2014.
4. "RSS worked overtime to take Modi wave to Northeast", *The Economic Times*, 18th May, 2014.
5. Srikanth, H. (1999), "Communalising Assam: AGP's Loss Is BJP's Gain", *Economic and Political Weekly*, Vol.34, No. 49, 4 December, p. 3413.
6. Mahanta, Nani Gopal (2014), "Loksabha Elections in Assam: Shifting of Traditional Vote Bases to BJP", *Economic and Political Weekly*, Vol. XLIX, No. 35, 30th August, p. 20.
7. For detail discussion, see Bijukumar, V. (2013), "Ethnicity and Regionalism in North-East India: A Study of Two Regional Political Parties – AGP and MNF", in Apura K. Baruah and Susmita Sen Gupta (eds.), *Social Forces and Politics in North-East India*, Guwhati: DVS Publishers, pp. 191-214.

Chapter - 9

Assam Assembly Election 2016: Triumphed BJP and Dwindled Congress

The election verdict of Assam Assembly brought some dramatic developments in the politics of the state. It not only brought down the three consecutive Congress governments led by Tarun Gogoi but also consolidated the electoral base of the Bharatiya Janata Party (BJP) in Assam. The BJP could form its first government in the North-East India through election with the alliance of the Asom Gana Parishad (AGP) and Bodoland People's Front (BPF). The verdict also gave some solace to the ruling party at the centre which failed to make much impact on the states like Kerala, West Bengal, Tamil Nadu and Puducherry where Assembly elections held along with Assam. The BJP's entry into Assam shed its image as a north Indian party and moved towards as an All India party. The Party made its presence across the state, region both in the Brahmaputra Valley and Barrak valley. In the Bengali dominated Barrak valley which comprises of districts such as Cachar, Karimganj and Hailakandi the BJP won 8 out of 15 seats leaving All India United Democratic Front (AIUDF) four, and the Congress three. The BJP made inroads into the Muslim dominated area as it won 15 seats in 49 Muslim-dominated constituencies in the state. Apart from winning all seats in Guwhati city, the BJP swept all 7 seats in Dibrugarh and all 3 seats in Karbi Anglong. Moreover, the BJP was able to penetrate in the tea belt showing its impressive win. Interestingly, for the first time in the history of Dima Hasao, the BJP candidate B B Hagjer won the 16 Haflong (ST) constituency. In the Barrak valley, the BJP's lone Muslim winner Animul Hague Laskar, a businessman, scripted history by wining from the Sonai constituency.

In the 126 seats in the State Assembly the BJP won 60 seats with a vote share of 42%, its alliance partner AGP secured 14 seats with a vote share of 8%. The BPF, another partner in the BJP alliance won 12 seats with a vote share of 3.9%. The BPF, former ally of Congress, initially moved towards the BJP for the development of Bodo Territorial Council (BTC). It has to be reminded that the BPF ended its ties with the Congress and withdrawn its ministers from the Gogoi government instigating Bodo tribals against Bangladeshi Muslim migration raising the bogey of threats from migrants. In 2011 election, the BPF won 12 seats and joined the Gogoi government and broken its alliance with Congress in 2014. Moreover, the anti-Muslim sentiment generated in Bodo areas of Assam describing it as anti-Muslim went in favour of the BJP.The three party pre poll alliances thus bagged 86 seats with two-third majority in the Assembly. The incumbent Congress party however could secure only 26 seats by winning 31% vote share. The AIUDF which claimed its base in the Muslim community won 13 seats with the vote share of 13%. It has to be reminded that in the 2011 Assembly election the BJP won only 5 seats against the 78 seats of the ruling Congress party. The AGP won 10 seats, the AIUDF won 18 and the BPF only 12. By aligning with BJP in the Assembly election, the AGP strengthened its position in the state. The AGP president Atul Bora elected to the Assembly in Bokakhat constituency. However, the AIUDF chief Dhubri and present Loksabha MP lost to the Congress candidate Wajed Ali Choudhury from Salmara south constituency.

Electoral Performance (Total Seats: 126)

Party	Seats Won	Vote Percentage
BJP	60	42%
Congress (I)	26	31%
AGP	14	8%
AIUDF	13	13%
BPF	12	3.9%

The BJP's surge in Assam in the Assembly election can be analysed in the context of its strategic approach in the state. Firstly, the BJP could muster the tacit support of the Bodos, the Tiwas and the Rabhas which enabled the BJP to make inroads to the minority areas. Secondly, the election saw a strong Hindu consolidation behind the BJP as both Bengali Hindus and Assamese Hindus supported the BJP. However, the Muslim vote (both Assamese and Bengali Muslims) split into the Congress and AIUDF. Thirdly, the BJP's prepoll alliance with the AGP and the BPF consolidated anti Congress votes in its favour. It has to be reminded that just before the announcement of the election the BJP sealed an alliance with the AGP and the BPF. Initially there were local protests from both the BJP and AGP in certain regions like Bongaigaon, Sivasagar, Sonitpur, Amguri and Tezpur against the alliance. However, the BJP leadership could overcome the dissent voices in forging the alliance. In the run up to the election, the BJP sealed an agreement with the AGP and the BPF to consolidate opposition vote against the ruling congress dispensation. In fact, such realist strategy of alliance building came in the context of two reasons. First, after its lost in Bihar Assembly election in October and November 2015 reverted the party's stand of 'going it alone' in the Assembly election. Secondly, the realization that the combined strength of the three party alliance can combat the congress. It has to be reminded that in the 2011 Assembly election, the BJP won 5 seats and the AGP got 10 and the BPF 12 altogether with a voting share of 33%. The BJP hoped that a grand alliance can dislodge the Congress regime which wields political power in the three consecutive terms in the State.Perhaps, the reasons for making an alliance rather than going it alone in the state was the realization of the party in the Bihar experience where it crumpled to strong Janta Dal United (JD(U)) and Rashtriya Janata Dal (RJD) alliance. The election verdict however proved that the alliance succeeded in preventing splitting the anti Congress votes. Fourthly, the BJP succeeded in bringing Tarun Gogoi's most trusted Himanta Biswa Sarma served as the minister of Health and Education in Gogoi government to the party, who infact the mastermind in the BJP's alliance with other two regional parties in the state. The seven of the ten sitting Congress MLAs who left parent party andwon on BJP tickets.

Further, inspite of the above factors which went in favour of the BJP's fortunes in the state, the BJP's victory more related to the systematic activities of the RSS in the state which has been quiet systematically working the tribal belt of the state for years. It has to be reminded that in 1979, the RSS founded its first school, Shishu Shiksha Samiti, in the state and about 500 Ekal Vidyalayas was created by the RSS in the state overtime. The RSS for a long time spreading its roots in the state by appropriating Assam's medieval saint Srimanta Sankardev for political gains. Sankardev led a reformist neo-vaishnavite movement against Brahmanism (Bhattacharjee, 2016). It also actively supported the anti-infiltration of Bangladeshi movements in the Assam movement of 1979-84 as it believed that illegal infiltration is a threat to national security.

Mosaic of Cultural Diversity

Assam is a complex society which constitutes Assamese Hindus, Bengalis, migrant Bangladeshis and tribal population considered to be a mosaic of ethno-cultural diversity. The Assamese Hindus are dominant in Brahmaputra valley and the Bengalis are dominant in the Barrak valley. Initially, the BJP's traditional stronghold is the Bengali dominated Barrak valley. As Srikanth argues that "although the BJP did not initially get the support of the Assamese Hindus, as early as in 1991, it could make a dent into the Bengali dominated Barak valley region, where it won parliamentary seats from Silchar and Karimganj constituencies (in 1999)" (Srikanth, 1999, p. 3413). However, in the recent past, in the Brahmaputra valley too, the BJP wooed the Assamese Hindus by raking up the issue of illegal migration of Bengali Muslims and its impact on the Assamese society. It accused the Congress of playing votebank politics of Bengali migrants. In fact, the BJP's promise to check illegal immigration presumably gained wider acceptability among the Assamese elite.

Among all the states in the NEI, Assam is considered to be the gate way of BJP to the rest of the states in the region. For quite some time, the BJP is turning its attention to the political developments in Assam and trying to occupy the opposition space vacated by the AGP. For instance, on 29th December, 2014, Amit Shah constituted a five member committee headed by its senior leader S S Ahluwalia to visit and review the condition of tribal victim of National Democratic Front of Bodoland -Songbijit (NDFB (S)) violence in Assam relief camps. More than seventy tribals were killed in the violence in Assam in attacks by pro Bodo militant groups in December 2014. In fact, few days before the visit of Shah in April, the BJP government was contemplating to delink Assam from the Land Boundary Agreement (LBA) with Bangladesh. The Protocol to the 1974 LBA, signed on 6th September 2011, paves the way for settlement of the outstanding land boundary issues between the two countries. The 2011 Protocol has been prepared with the full support and concurrence of the State governments concerned – Assam, Meghalaya, Tripura and West Bengal. As agreed upon through several rounds of negotiations started during UPA-II, Assam is set to lose around 268.39 acres in the final arrangement with Bangladesh under LBA, but does not get any land in return. West Bengal is supposed to lose 1,957 acres, but get 2,398 acres, while Meghalaya will lose 41 acres and get 250 acres in return from Bangladesh. Assam giving up land is part of settling a disputed 6.1 km stretch that's been with Bangladesh since Partition. For quite some time, this is an emotive issue in Assam's polarised and volatile politics and BJP's Assam unit has always opposed the land loss. The BJP top brass considers Assam, a major Northeastern state that goes to polls next year, a winning prospect and these poll calculations may result in delinking LBA with Bangladesh for now. Due to the growing resentment against the LBA in Assam, the BJP is revising the actual plan and accordingly the Indo-Bangladesh LBA will now involve only West Bengal, Tripura and Meghalaya on the Indian side. The Constitution Amendment Bill to ratify the Indo-Bangladesh Land Boundary Agreement is likely to be introduced in Parliament with a major change by delinking Assam.[1]

Emergence asa Political Alternative

Before 1991, the BJP was not a significant force in the electoral politics of Assam. In 1991 Assembly elections, the BJP won 10 seats out of 48 Assembly seats it contested securing a vote share of 6.4%. In the 1991 general election, the BJP won two seats with a vote share of 9.6 per cent. In the 1996 general election its vote share went up to 15.9% with one seat. However, in the Assembly election in 1996 it could manage 10.4 per cent votes winning 4 seats. In 2001 Assembly election with the alliance of AGP the party bagged 8 seats and 35.8 per cent seats. In 2004 general election the BJP won 2 seats and the 2006 Assembly election won 12 seats with a vote share of 11.98 per cent. Like elsewhere in India, initially, the BJP allied with the regional party, AGP in 2006 assembly election and 2009 general election. In the 2014 general election by winning 7 seats (of the total 14 seats) and securing a vote share of 36.86% the BJP gradually emerged as a credible alternative to Congress in the 2016 Assembly election.In February 2015municipal polls the BJP made a clean sweep winning 21 municipal boards and 24 town committees compared to 2009 elections when it won only at 5 municipal boards and 11 town committees.

The BJP's growth in the state politics can be seen in the context of the anti-incumbency against the three consecutive term of the Congress government and the declining prominence of AGP as an ethno-regional party. In the recent past the state is witnessing the erosion of ethno-regional nationalism championed by the AGP in the eighties. It is to be reminded that the Assam movement (1979-84) sowed the seeds of ethno-regionalism which witnessed the emergence of AGP making inroads into state politics eroding the Congress mass base. The AGP which came into power with the cause of 'Asomiya Nationality' and the issue of illegal migration, in course of time, diluted its stand on Illegal Migrants Determination by Tribunal IM(DT) Act, 1983 due to compulsions of electoral politics. As a result, there was a growing disillusionment among the Hindus against the AGP, this created a fertile ground for the BJP in Assam. Over a time, the BJP used the issue of illegal migration of Muslims for expanding its mass base in the state. As Srikanth argues that "the politics of regional identity had kept Hindutva at bay in Assam for over two decades. But the AGP government's poor performance and the bogey of Muslim fundamentalism led Bengali and Assamese caste Hindus to the BJP" (Srikanth, 1999, p. 3412). As a result, the AGP, the prominent regional political force is declining its space in the state. Moreover, AGP's alliance with BJP in the 2006 Assembly and 2009 Loksabha election cost more to the AGP. The BJP could grow at the expense of the decline political space of the AGP. It is argued that the traditional support base of AGP – the Assamese Hindus, the Assamese Muslim and tribals – gradually shifted their allegiance to other political parties (Mahanta, 2014, p. 20). The regional agenda of theAGP, especially detection and deportation of illegal Bangladeshi migrants were hijacked by the BJP. In the recent past, many leaders of the AGP joined the BJP adding further boost to the BJP in the state. In December 2015, the BJP constituted its campaign panel for the Assembly elections 2016 with number of former All Assam Students Union (AASU), AGP leaders.

Diminution of the Congress

The three consecutive term of the Tarun Gogoi governmentwitnessed strong wave of anti incumbency and charges of corruption. During the tenure of the Gogoi regime witnessed many clashes in the Bodo areas in the State especially between Bodos and Muslims. The growing resentment against containing frequent clashes and the civil administration's failure to rehabilitate the victims of clashes added further blow to the Gogoi administration. When the Assembly election was approaching and the BJP was chalking out its strategy to win the Assembly election in the state, the Congress faced disarray within the party and the government. In the recent past, many Congress legislators joined the BJP. In August, 2015, an embarrassment to the state Congress, former Minister Himanta Biswa Sarma joined the BJP. Himanta who was Tarun Gogoi's trusted aid disillusioned with the Congress due the realization that his political ambition to become the Chief Minister of the state was dashed by the Congress as the Gogoi is promoting his son Gaurav Gogoi. While contesting such argument Assam Congress leader Kishore Bhattacharjee said that "Gaurav's entry into politics has no role in their differences. It started way back when (now Congress MLA) Pijush Hazarika was elected the Assam Pradesh Youth Congress

President in June 2008. Then there were speculations in 2012 that Tarun Gogoi would resign as Chief Minister and become the country's Vice-President, Sarma was really hoping to become the Chief Minister".[2] Further, a section of Congress questioned chief minister Tarun Gogoi for promoting his son, the Lok Sabha MP from as his political heir in the state.

The Repeal of IM(DT) Act, 1983

The appointment of Sarbananda Sonowal, the Union Minister of State for Sports, as the president of the State BJP gave further boost to the saffron party. Sonowal, the former leader of the AASU and subsequently MLA of the AGP switched over to the BJP some time back, is a crusader against illegal migration of Bangladeshi in Assam. In 2012, he accused the illegal migrants of deteriorating the life of the indigenous people of Assam. He said that in the last 32 years the indigenous people of Assam have been cornered and pushed to the status of minority due to the huge influx of illegal immigrants from Bangladesh.[3]

The illegal migration from Bangladesh is a sensitive issue in Assam as it developed far reaching consequences in the political, economic and socio-cultural life of the people.It is one fo the biggest issue in the Assam Election since 1985. As it stated earlier, the Assam movement which put the demand for the detection and deportation of illegal migrants (often used as 'foreigners') in the state. In its effort to end the movement the Indian government formulated the IM (DT) Act 1983 to protect the interest of Assam. According to the Act, anybody settled in Assam before March 25, 1971 was a legal citizen. However, rest of India, the cut of date for acquiring Indian citizenship is July 9, 1948. Further, the person accused had to do nothing to prove his/her citizenship whereas the compliant had to prove that someone was illegal. The Act also provides special protections against undue harassment to the minorities affected by Assam Agitation. The Act is applicable only to Assam while rest of the states in India is covered by the Foreigners Act, 1946. The Act it was viewed that the provision designed to make it difficult for authorities to identify, leave alone, deport illegal Bangladeshi from Assam.

In a petition filed by Sarbananda Sonowal, who was with AGP contended that the IM(DT) is only encouraging vote bank politics without addressing the problem of illegal migrants. In July 2005, the Supreme Court observed that the Act was the biggest barrier to deportation of the illegal migrants from the state. The Supreme Court in its 114 page judgment stated that "the Act has created the biggest hurdle and is the main impediment or barrier in the identification and deportation of illegal migrants". Further, it observed that, "the presence of such a large number of illegal migrants from Bangladesh, which runs into millions, in fact an aggression on the state of Assam and also contributed significantly in causing serious internal disturbances in the shape of insurgency of alarming propositions".[4]

The repeal of the IM (DT) Act by the Supreme Court in 2005 further communally polarized the state. When both BJP and AGP welcomed the court verdict, the Muslim communities expressed their anguish. The BJP claimed that 'discriminatory' Act failed to effectively identify and deport illegal migrants in the state and the Supreme Court observation was a setback to the Congress which is using this as a vote bank politics. After the Supreme Court verdict, the BJP took out a rally in Guwhati in July 2005 demanding the deportation of all illegal Bangladeshi nationals from Assam. It has to be reminded that the RSS and the BJP supported the Assam movement to end the illegal migration in the state. Over a time, the Party shared the sentiments of the AGP on the issue of illegal migration and supported this provision in the Assam Accord of 1984 between the AASU and the Rajiv Gandhi government.

The Supreme Court's invalidation of the IM(DT) Act was viewed the AIUDF as the inability of the Congress to defend the Act. However, foreseeing the possible minority resentment against theCongress which had to face the Assembly election in 2006, the Prime Minister, Manmohan Singh constituted a Group of Ministers to examine the fall out of the repealing of the IM(DT) Act, particularly its impact on minorities. The BJP and the AGP criticized this action and describes as the backdoor entry of the Act.

Even after ten years of the repeal of the IM(DT) Act, the issue continues to haunt the politics of the State. The BJP accused the Congress of following a policy of appeasement which created grave security implications for the country. It says the large scale intrusion of illegal Bangladeshi immigrants has significantly altered the demographic complexion of North-Eastern states and has serious long-term political, social and economic implications.[5] In September 2012, Ram Madhav, the RSS leader once said that, "we need to detect and defranchise the Bangladeshi infiltrators from the country. There is very little done by the central government to deport them, just 1 per cent per 5 days, though the rate of infiltration is about 6, 000 per day"[6]. The BJP's Vision Document released before the General Election 2014 contained a separate section on North East which promised to put an end to infiltration from Bangladesh and vigorously pursue the 3 D – formula – Detect, Delete and Deport (illegal migrants from Assam).[7] The BJP's Assam Vision Document for 2016 Assembly election also promised to crackdown on infiltration and to seal the Indo-Bangla border. It accused the Congress of destroying and changing the demography of the state by encouraging infiltration. The document also promised stringent action against industries and business which employ illegal migrants.

In his visit to Assam on 26th April 2015, the BJP president asserted that "Bangladeshi infiltrators have taken away everything. They have taken away land of the Assamese people. They have taken away your jobs. They have eaten into the development funds. Yet the Congress government does not have the guts to touch them. It is only the BJP which can free Assam from the clutches of the Bangladeshis,"[8] He also took credit for the process of updating the National Register of Citizens currently going on in the state and said the NDA government had earmarked Rs 140 crore to the state for this purpose. In his opinion, "once the NRC is revised and updated, all the Bangladeshi infiltrators will be exposed". Accusing the Congress of not stopping illegal migration as it is playing vote bank politics, the BJP president promised to stop illegal migration of Bangladeshis into Assam.[9] Setting the agenda for the campaign for the Election, Shah was categorical that "next elections will be fought on this issue. Assam poll will be for freeing the state of illegal Bangladeshi migrants. Assam polls will also be for development of Assam and North-East". [1010]*Ibid*

The BJP often depict majority of the Muslims as "illegal Immigrants" from Bangladesh which cause imbalance to the state demography and socio-cultural mosaic of the state.

Setting aside its national agenda and issues, the BJP was able to rake up regional issues such as illegal migration, detection and deportation of foreigners which were once raised by the AGP. In fact, the BJP hijacked the regional agenda of AGP, especially on the issue of illegal migrants. However, though BJP wakes up the migration issue, it only focuses on the Muslims not the Bengalis Hindus whom it considered as their supporting base.The BJP while criticizing the illegal migration from Bangladesh, in the recent past took another turn in this issue. The Party now welcoming the migration of Hindus from Bangladesh stating that those Hindus who face religious persecution in that would be accommodated to India and would be given citizenship. Shah in his visit to the state even asserted that the BJPwould provide all support to Hindus who came to India due to religious persecution and promised that the Hindu refugees from Bangladesh will be given Indian citizenship if the BJP comes to power in Assam in

2016 Assembly election. The communal fervor of the BJP is explicated when it was critic of Muslim migrants, and taking the burden of supporting Hindus who came to India because of the so called harassment and religious discrimination. The saffron party's surprise move, however created certain resentment in the state when organizations such as the AASU and the Assam Jatiyatabadi Yuva Saba Parishad (AJYCP) who alleges that it is in fact diluting its stand on Bangladeshi migration problem. However, some sections of the state BJP feel that this would lead to the alienation of Assamese educated and middle class away from the party.

For quite some time, Assam is passing through a critical political juncture in which the linguistic chauvinism and ethnic regionalism which dominated for decades were overshadowed by the growing tendencies ofcommunal mobilization. The growing communal polarization between Bodos and the Muslims minority groups leads to frequent ethnic killings. The Bodo Kacharis which constitute the largest tribal group in Assam and which account for 38 per cent of the total population of the state were instigated against the Muslim population in the Bodo areas of the state. However, the BJP's communal polarization between migrants Muslims and Assamese speaking Hindus and the tribal communities and migrants made political dividends to the BJP.

Conclusion

The astounding victory of the BJP in Assam gave some relief to the ruling dispensation at the centre after its stunning defeat in Delhi and Bihar Assembly elections. Rather than seeing as a victory for the Narendra Modi, it can be seen as a result of communal polarization, strong anti incumbency and the vacuum created by the regional forces and secular alternatives in the state. In a closely fought election, regional issues rather than national issues figured throughout the election campaign. The emotive issue of illegal Bangladeshi migration once again assumed centre stage in political domain and gave more political dividends to the BJP. However, the real outcome of the first ever BJP government in the North-East depends on its approach towards the preserving the cultural diversity of the state.

Notes

1. *The Economic Times,* 13th April, 2015.
2. *The Assam Tribune*, 28th August, 2014.
3. see *Organiser* 16th September 2012.
4. "IMDT Act is the biggest barrier to deportation, says Supreme Court", *The Hindu*, 14th July, 2005.

5. see BJP (2006), "Achievements and Looking Ahead; 1980- 2005", Vol. 9, New Delhi.
6. see *Organiser* 16th September 2012.
7. see BJP (2014), *Vision Document*, 2014.
8. "Amit Shah in Guwahati: Get ready to 'oust Congress' in 2016 Assam assembly polls", *The Indian Express,* 28th April, 2015.
9. "Only BJP can free Assam from illegal immigration, Amit Shah", *The Economic Times*, 27th April, 2015.
10. *Ibid.*

References

Bhattacharjee, Malini, 2016; 'Tracing the Emergence and Consolidation of Hindutva in Assam', *Economic and Political Weekly*, Vol. LI, No. 16, 30, 16 April, pp. 80-87.

Mahanta, Nani Gopal, 2014; 'Loksabha Elections in Assam: Shifting of Traditional Vote Bases to BJP', *Economic and Political Weekly*, Vol. XLIX, No. 35, 30 August, pp. 19-22.

Srikanth, H, 1999; 'Communalising Assam: AGP's Loss Is BJP's Gain', *Economic and Political Weekly,* Vol. XXXIV, No.49, 4 December, pp. 3412-3414.

Chapter - 10

Manipur Assembly Elections 2017: BJP's Ascendency in the Periphery

The thumbing victory of the Bharatiya Janata Party (BJP) in the 2017 Assembly election in Manipur added another jewel to the crown of BJP in North East Region of India. Although emerged as the second-largest party to the incumbent Congress, the BJP could form the government for the first time in the state, with support of smaller parties like the Naga People's Front (NPF), National People's Party (NPP), Lok Janshakti Party (LJP) and independents. The BJP not only dislodged the incumbent Congress regime's effort to form its government for the fourth consecutive term, but also sharpened its plan to bring a Congress *mukht* Northeast India. The Assembly election was held in the context of mounting social unrest and political volatility created by the agitation for the demand of Inner Line Permit (ILP) by the Meiteis and the economic blockade imposed by the United Naga Council (UNC) against the creation of new districts in Manipur. Phanjoubam aptly captured the situation as a 'voting in a season of discontent' (Phanjoubam 2017). Amid these political unrests, the state witnessed an electrifying election campaign of national leaders, including Prime Minister Narendra Modi, the BJP President Amit Shah and the Congress Vice-President, Rahul Gandhi. During the campaign it was obvious that for the Congress, the incumbent Chief Minister Ibobi Singh was its chief ministerial candidate, and the BJP it did not project anyone for the top job.

The two-phase election held in March witnessed a massive turnout of 84 per cent. The keenly contested election produced a fractured verdict in which the Congress emerged as the single largest party winning 28 seats with the vote share of 35.1 per cent in the 60-member Assembly. It has to be reminded that in 2012 Assembly election, the Congress retained power for the third consecutive term with the massive majority of 42 seats. In this election, however, the Congress vote share declined to 35.1 per cent from 42.80 per cent. The BJP, which drew blank in the previous Assembly elections of 2012, though it contested 19 seats, was able to capture 21 seats with a vote share of 36.3 per cent this time (Table 1).

Table 1: Trends of 2017 Assembly Election

Party	*Seats*	*Vote Share (in per cent)*
Indian National Congress (INC)	28	35.1
Bharatiya Janata Party (BJP)	21	36.3
Naga Peoples Front (NPF)	4	7.2
National People's Party (NPP)	4	5.1
Lok Jan Shakti Party (LJP)	1	2.5
All India Trinamool Congress (AITC)	1	1.4
Independent	1	5.1

Source: Election Commission of India.

Hill—Valley Divide and the Social Chemistry

A proper understanding of the Hill—Valley divide, the social composition and the geographical distribution of the communities in the state is critical for a meaningful analysis of electoral politics of Manipur. All such issues always influence the nature and outcome of electoral politics of the state substantially.

The northeastern state of Manipur, having area of 22,327 square kilometres, was incorporated into the Indian Union in October 1949. It achieved full statehood in 1972. Manipur has 352 km long international border with Myanmar in the south-east. It is also known for its Hill—Valley divide. The Hill comprises five districts—Senapati, Tamenglong, Churachandpur, Chandel and Ukhrul, where the tribal communities inhabit. The Valley consists of Imphal West, Imphal East, Bishnupur and Thoubal. It has two constituent parts – one of which is in Imphal valley in the heart of the state and the other is Jiri valley in the west beyond the pale of hill ranges bordering the Cacher District of Assam.

Manipur is not a tribal state, and not under the Sixth Schedule of the Constitution, where the minority tribal communities have autonomy in the state. It is a highly pluralised society with a complex ethnic composition. Manipur has three major ethnic groups such as Meiteis, Kukis and Nagas and the smaller groups like Mizos, Zomi, Chins, Paites, Hmars, etc. The

Meiteis resides in Valley, which constitutes only 10 per cent of the state's total area, including four districts such as Imphal East, Imphal West, Thoubal and Bishnupur. According to the 2011 Census, the Valley districts account for 61.54 per cent of the state's population, while the Hill districts constitute 38.46 per cent of the total population. Thus, Manipur is seen as an appropriate example of maintaining ethnic boundary within the territorial boundary (Bijukumar 2017: 14). The Hill—Valley divide and the recurring conflict between the people of Hill and Valley are not merely an ethnic or territorial one, but have social, economic and political dimensions.

According to the 2011 Census, the Hill districts witnessed rise in the decadal growth rate (2001—11) as Senapati (25.16 per cent), Tamenglong (25.69 per cent), Churachandpur (19.03 per cent), Ukhrul (30.07 per cent), and Chandel (21.72 per cent). On the other hand, the districts in the Valley witnessed below 20 per cent in the population growth rate as Imphal West (15.82 per cent), Imphal East (14.63 per cent), Bishnupur (15.36 per cent) and Thoubal (15.48 per cent). According to 2011 Census, the Scheduled Tribe (ST) population was 11.67 lakh as against 7.41 lakh in 2001 Census. About 95 per cent of the ST population is found in the Hill districts of Manipur, while the remaining 5 per cent are in the Valley districts. Religiously, the Meiteis, the dominant ethnic group in the Valley, are Hindus and the tribals in the Hill areas are largely the Christians. The Hindus who constitute about 46 per cent of the total population are also settling in the Valley. Most of the tribes are Christians and they are mostly settling in the Hills.

As per the 2011 Census, there has been a decrease in the percentage of Hindu population (5.91 per cent) during 1991—01, while the Christian population increased to 17.70 per cent. Since 1971, there is a declining trend of population in the Valley and increasing trend in the Hill areas. For instance, in 1971, the Valley population was 67.40 per cent as against the Hill population of 32.60 per cent. In 1981, the Valley population declined to 65.57 per cent as against the rise in the Hill population to 34.43 per cent. In 1991, the Valley population declined by 64.56 per cent against the rise in the Hill population of 35.44per cent. In 2001, the Valley population was 61.54 per cent and the Hill area population was 38.46 per cent. In 2011, the Valley population further declined by 57.21 per cent and the Hill population rose up to 42.79 per cent (Table 2).

Table 2: Trends in Population Growth in the Hill and Valley Regions

Year	*Valley (in per cent)*	*Hill (in per cent)*
1971	67.40	32.60
1981	65.57	34.43
1991	64.56	35.44
2001	61.54	38.46
2011	57.21	42.79

Source: Government of Manipur, Economic Survey, 2015—16.

Social Division and Electoral Constituency

Of the 60 assembly seats in Manipur, 40 represent the Valley and 20 the Hill areas. Among the 40 constituencies, 39 are general and one constituency (Sekmai) is reserved for the Scheduled Caste. Of the 20 constituencies in Hill areas, 19 constituencies are reserved for the hill tribes and the lone constituency (Kangpokpi), considered to be largely populated by the Nepali population in the erstwhile SADAR (Selected Area Development and Administrative Region), is general. In these 19 constituencies, Nagas normally hold sway in 11 to 12 constituencies and rest are generally won by the Kukis and allied tribes. Partiality is also felt in the constituency delimitation process. It was often alleged that even though population in the Hill areas are growing, adequate number of constituencies are not created. On the other hand, the population is declining in the Valley over the decades, but with no change in the number of constituencies. This disproportion in growing population and inadequate number of constituencies is a great concern for the tribal communities, as they feel that it leads to imbalance in the power structure of the state.

Simmering Discontent among the Meiteis

Although the Meiteis dominate the Valley and have decisive influence in the politics of the state, they often develop a sense of alienation in the region due to the growing infiltration of outsiders and the changing geographical and demographical equations in the state. The Meiteis allege that they cannot buy lands in the Hill areas, while the tribals can possess land in the Valley. Interestingly, as per the constitutional provisions, the outsiders, including the Meiteis need the permission of the Hill Area Committee (HAC), while those in Hill areas can buy land in the Meiteis-inhabited areas. Over the period of time, the Meiteis believe that their control over land is shrinking due to the tribal inhabitance in the Valley as well as the migration of the outsiders such as Biharis, Marwaris, and Punjabis for business purpose. According to the Meiteis, the north Indian population outnumbered the indigenous Meiteis in the district of Bishnupur. Considering this as a grave situation, the Meiteis demand more protective measures from the state fearing that they are losing their land and resources to the outsiders including the tribals from the Hill areas. The growing sense of getting reduced into a minority in the Valley forced the Meiteis to demand ILP to restrict the entry of the outsiders into the region under the aegis of the Joint Committee on Inner Line Permit System (JCILPS), an umbrella organisation of 30 groups, which subsequently witnessed violent protests in the middle of 2015. The JCILPS' intension to uphold the cause of the indigenous people of the state is often questioned by the tribal communities. Even though the Meiteis frequently assert that these bills would not affect the tribal communities, there has been growing resentment by the tribals against these bills. Those who are supporting the demands of Meiteis and these bills argue that the demand for ILP is yet another way to protect the interest of the indigenous population due to the massive flow of non-indigenous population.

Sense of Deprivation among the Tribals

The Hill-area tribals, on the other hand, also have a sense of deprivation as they allege that most of the employment opportunities in the state are monopolised by the Meiteis. In the arena of political representation, out of 60 seats in the Legislative Assembly, 40 are represented by the Valley people and 20 by those from the Hills. Naturally, in the state legislative assembly and in the government, the Meiteis have decisive majority which also is manifested in the policy making process. Development is more concentrated in the Valley leaving the underdevelopment and impoverishment in the tribal areas. The relative deprivation of the Hill tribes are more glaring as they lack better schooling, health and housing facilities in the state. The Hill tribes even allege that there are concerted efforts of the Meiteis to grab their land and resources in the tribal regions adjacent to the Valley. However, the inter-community conflicts among the tribal communities such as Nagas and Kukis often act as a stumbling block for the unity of the tribals in their fight against deprivation and to demand more avenues from the state. As Roluahpuia argued "contrary to the claims of the JCILPS, the tribals were wary of the fact that these bills will provide leverage to the Meitei demand for uniform land laws as in the case of MLR&LR Act and deny the tribal rights over their land and identity" (Roluahpuia 2016, p 6). The tribal communities in the Hill areas feel that these would endanger their social life rather than the non-tribals from the outside. Although there are internal conflicts among the tribal communities in the Hill areas, often pitting a united front against the Meiteis, they have blocked the demand for ST status of the Meiteis.

Election Context

As it was stated earlier, the Assembly elections were held in the context of the agitation for demanding ILP and the United Naga Council's (UNC) long economic blockade against the creation of new districts in Manipur. The pressing demand by the JCILPS compelled the Ibobi Singh government to enact three bills on 31 August 2015. These bills include: a) the Protection of Manipur People Bill, 2015; b) the Manipur Land Revenue and Land Reforms Bill (Seventh Amendment), 2015; and c) the Manipur Shops and Establishments (Second Amendments) Bill, 2015. According to Ngaihte, "these three bills were the culmination of a two-month long agitation by the Meitei people in the Imphal valley for introduction of an Inner Line Permit (ILP) system to regulate and curtail the entry of 'non-Manipuris' into Manipur" (Ngaihte 2015).

The passage of these bills, which are related to the ILP, invited sharp criticisms and violent protests from the Hill tribes like the Nagas and Kukis. The protesters felt that many provisions of the bills make them alien in their native land as the intention of the bill is to 'snatch away tribal lands' and to infringe their rights. They even questioned the key provision of the bill with regard to the 1951 cutoff date for defining who is 'Manipur People'. Questions were also raised regarding the bills not been debated and consulted widely with all cross section of people of Manipur and communities living there, and many felt that it was a move against 'outsiders' by Manipur people. Alarmed by the intrusion into their identity and land rights, the tribal communities demanded the protection of their rights according to the Sixth Schedule of the Constitution. It is argued that 'the hill people fear that the three bills will erode their exclusive right over Hill lands accorded to them first by the British's policy of segregation, and then inherited by independent India' (Phanjoubam 2016: 14). After the enactment of the Bills in the Legislature on August 2015, violent protest by the Manipur Tribals Forum (MTF) erupted in Churachandpur District, where houses of the members of legislative assembly and parliamentarians were burned and the outrage subsequently witnessed the death of nine young protesters in September 2015.

The economic blockade against the creation of new districts started with the Congress government's move to create two districts—Kuki-dominated Sardar out of Senapati district and Jirbam out of Imphal East District. The UNC considered Senapati a part of the Naga ancestral homeland. According to Phanjoubam, "the UNC considers four of the seven split districts to be a part of the ancestral Naga homeland and was quick to accuse the Manipur government of splitting this homeland…" (Phanjoubam 2017). However, the Congress government discarded the UNC's plea and further went ahead with seven districts by splitting seven districts. The economic blockade called by the UNC adversely affected the everyday life of the people—rising prices of essential commodities, petrol and cooking gas.

BJP's Emergence and Mobilisation

The advent of BJP in the state was marked by the by-elections to the two Assembly constituencies in November 2015, where the BJP candidates defeated the ruling Congress candidates. It has to be reminded that in the 1995 Assembly election, the BJP won a single seat and in 2000 Assembly election it won six seats (including four in Valley and two in the Hills), but drew a blank in the 2004 election. However, in the 2015 by-election BJP candidates Khumukham Joy Kishan Singh in Thangmeiband Assembly constituency and Bishwajit Singh in Thongju Constituency defeated the Congress candidates, thereby adding another feather in the crown of the party in the region. It needs mention that for some time the BJP is wooing many regional leaders of other parties and prominent figures of the state to its fold. In September, RadhabinodKoijam, the former Manipur Chief Minister, Okran Joy Singh, the former leader of the Manipur People's Party (MPP) and YumnamJoykumar Singh, the former Director General of Police (DGP) joined the saffron party.

After the ascendency of the BJP government at the Centre in May 2014, Manipur was one of the attractions for the BJP in the NEI apart from Arunachal Pradesh and Assam. Way back, in his maiden visit on 18 April 2015 in the Congress-ruled state of Manipur, Amit Shah appealed the people to "elect BJP, get benefit" emphasising the need for BJP governments both in the state and at the centre for the better development of the state. In a dig to Congress, the BJP president pleaded for making North East a 'Congress –free Zone', where the people of Manipur has a decisive role. The BJP president said that apart from corruption, it was the Congress government that was holding Manipur back from progress and development.[1]

In the civic elections too, the BJP emerged as a potent force in the state. In the January 2016 municipal and nagar panchayat elections, the

BJP won 62 seats in the 278 member municipal council. In the 27-member Imphal Municipal Corporation elections held on 2 June 2016, the BJP emerged as second largest party winning 10 seats after the Congress, which could secure only 12 seats. The three consecutive years of the Obobi government was marred by allegations of fake encounters, corruption and human rights violations. In a further boost to the BJP's ambition in the state, on 24 May 2016, the four Naga Peoples Front (NPF) legislators in the Manipur Assembly joined BJP leading to the formation of North-East Democratic Alliance (NEDA) in Guwahati in the presence of Amit Shah and Ram Madhav. Himanta Biswa Sarma, the former Congressman and the current BJP Minister in Assam, was elected as the Convenor. The objective of the Alliance was to strengthen the party's base in the region, but outwardly it claimed that the intension of the NEDA was on the agenda of the overall development of the region. After successfully dislodging the Congress regime and installing a rebel Congress-led government with the outside support of the BJP in Arunachal Pradesh and forming its first government in Assam, the BJP gradually focused on Manipur.

Communalising Dwindling Hindu Population

Although BJP's presence in the state was relatively recent and low profile, the Rashtriya Swayamsevak Sangh (RSS) has strong roots in the Manipur. In fact, the long and systematic work of the RSS played a vital role in the electoral victory of the BJP. The BJP general secretary in charge of NEI admits that the commendable role of RSS in the electoral success of the Party in Manipur. Manipur is often described as a Hindu enclave surrounded by Christian population on all sides. The Meiteis who are mostly Vaishanavites claims to be the descent of Lord Arjuna, having more attachment to the RSS. In fact, the Hindu Meitei under the leadership of Maharaja Churachand Singh formed the Nikhil Hindu Manipuri Mahasabha in 1934 to regulate their religious activities. The RSS often raises the issues of dwindling Hindu population to mobilise the Meiteis to the BJP fold. It is alleged that the reason for dwindling Hindu population is the high fertility of Christians compared to the Hindus and conversion to Christianity. An article in the 4 January 2015 issue of the RSS' mouthpiece, *Organiser*, has offered some statistics in support of this argument. It says, 'There was a 5.2 per cent decadal (1991—2001) growth in Hindu population of Manipur. However, at the same time, Christians grew by 36.6 per cent and Muslims by 43.1 per cent'. It further adds, "North-eastern states, excluding Assam, recorded 50.6 per cent growth in Christians and 42.4 per cent growth in Muslims (in the same period)." The Sangh Parivar, which engages in *gharwapsi* (homecoming), often raises the issue of reduction in Hindu population in the state. In a resolution adopted in the RSS' Akhil Bhariya Karyakari Mandal in Ranchi in October 2015 claimed that in Manipur the share of the "religions of Bharatiya origin" was over 80 per cent in 1951, but came down to 50 per cent in 2011."[2]

BJP's Twin Strategy

The BJP often uses the dwindling Hindu population in the state to woo the Meiteis in its fold. However, it does not antagonise the tribal population in the Hill areas. In fact, the BJP wanted to allay the growing apprehension that it may go with the Meitis jeopardising the interest of the tribal population. On the other hand, the BJP's strategy was to appease major ethnic communities in the state such as the Meiteis, Nagas and Kukis. In the recent past, the BJP was able to make inroads into the tribal constituencies especially in the Naga-inhabited areas. The party uses the much acclaimed Naga Peace Accord of 2015, though the provisions of the accord were not made public, as a rallying point for its Naga mobilisation. Like the mobilisation of the Nagas, the BJP did not take an antagonistic strategy against the Kukis in the state. The Assembly election 2017 shows that the BJP made strong presence even in the Kuki-dominated areas. The majority of the Kukis were traditionally the support base of the Congress. In this election, there was a division within the Kuki extremist organisation. While the Kuki National Organisation extended its support to the Congress, the United People's Front—a conglomeration of Kuki extremist groups—supported the BJP. As a result, the BJP managed to get three Kuki MLAs. The verdict further proves that the BJP's electoral support extended to all major communities such as Meiteis, Nagas and Kuki, and both in the Hill and Valley. Of the 40 Assembly constituencies in the Valley, the BJP won 16 seats including the lone SC constituency. In the 20 constituencies in the Hill areas, the BJP won four seats—Tamenglong, Thanlon, Henglep and Churachandpur. The lone general constituency (Kangpokpi) was also wrested by the BJP. In the government formation too, the BJP strategically went ahead of the Congress. Although the Congress emerged as the single largest party, the BJP early jumped into the formation of the government. In fact, it was alleged that the state governor Najma Heptulla by acting on behest of the centre invited the BJP, ignoring the Congress, the single largest party, which she felt can provide a stable government in the state. The BJP initiated talks with the smaller parties and the independents, before the Congress. It was able to even defect the Congress legislator Shyam Kumar.

Sharmila's Defeat and the Women Question

The Assembly election also witnessed the humiliating defeat of Irom Chanu Sharmila who spent 16 years on hunger strike against the draconian Armed Forces Special Powers Act (AFSPA), 1958. It has to be reminded that a few weeks before the elections, Sharmila called off her hunger strike to contest the Assembly elections to take her cause in a parliamentary way. She formed her political outfit named the People's Resurgence and Justice Party (PRJA) and contested against the Chief Minister, Okaram Obobi Singh in the Thoubal constituency. However, her clout of the agitation politics could not translate into reaping benefits in parliamentary politics as she secured only 90 votes. The humiliating rout of Sharmila goes beyond the electoral chemistry of success and defeat. It needs to be analysed with proper insight and the deeper malaise in the society. The defeat of Sharmila explicates the deep-rooted patriarchy in the society and its bearing on the electoral politics in Northeast India in general, and Manipur in particular.

Like other parts of the Northeast India, though women actively participate in agitational politics and were in forefront of many movements, their representation in the parliamentary politics is often dismal. Although women in the region explicitly appear in public sphere, in contrast to the rest of the women in mainland India, there exists robust patriarchal values, which prevent their entry into parliamentary politics. In Manipur, women played a vital role in all spheres of life. In the 1970s, Manipur women waged a movement against liquor. In the late 1970s, the Meira Paibi (Women Torchbearers) Movement played a significant role in protecting people from social evils like drug, rape, murder, etc. The Manipur Mahila Sammelan was in the forefront of the movement for the statehood for Manipur. The Manipur women organisations also fought against the human rights violations by the armed forces using the AFSPA.

The 16-year-old struggle of the Sharmila was historic not only in terms of its duration, but also as a response to the state repression and the intersectional oppression of ethnicity and gender. It is often argued that the gender identity coupled with ethnic identity bring more oppression and discrimination of women in the NEI. This oppression is mainly classified into internal and external. The internal oppression occurs out of intersection of gender and ethnicity. For instance, how the armed forces engage in raping and murdering the tribal women. The state and its machinery play a vital role in intersectional discrimination and oppression of women. In the counter insurgency operations, state commits various kinds of human rights violations, wherein the women are the worst sufferers. Internally, the tribal women due to their ethnic identity and cultural specificity confront with multiple forms of oppression and discrimination in comparison with non-tribal women. In other words, ethnic identity combined with gender identity brings more oppression of women by the state. In the name of counter insurgency, the Indian state applies draconian acts like the AFSPA, 1958 to kill innocent civilians declaring them as terrorists. Under the provisions of this Act, the state government declares an area as 'disturbed' and gives extraordinary power to the armed forces to arrest any person with suspicion. In most cases, the arrested person is killed by the security forces depicting him or her as terrorist. In this gruesome act of the security forces, women became the scapegoats as the Act gave an opportunity for the armed forces to commit violence against women in the form of rape, abduction, sexual exploitation, etc. In this context, the gender identity intersecting with ethnic identity turn into causality for women.

During insurgency and the resulting counter insurgency operations by the state atrocities against women in the forms of molestation, rape, abduction take place. The intersectional oppression of women comes in the forms of sexual subjugation by the security forces. The intersection of gender and ethnicity often becomes a causality in the extremist activities by the non-state actors and the counter actions against them by the state. The tribal women are the worst victim of intersectional discrimination during the counter insurgency operations by the state. It shows both masculine and racial superiority of the Indian state in general, and the armed forces in particular. The tribal women are locked into trauma of the intersectional discrimination of gender and ethnicity. The atrocities against women result in their impoverishment, thereby adversely affecting their capabilities. It is argued that "counter-insurgency measures organised by the security forces often accompanied extremely gender insensitive measures aimed at the decapitation, maiming and heaping of indignities over the body of Manipuri women" (Arambam 2007: 359).

The repressed sexuality of the tribal women is an alarming trend in the civil society of the NEI. Rape committed by security forces destroys the virginal modesty of the tribal women. The resistance to AFSPA mainly came from the women who felt that it would exploit their gender and ethnic identity. In October 2003, a school girl N. Sanjita committed suicide after she was raped by the Grenadiers at Jiribam in Manipur creating widespread protest by the tribal women. On 15 July 2004, dozens of naked tribal women in Manipur protested in front of the headquarters of the Assam Rifles carrying the banners that read, "Indian Army Rape Us", "Indian

Army take our Flesh". The protest cropped up against the Indian security forces that allegedly abducted, raped and killed a tribal woman named Thangjam Manorama Devi. The hunger strike of Irom Sharmila, a tribal woman in Manipur, for repealing the AFSPA is another example of intersectional discrimination and oppression between gender and ethnicity. Sharmila launched her fast unto death immediately after the 'Malom Massacre' by the security forces in November 2000.

Throughout the fast extending over more than 16 years, Sharmila was often seen as the epitome of the resurgence of oppressed sexuality of the Manipur women. However, when she called off her agitation and took the parliamentary ways to address the issue of state repression through AFSPA, the people of Manipur rejected her proving that parliamentary politics as a site of male bastion. However, others would feel that Sharmila failed to realise the basic political sensibility of electoral politics that winning an election is not based on a single issue alone (in Sharmila's case, the human rights violation under the AFSPA), but attracting the electorate with multiple issues which are impoverishing their everyday life. As Phanjoubam argues:

Sharmila's humiliating defeat, then, is certainly not a question of Manipuris ceasing to respect her or not being grateful for her superhuman contribution to their struggle. It was, instead, a statement acknowledging that politics is much more complex than a one-agenda resistance campaign. The elections were not just about liking or hating the AFSPA. People's voting decisions are determined by issues pertaining to multiple insecurities, such as unemployment, falling standards of living, a drop in the quality of education and the existential threat to the state on account of deep divisions between ethnic communities — AFSPA is just one among several insecurities.[33]"

The defeat of Sharmila further worries the skewed representation of women in the state assemblies in the northeast India in general and Manipur in particular. In the newly elected Assembly, for instance, only one woman could enter. In the Kangpokpi, the only general seat, which was earlier with the Congress, in the Hill areas, Nemcha Kipgen of the BJP won the election.

Conclusion

The verdict of the Manipur election shows the BJP's political manoeuvre to deal concrete situations with appropriate strategy of mobilising contending social constituencies, which has proved success. The party's strategy of mobilisation of both the Meiteis and the tribal communities on different issues dashed the Congress' electoral chances in the state. The fortunes of the Congress were adversely affected by the resentment aroused of the ILP agitation and movement against the creation of the new districts by the UNC, in addition to the strong anti-incumbency and allegations of fake encounters, corruption and human rights violations. In the post-election scenario, though the Congress emerged as the single largest party, the BJP went ahead in fine-tuning its strategy to counter Congress ascendancy in the state making minor defection in the Congress and winning the support of the floating independents. However, the real testing point for the BJP government lies in finding out durable solution to the Naga issue without touching the territorial integrity of Manipur.

Notes

1. "Elect BJP, Get Benefits, Shah Tells Manipur-BJP Chief Addresses Imphal Rally," *The Telegraph* 19 April 2015.
2. See "Review Policy to Check Muslim, Christian Population: RSS Resolution," *The Indian Express,* 1 November 2015.
3. "A Defeat Forehold," *The Indian Express*, 20 March 2017.

References

Arambam, Lokendra (2007): "Peace Process in Manipur: Armed Conflict, State Repression and Women," in Anuradha Dutta and RatnaBhuyan (eds.), *Genesis of Conflict and Peace, Understanding Northeast India: Views & Reviews.* Vol I, Akansha Publishing House, New Delhi, pp. 343—366.

Bijukumar, V (2017): "Indigenous Assertion and the Politics of Retaliation: Hill-Valley Conflicts in Manipur," *Man and Society: A Journal of North-East Studies*, Vol XIV, Summer, pp. 7—26.

Ngaihte, Thangkhanlal (2015): "Manipur: Decoding the Rift between the Meiteis and the Hill Tribes," *The Indian Express*, 21 September.

Phanjoubam, Pradip (2016): "Manipur and Mainstream Media: Lost in the Rhetoric," *Economic & Political Weekly*, Vol 51, No 30, pp. 12—15.

Phanjoubam, Pradip (2017): "Voting in a Season of Discontent," *The Hindu*, 18 January.

Roluahpuia (2016): "Media in Conflict or Conflict in Media: Examining Media Coverage of Conflict in Northeast India," *Asian Ethnicity*, 12 August.

Chapter - 11

When Lotus Bloom in Periphery: Assembly Elections in Meghalaya, Nagaland and Tripura, 2018

The assembly elections 2018 in Meghalaya, Nagaland and Tripura scripted a new history in the politics of these states in particular and the Northeast in general. The BJP, till now, was not a decisive voice, emerged as an alternative political force challenging the hegemony of the Congress, the Left and the ethno-regional parties. Though in Meghalaya and Nagaland, it emerged as a second fiddle to the regional political parties and thereby able to be a part of the governments by regional forces, in Tripura, the BJP could secure two-third majority of its own, though it had a pre poll alliance with the tribal party of Indigenous People's Front of Tripura (IPFT), demolishing a quarter rule of the left front in the state.In the left ruled Tripura, the BJP could mobilize both the indigenous tribal communities and the dominant Bengali communities to its fold on various grounds. In the mostly Christian dominated states of Meghalaya and Nagaland, the BJP could make inroads into different ethnic communities through diverse appeals and political promises. Such an electoral and political upsurge of the BJP is the logical conclusion of its attempt to outbuilding its overall image of Hindu and North Indian Party. For quite some time, northeast India is a dream for the party not only for electoral goals but also for its political goals and ideological imperatives. Strategically this region shares international boundaries with China, Bangladesh, Myanmar, Nepal. Often cross broader migration take place, and the issue is highlighted by the BJP. Ideologically for BJP, the region is important as it is largely dominated by the Christians in some ways. The RSS considered that the age-old belief and practice that the Janjati communities of the North East are an integral part of greater Hindu Samaj. The North East also witnessed the intensive work of RSS particular and particularly the exponential growth of sakas.

The electoral strategy and mobilization of BJP not only based on its skill of social engineering in the ethnically diverse region but also its rhetoric of development. For its mobilization strategy, the party often cites the initiative taken by the Vajpayee government 2001 to set up Development of North Eastern Region (DONER) in 2001 for the development of the North East. In the run up to these Assembly elections, the Union government announced a slew of development projects to woo cross sections of the people in NEI. In December 2017, in the run up to the election in three Northeastern states, a slew of development projects announced by the Prime Minister Narender Modi which includes 90,000 crore road project connecting all the Northeastern states. In fact, for quite some time, the BJP is using the much fanfare Act East Policy for its mobilization in the region. In 2014, Modi stated that those who believe in Vastu Shastra say that Northeast is the part that should be taken most care for prosperity of the house. Similarly, India will prosper only if its northeast region gains. Therefore it is time to offer lotus (BJP) to this Ashta Lakshmi.[1] The BJP's appeal to development in Meghalaya and Nagaland, the two Christian dominated states – inspite of the issues such as the beef ban and atrocities against the minorities, could win political dividends for the party.

Meghalaya – Theatre of Fractured Verdict

Meghalaya has a history of fractured mandates and unstable governments since 1978 with coalition politics characterized by the ditching party loyalty. The verdict of assembly election in the hilly state of Meghalaya reiterated that the people never give majority to a single party in the state, except in the first assembly election in 1973. Only in the first election, the APHLC got an absolute majority with 32 out of 60 seats. In 1976, the All Party Hill Leaders Conference (APHLC) merged with the Congress. Many times the Congress was managed to form government with the support of smaller parties and independents often leading unstable governments. Since then no political party could win majority of its own in the Assembly often leading to defections and mergers which caused sturdy political instability in the state. Though, the Congress which was ruling the state for the last ten years, emerged as the single largest party with 21 seats in the sixty-member assembly, it could not form the government. On the other hand, the National People's Party (NPP), an ally of NDA at the center, muster the support of smaller parties and the BJP could form the government. Conard Sangma, the incumbent Lok Sabha MP from Tura constituency emerged as the leader of the NPP legislative party formed the government with the help of UDP, HSDP and BJP. The new government secured the support of 34 MLAs (NPP-19, UDP-6, HSDP-2, PDF – 4, BJP-2).

On 27 February, 2018 Meghalaya went for the poll to elect its 60-member assembly of which four non-reserved assembly constituencies – three in Shillong and one in Tura- and rest are reserved for the STs. In the keenly contested election, the voter turnout was 85% compared to 87% of the previous one. Prior to this, the campaign engrossed on multitude of issues, allegations and counter allegations. While the national issues rarely find adequate attention, the local issues related to state and ethnic communities were raised by the contending political formation throughout the campaign. The Congress at some point of time raised the issue of the denial of visa to the Baptist World Alliance leaders by the Consulate General of India in Johannesburg. Unlike other states in NEI, the BJP had many hurdles in Meghalaya. Its Hinduvta agenda often cannot be operated in the hilly state with deep rooted influence of Church and other ethno-regional organisations. This reality forced the BJP toraise the developmental paralysis and the corruption under the one-decade rule of the Congress government in the state. During the campaign, the BJP promised good governance, offering job opportunity, connectivity between north east and ASEAN and strengthening the Act East Policy. In the largely beef consumed state, the BJP set aside the beef issues rather focused on development issues.

In the 60-member Assembly, the INC emerged first position with 21 seats followed by the NPP which secured 19 seats, UDP 6, PDF 4, BJP 2, NCP 1, KHNAM 1 and independents 3. The People's Democratic Party (PDF) won new entrant with 4 seats. In the Khasi Hills, of the 36 seats, the Congress won 11 seats and in Garo Hills it could secure only 10 seats. In the Garo Hills, the NPP won 11 seats. It proves that the NPP wave fails in Garo Hills as the Congress was able to hold its positions in its strongholds. In the Khasi Hills, the NPP could win only 8 seats. The BJP could win only two seats in the state mainly from the Pynthorumkhrah and South Shillong in East Khasi Hills. The NPP though a new entrant in the state politics, it could emerge as the second single largest party without forging any alliance in the election even with the BJP to whom it allied at the centre. The NPP could reach out three major Hill areas of the state – Khasi, Garo and Jaintia. However, it has to be reminded that some of the Congress sitting MLAs who shifted their alliance to the NPP ahead of the election. The NPP had strongholds in the Garo Hills spreading its influence in Khasi-Jaintia Hills. It was formed by late P A Sangma in 2013 after leaving NCP, to consolidate tribals across the country under one political frame work. Since then, the party was able to show its impressive presence in certain states as it has MLAs in Rajasthan, Manipur and Nagaland. In Meghalaya, over the last two years, 13 ruling Congress MLAs ditched to the NPP after resigned from Assembly and joined the NPP.

Party Performance in Meghalaya Assembly Election 2018

Party	*Seats Won*	*Per centage of votes*
Indian National Congress	21	28.5
National People's Party	19	20.6
United Democratic Party	6	11.6
People's Democratic Front	4	8.2
Bharatiya Janata Party	2	9.6
Hill State People's Democratic Party	2	5.3
Nationalist Congress Party	1	1.6
Khun Hynniewtrep National Awakening Movement	1	0.9
Independent	3	10.8

Source: Election Commission of India

Lateral Entry of BJP in State Politics

The verdict of the elections was the projected as the victory of the BJP by its national leadership, but a postmortern analysis of the election shows that it was a victory of regional players and ex-Congressmen. Instead of BJP, the regional parties assumed key role in the fractured mandate. Of the 47 seats it contested, the BJP could win only two seats in the state mainly from the Pynthorumkhrah and South Shillong in East Khasi Hills. Even though, with much fanfare created by the BJP, it could not do impressively in the Garo Hills, the strong holds of the NPP. The BJP drew blank in the Garo Hills. Of the 23 seats in Garo Hills, it could not get one seat though party mobilization and campaign focused on the region. Inspite of the fierce campaign unleashed by Prime Minister and Amit Shah, the Party could second position only in two constituencies in Garo Hills – Ampati and South Tura.

However, the marginal numerical strength of the party in the Assembly cheers the party as it could enter a largely Christian inhabited state. Over the years the BJP, which is often described as Hindu and anti-Christian party, was able to penetrate into the Christian dominated state with the support of regional parties and local leaders. In the 2013 assembly election, the BJP contested in 13 seats but could not win a single seats and its vote share was just 1.27%. Unlike Assam, Arunachal Pradesh and Manipur, the party does not have substantial base and on this realization, it looked for alliances and social groups for its expansion.In the 2014 general election the BJP entered into an alliance with National Peoples Party (NPP) of Purno A. Sangma. It has to be reminded that Sangma who quit NCP, a constituent of the United Progressive Alliance (UPA) government at the Centre, few months before the election before forming the NPP and later formed a tactical electoral understanding with the NDA. In the 2014 general election, the Garo inhabited Tura seat was won by the Garo veteran Sangma by securing 22.84% of votes with the support of the BJP. However, political mobilization of the BJP got a boost after the 2014 general election. In October 2015 in the Garo Hills Autonomous District Council (GHADC) the BJP won one seat in Zikzak constituency in alliance with NPP.

By winning two seats in the assembly and being a part of the NPP led coalition in Meghalaya, the BJP felt that it could reverse earlier sentiments of Christians and ethnic communities in its favour. It has to be reminded that with great hope of boosting the party organization by wooing Hindu Nepalese and Bengali population in the state, the visit of the BJP President in the Congress ruled state of Meghalaya on 22nd April, 2015 was greeted with bandhs by outlawed extremist organizations such as the Hynniewtrep National Liberation Council (HNLC) and massive protest by Non-Governmental Organizations such as Thma U Rangli-Juki (TUR), Hynniewtrep National People's Front (HNPF) and Khasi National Union (KNU). The ethnic organizations even organized beef party to protest against the BJP governments move to ban beef which is the favourite food for the tribals in the state. The three regional parties in the State – United Democratic Party (UDP), Hill State People's Democratic Party (HSPDP) – voiced their concern on issue of ban on cow slaughter in separate meetings with the BJP national president Amit Shah. Amid growing resentment against the BJP government on the issue of banning beef, Ram Madhav, the BJP general secretary who accompanied Shah stated that "there is no such proposal to ban cow slaughter in the Northeastern states".[2]

Failing to polarize communally on emotive issues like elsewhere in the region, the BJP relied on the bogey of 'development 'in the state to mobilize its support base. The BJP President in his maiden visit to the state on 22nd April, 2015 asserted that the BJP government initiated construction of hostels for the welfare of North East students in Bangalore, Delhi

University and Jawaharlal Nehru University. Further the BJP leader Nalin Kohli made it clear that BJP is not an anti-Christian Party but a development –oriented party.[3] The Prime Minister Narendra Modi's visit to Shillong in the last week of May 2016 to attend the 65th NEC plenary session meeting can be seen in this context. Though the visit was entirely official, a section of the political class believes that by reiterating the developmental mantra, BJP was wooing certain sections of the society and thereby attempted to emerge as a potential alternative to the Congress in the state.

After engineering defection and overthrowing the Congress regime in Arunachal Pradesh and Assam, the BJP posed a challenge to the Congress government in Meghalaya. The BJP was desperately looking for a change from the Congress led Mukul Sangma government. In a prelude to make state free from the Congress, the BJP showed much interest in the internal squabbles with the state Congress. It has to be reminded that though the Congress in the state is vulnerable to factional squabble for a long time, the recent one was due to the defeat of the Congress candidate to Conrad K. Sangma of NPP in the Tura Loksabha bi election. The Garo Hills in which the Tura constituency belongs was considered to be the stronghold of the Chief Minister Mukul Sangma who was picked up by the central leadership of the Congress party to counter the influence of the Garo strongman, Purno Sangma. Though in the 2013 state assembly election Mukul could erode the base of the Purno, in the 2014 Loksabha election and the 2016 by-election, he was miserably failed to canvass the Garos to the party. Interestingly, Mukul was able to garner support in favour of his wife, Dikkanchi D. Shira, the sitting MLA as the candidate of the bieletion. In the election, the mandate was in favour of Conrad K. Sangma, the younger son of late Purno Sangma as the Garo people endorsed the family politics of Purno s once again over that of Mukul. The electoral defeat rekindled the factional politics in the state as D D Lapang, the MPCC president and the former Chief Minister and Vincent Pala, the MP from Shillong constituency demanded leadership change in the state. In his three page letter to party president Sonia Gandhi and the Vice President Rahul Gandhi, Mukul Sangma calaimed that "the BJP is campaigning in Shillong and are in connivance with cabinet ministers and looking to sir trouble for the state government".[4]

While the internal bickering of the ruling Congress and the shaky government further gave a boost to the electoral strategy and political mobilization of BJP in Meghalaya. Moreover, the ascendancy of BJP government in neighbouring Assam in 2017, accelerated the BJP's inclination towards the state.Further, Hiamanta Biswas Sarma, the convener of NEDA and the BJP turned Congress politician in Assam masterminded defection in the Congress and choked out the electoral strategy for the party. The BJP was able to defect two sitting Congress MLAs to the party. Moreover, in the run up to the election, the BJP deputed K.J. Alphons Kannanthanam, its Christian face and the Union Minister for State to coordinate its activities even before the election declared in the state. The former bureaucrat who belonged the Syrian Christian community in Kerala was made the party's election-in-charge for Meghalaya hoping dispel its image as anti-Christian.

The verdict of the Assembly election set certain trend in the politics of the state. Firstly, it witnessed the reassertion of political dynasty as both the Congress and the NPP relied on family politics. Agatha K. Sangma elected from South Tura constituency and elder brother James Sanga from Dadangre constituency. Secondly, there was a marginal dip in the vote share of the Congress in Khasi and Garo Hills compared to the 2013 Assembly polls. In the Garo Hills, the party secured 31.7 % voted against 31.8 in 2013. In the Khasi Hill the vote share reduced to 29.1% compared to 36.3% in 2013. Interestingly, in the Jaintia Hills, congress secured 19.3% votes compared to 14.8% in 2013. Though Congress lost many siting seats to NPP, BJP and other smaller regional parities, it wrested seats in urban areas such as East Shillong, Nongthymmai, West Shillong, Mawlai. The NPP's voter share was considerably increased across the three Hill areas compared to 2013. For instance, in Garo Hills it secured 27.7% votes compared to 20.14% in 2013, in Jaintia Hills the party could muster a quantum jump of 32.01% (9.6% of 2013) and in Khasi Hills 16.2% against 10% in 2013. Thirdly, In the matrilineal society of Meghalaya, only three women elected to the legislature, compared to the tally of five in the 2013 election. In the 60-member Assembly, 32 women contested elections could win only 3 seats. The Congress gave ticket to 7 women candidates, NPP 5, BJP 2, Garo National Council 2, HSDP 2, NCP 1, PDF 2, UDP 1 and independents 10. Lot of women contested as independents rather than holding party ticket. In most cases, many mainstream political parties consider them as not "winnable candidates". The Congress candidates Amparean Lyngdoh and Dikkanchi D Shira, wife of former Chief Minister Mukul Sangma could entry into the assembly. The NPP got only one women MLA, Agatha Sangma, the sister of present chief minister. Fourthly, morethan the victory of the BJP, the invisible hand of RSS in its sustained mobilization and incessant activities is recognized by various quarters. Though BJP is a new phenomenon in state politics, the RSS is not an alien to the state, as it started its activities in the state way back in 1946 under Vasantrao Oak in Shillong. Over the years, the RSS put strong effort to mobilize Christian population even the clergy belong to Christians. On 15 December, 2016, RSS conducted a "Know RSS" programme and invited 300 teachers among which 125 were Christians.

Nagaland – Stitching new Alliance

The assembly election produced a fractured mandate in another Christian dominated state of the Northeast. In the 60-member assembly, though the NPF emerged as the single largest party with 27 seats the BJP-NDPP alliance could form the government. The BJP-NDDP combine secured 29 seats with a voting share of 48.3%. The BJP was the allay of NPF for a long time. Close to the election, the BJP serves its 15-year-old ties with the NPF and made an alliance with the newly formed Nationalist Democratic Progressive Party (NDPP) under the leadership of former chief minister Neiphiu Rio.Striking an alliance with NDPP, it could dislodge the NPF government which was in power since 2003, except for a three-month period of president's rule in 2008. The Congress virtually washed out as it could not win even a single seat in the Assembly. It is to be reminded that the Congress ruled the state for five terms in the past and since 2003 when it was in opposition.

Perhaps, the biggest gainer is the BJP which contested 20 seats and won 12 seats and emerged as the third largest party after the NPF and the NDPP. The BJP's vote share rose up to 14.4% compared to 1.75% in 2013 with only one seat. The BJP could end the 15 years of NPF rule in the state with the alliance of NDPP. Though, during the election process, the Nagaland Baptist Churches Council (NBCC) in an open letter appealed for the rejection of Hindu nationalist politics of BJP and cautioned of BJP's cynical design in the state in the form of spreading Hindutva in the state, the BJP could muster impressive victory and be part of the new coalition government.

Party Performance in Nagaland Assembly Election 2018

Party	*Seats Won*	*Per centage of votes*
Naga People's Front	27	38.8
Nationalist Democratic Progressive Party	16	25.2
Bharatiya Janata Party	12	15.3
National People's Party	2	6.9
Janata Dal (United)	1	4.5
Independent	1	4.3

Source: Election Commission of India

In the 2014 general election, the NPF leader and chief minister Neiphiu Rio won the lone Lok Sabha seat with the support of BJP hoping his 'greater role' in the national politics. After Rio elected to Lok Sabha, T R Zeliang took over the helm of affairs of the state. On 27th April, 2015, shortly after the visit of Amit Shah, the Nagaland chief minister T R Zeliang inducted the BJP legislator, Paiwang Konyak as a minister in the state cabinet. In the current state Assembly, the opposition presence is virtually blank adding a boost to the NPF and the BJP. All 60 MLAs are part of the DAN led by the NPF. In November, 2015 with eight Congress MLAs joined NPF, virtually no opposition in the current Assembly in Nagaland. It has to be reminded that three NCP MLAs joined the BJP which is already a part of the NPF-led DAN. The migration of Congress MLAs was the culmination of the growing dissidence activities in the Congress for some time. However, the Chief Minister hoped that it would strengthen the Naga peace process and the positive response to the Naga Peace Accord between the Government of India and the National Socialist Council of Nagalim (Issac and Muivah) in August 2015.

Unlike rest of the states in North East, the ruling Naga People's Front (NPF) is alliance partner in the NDA at the centre and the BJP was an ally of the NPF led Democratic Alliance of Nagaland (DAN) in the state. This political reality often prevented the national and state leadership of the BJP to refrain from attacking directly to the state government. The BJP President Amit Shah in his visit to the state on17th April, 2015 while highlighting the BJP-led government's initiative to develop the North Eastern region also sent a strong message that the Centre "will not tolerate corruption at any cost". Highlighting the general trends and without directing attacking the state government the BJP president asserted that "NE states including Nagaland does not lack funds and central assistance but corruption at many levels has hampered the developmental projects meant for the grass root level. Developmental policies and funds provided by the Central government for developmental purposes do not reach the people."[5]

Triumph of a Counter-Narrative

Though political pundits gave different shades of the victory of the BJP in Nagaland, it is in fact, the victory is the outcome of a new counter-narrative scripted the Hinduvta forces in the state. Nagaland is a state with huge Christian population (87.93% according to the 2011 Census) and Christianity peeped into the socio-cultural and religious life of the people since the British period itself. However, for the Hindutva forces the Nagas are not Christians and the traditional Nagas were the followers of eternal Hindu Dharma. The sang parivar outfits took keen interest in Nagaland for quite some time back. In 2015 March, a Hindu Sammelan was organized in Dimapur to commemorate the golden jubilee of the Vishwa Hindu Parishad. Though throughout the election campaign the BJP and the Prime Minister Narender Modi focused on corruption and development, the verdict is the outcome of its systematic effort to reinterpreting the culture and personalities of Nagas.

In the largely Christian populated Nagaland, the BJP constructs a counter narrative to Christianity to strengthen its base. The BJP's attempt to glorify the Naga spiritual leader and freedom fighter 'Rani' Gaidinliu by constructing a memorial museum-cum-library in Kohima can be seen in this direction. Gaidinliu (1915-1993) fought against the British and imprisoned by the British in various jails in North East. She composed over 300 song including hymns, patriotic songs, poems. Gaidinliu who was described by the British as the "Terror of North East" involved in an armed struggle against the British. In fact, Nehru was fond of Gaidinliu and called her 'Rani' because she took anti-Naga stand in Naga self-determination movement. It has to be reminded that the Naga movement was in fact the first movement which India faced after independence and tested Nehru's ability as an nation builder. In fact, Nehru wanted to counter the Naga movement forced him to praise Gaidinliu.

Gaidinliu who belonged to the Zleiangrong community also resisted the conversion of Nagas to Christianity and defended traditional Naga religion of animism called "Heraka". It is estimated that today there are around 20, 000 Heraka followers who are scattered in parts of Nagaland, Manipur and Assam. It has to be reminded that to weaken the protest of Zleiangrong community – the British divided them into three states- Manipur, Assam, Nagaland (then Naga Hills). The Zeliangrong Heraka Association (ZHA) opposes the 'westernisation' of the Naga culture and protecting the indigenous religion, culture and language. It also critical of western hedonism and consumerism and reasserting communitarian values in the place of western values. Gaidinliu wanted to bring indigenous Naga groups such as Rongmei, Zemi and Liangmai tribes and campaigned to bring them into one ZHA to save them from religious conversion to Christianity. In December 2014, Modi visited Nagaland during the famous Hornbill and which coincided with the conclusion of Gaidinliu's birth centenary celebration (26th January 2014 to 26th January 2015). The Prime Minister in his speech in English and wearing Naga traditional dress emphasized the Naga pride. At the end of his address Modi preferred to use the Naga nationalist slogan "Kuknalim"(Victory to Nagalim/Nagaland) instead of his usual nationalist chant "Jai-Hind" (victory to India). The ZHA submitted a memorandum to the Prime Minister demanding that their leader Gaidinliu must be honoured and recognized. The larger demands include: bringing new coins to commemorate the birth centenary of Gaidinliu; opening of a central university in Nagaland with her name and setting up of a department dedicated to the promulgation of the "eternal religion and eternal culture of Nagas", renaming of Naga Nagaland's only airport as "Rani Gaidinliu Airport"; installing Gaidinliu's portrait in Nagaland Assembly, the official offices of Chief Minister, Governor and other ministers. Subsequently, the Centre released coins of Rs.5 and Rs. 100 denominations with her images on them to commemorate her birth century. In fact, a strong protest came from the Naga community itself as many Naga tribes see her as anti-Naga as she betrayed the Naga national movement for a sovereign state. The organizations such as the Angami Public Organization (AYO) opposed any move to glorify Gaidinliu.[6] Nagas, on the other hand, never recognize her as a spiritual leader and described Gaidinliu as an outside and a cult leader who had opposed Naga nationalism and the advent of Christianity in the state. The Nagas view Gaidinliu as an outsider and call her the cult leader.[7]

In the past, the BJP was trying to gain foothold in the state by glorifying Gaidinliu who opposed conversion to Christianity. Though Gaidinliu fought against both British and Christian missionaries, the BJP is only highlighting her opposition to the Christianity and thereby it is attempting to create communal polarization among the Nagas in the state.[8] The BJP, in fact, wanted to appropriate Heraka (the indigenous faith based on animism) with Hinduism against Christianity by projecting her as the "spiritual leader" of Nagas against Jesus. The Hinduvta forces are hobnobbing with indigenous religious movement such the Zeliangrong Heraka Association (ZHA) to Hinduise it against the Christian associations. By opposing a challenge to Christianity and rejecting the missionary work ZHA asserts the Heraka identity. It has to be reminded that the Hinduvta forces always stand for Bharatvarsha, the larger Hindu imagination. The Akhil Bharatiya Vanavasi Kalyan Asharam (ABVKA) is supporting the activities of the ZHA. The Sangh Parivar now claims that Heraka as the part of the larger Hindu family. It is argued that "since many of the practices of the Heraka are derived from Hinduism, the Sangh parivar has declared them to be vanavasi (forest-dwellers) and sought to assimilate them into the Hindu fold" (Dangmei, 2013: 27). In appropriating Heraka with Hinduism the Hindutva forces are countering the dominant Christian narrating by constructing a counter alternative premised on Hindutva (Bijukumar, 2017).

The Assembly election 2018 also manifested another trend in the Naga society and politics. Though five women contested election but could not win a single seat endorsing Assembly is a male bastion and electoral politics is far from gender friendly. However, this trend is nothing new and since 1963, when Nagaland attained statehood, it has not elected a single woman to the Assembly. The late Rano M. Shaiza is the only women elected to Loksabha from Nagaland in 1977. In 2017, large scale protests erupted against reserving 33% seats for women in urban local body elections. In Naga society, which is explicitly seen as gender friendly, political representation of women is a question mark. The Naga Hoho, the traditional body of the Nagas largely a male body and the customary laws are strengthening patriarchy. (Hausing, 2017). Though, in the civil society action, the organizations such as Naga Mothers Association was strong in agitationpolitics, political representation is a distant dream for them.

Tripura–Setting Red Sun

Perhaps, the BJP's resounding victory in the 2018 Assembly elections came from the communist ruled state of Tripura as the party with the alliance of Indigenous People's Front of Tripura (IPFT) could demolish the twenty-five years rule of the communists. Unlike assemblyelections in Meghalaya and Nagaland, the BJP's desire for power in the relatively smaller state of Tripura, goes beyond mere capturing power, but an ideological contestation between the Marxists and the Hindu nationalists. The BJP's slogan of *Chalo Paltai* (Let's Change) invoked a magnetic effect on both the dominant Bengali and the indigenous tribal communities. In the state, with 60 constituencies, thirty for the general, twenty for the ST and ten for the SC, the party could capitalize the discontent of both the Bengalis and the tribals and could able to catch the imagination of the cross sections of the society. In the 2018 election, the BJP contested in 50 seats and 9 seats went in favour of the IPFT, the Congress on the other hand contested 51 seats, the CPM put up candidates for 57 seats and 24 seats went for the Trinamol Congress. In the election verdict, the BJP secured more than absolute majority by winning 35 seats and the ruling CPIM could secure only 16seats. The IPFT which inked a pre-poll alliance with the BJP secured 8 seats the Congress drew a blank. Though BJP secured 35 seats and its percentage of votes against CPIM was marginal as the BJP vote share was 43% against CPIM's 42.7%.However, the BJP had a great sigh of relief that its vote share shoots up compared to the 1.5% in the 2013 Assembly polls.

Party Performance in Tripura Assembly Election 2018

Party	*Seats Won*	*Per centage of votes*
Bharatiya Janata Party	35	43
Communist Party of India (Marxist)	16	42.7
Indigenous People's Front of Tripura	8	7.5
Indian National Congress	0	1.8

Source: Election Commission of India.

Breaking the Saga of the Communist Rule

The astonishing victory of the BJP, in fact, ended the saga of communist rule in the state. It has to be reminded that in January 1972, Tripura attained full statehood along with Meghalaya and Manipur and the second largest state in the North East after Assam having a literacy rate of 87.22%. In 1977 the left front government formed its first government and repeated the same in 1983, 1993, 1998, 2003, 2008 and 2013. During 1988-1993, the Congress ruled the state with the support of the Tripura Upajati Juba Samity, a tribal party. In 1998, Manik Sarkar became the chief ministerbeating the anti-incumbency wave and crafting the consecutive victory for the communist party. For the last twenty-five years of the communist rule, the government was able to bring peace in the once trouble torn state.It has to be reminded that in the 1990s, the state witnessed turbulent years in Tripura's history as it witnessed abduction and killings. By transforming the state from militancy to normalcy, the strengthening of the public distribution system and the implementation of other welfare policies of the state, the left front was able consolidate its mass base. The communist regime as able to maintain social harmony between the majority Bengali and the minority indigenous tribal communities, even though its popular support largely came from the Bengalis. It has to be reminded that 80 per cent of the state's 37 lakh people are Bengali-speaking Hindu, mostly migrated from Bangladesh. It is often argued that while left in Kerala is rooted in the social reform movement, the left in West Bengal was rooted in trade union movement, in Tripura it was based on the support extended by the immigrant Bengali community.

Simmering Tribal Discontent

The social balance and harmony between the Bengalis and the tribal communities depleted over the years of the left front. It has to be reminded that around 60% of Tripura's total areas Hilly inhabited by the tribal community called Tripuris and the tribals constitute around 20% of state population and a dominant factor in around 20 constituencies. A simmering discontent engulfed among the tribal communities as they felt that the communist regimes unduly titled towards the dominant Bengali community denying their employment opportunities and other material benefits. The IPFT often rises the systematic margianlisation of the indigenous communities at the hands of the Bengalis. In fact, such a marginalization traced back to the 1960s, when large portion of tribal lands were transferred to non-tribals. It has been observed that, "the Tripura Land Reforms and Land Revenue Act was passed in 1960 to stop land alienation from tribal to non-tribal communities.However, the steady inflow of migrants has complicated this problem" (Debbarma and Debbarma, 2009: 173). Added their worries, the non-tribal money lenders gave tribals loans against land with in exorbitant rate of interest. In addition to the material deprivation, there was a growing feeling of cultural impoverishment on the side of tibals due to illegal migration. On 10 June, 1967, Tripura Upajati Juba Samiti was formed to revive the traditional cultural symbols and practices of the tribals against the Bengali culture. Since 2009, the IPFT is demanding the separate state called Twipra, for the tribals by carving out the TTAADC (Tripura Tribal Area Autonomous District Council) from Tripura. During the consecutive left front rule, unemployment emerged as the grave problem among the tribal community. In 2017, the state witnessed violent activities like blockade and bandhs by the tribal organizations to press the demand for unemployment.

Political Capitalising ofDiscontent

The BJP's in its campaign also high lightened the insensitiveness towards the condition of tribals in the state. The BJP could garner the simmering discontent of the tribals in its favour. The BJP was able to channelise the ethnic animosities between the Bengalis and tribals in their favour. It was able to create a misconception that during the twenty-five years rule of CPI(M) the Bengalis were mostly benefited at the cost of the tribals as there was minimal representation of tribals in Ministry and government services. However, it adopted a pragmatic strategy of striking a political balance between the Bengalis and the indigenous tribal communities in tis mobilization strategy. Without antagonizing the interests of the Bengali community, it was able to champion the cause of tribal community, who over time became minority in their own land due to the migration of Bengali community and their access to resources and political power in the state. During the 2018 election campaign, in the development front, the BJP promised special economic zones for food processing, bamboo, textile and information technology sector. Close to election,

Himanta Biswa Sarma, the convener of the NEDA, stitched the alliance between the BJP and the IPFT. Going along with the IPFT, it once again underlined the need for aligning with the smaller parties and make use of the resources. It also broke the class politics of the left with the pragmatic use of identity politics as the BJP was also utilitised both ethno regionalism and Hindu nationalism to achieve the political power. While, in the election campaign, the left heavily relied on the personal image of the chief minister, Manik Sarkar as the "poorest chief minister" in India, the BJP also highlighted the non-implementation of the Seventh Pay Commission and the state employees are getting their salaries according to the fourth pay commission. In fact, the BJP's vision document promised the implementation of Seventh Pay Commission and thereby winning the support of the employees too. As a result, a sizeable Bengali Hindus shifted their loyalty to the BJP. Thus, the demographic composition was used by the BJP to firm its footsteps in the state.

The BJP's campaign strategy, communal polarization and the bogey of development, was in fact resounded in 2015. While concluding his ten days tour to all eight North-Eastern states the BJP president on 27th April, 2015 Shah asserted that 'People of the country have remove the Communists from other parts of the country, now the turn has come for the people of Tripura to remove them from the only state of the country', Amit Shah said, "The left front govt. in Tripura has brought no development to the state rather than corruption, scams and deprivation for the common masses." In a dig at the Marxist government in the state, Shah said that "the days are not far when their last boat will sink in the sea. In order to join the mainstream of development process of the country, regime change in Tripura is necessary". Alleging massive corruption in MGNREGA, Shah made a clarion call to the people of Tripura to topple the Left Government in 2018 Assembly election and the BJP can provide good governance and development in Tripura.

Appropriation of Tribal Kings

In Tripura, the BJP is engaging in the process of appropriating Maharaja Bir Bikram Kishore Manikya Bahadur (born on 19th August, 1908 and died on 17th May 1947), the last tribal ruler to the Hindu fold. Such argument is strengthened by the recent decision of the Union government to install 184 feet bronze statue of Bir Bikram Kishore, the 184th king of Tripura's Manikya dynasty which ruled Tripura for more than 300 years. In fact, such appropriation comes in the light of the BJP's indictment of both the Congress and left in the state of not giving due recognition to the King's contribution to Tripura's development.

It has to be reminded that Bir Bikram Kishore, who ruled Tripura between 1923 to 1947, merged Tripura with independent India. Commonly described as the architect of modern Tripura, the king initiated land reformed and reserved land for the indigenous Tripuris in the last 1930s, and set up schools, colleges and airport. Adorned at the age of sixteen and died at the age of 39, the King also played critical role in the formation of the present TTAADC. However, the premature death of Bir Bikram Kishore engulfed political uncertainty in Tripura as his son, Kirti Bikrm Kishore Manikya was too young to become the King forcing Kanchanprova Debi, his mother and widow of Bir Bikram Kishore to become the Regent who ruled on behalf of his younger son. In fact, the Regent signed the agreement of accession on 13 August, 1947 and on 15 October, 1949 Tripura merged with the Indian Union.

On 19th September, 2013, on the occasion of the golden jubilee of the Tripura Legislative Assembly, speaking in a seminar in Agartala, the Chief Minister Manik Sarkar revealed that the members of Trupura's Manikya Royal family under Bir Bikram Kishore wanted to merge with then East Pakistan (now Bangladesh). However, sensing the public sentiments, Bir Bikram Kishore before his death expressed his desire to keep Tripura with the Indian Union. He also revealed that Bir Bikram Kishore was also planned its integration with Assam. It has to be reminded that the State Reorganisation Commission constituted in 1953 proposed to merge Tripura with Assam. However, the proposal was finally dropped and Tripura became a Union Territory on 1 November, 1956 and achieved statehood in 1972.

The BJP's appropriation of Bir Bikram Kishore can be seen in the larger context of the wooing tribal community in its fold. The BJP, in fact, is using the tribal indigeneity to counter the consolidation and domination the Marxist regime in the state. It is also hoping that the appropriation of Bir Bikram Kishore would bring more political dividends in its favour as well as to counter the emergence of Trinamol Congress which is replacing the Congress, the principal opposition in the state.

The Great Community Divide

The victory can be seen as a collective work of Ram Madhav, Himanta Biswa Sarma and Sunil Deodhar. The BJP could make massive inroads into the congress vote share. For instance, in 2013 assembly election the Congress got 36.5% and in the 2018 it considerably reduced to 1.8%. The

Congress tally in the Assembly reduced to zero against 10 in the 2013 election. The Congress's vote share among various communities decreased dramatically in the 2018 election. For instance, among the general community the vote shared reduced to 2.2% compared to 45.6% in 2013. The vote share among the SC's is 1.3% compared to the previous tally of 44.1% in 2013. Among the STs, the Congress could garner only 1.4% vote share against 43.4% in 2013.

The BJP also could take away some slice from the CPIM's pie, which is manifested when its vote share reduced to 42.6% compared to its 2013 tally of 48.11%. The reduction in the voting share of the CPIM was across the communities in the state. For instance, among the tribals, there was dip in the vote share for the CPIM to 46.3% compared to the 53.5% in 2013. In the Scheduled Castes which constitute around 17.8 % of the population, the CPIM's voting share reduced to 46.3% in contrast to 53.5% in 2013. Among the general community too the dip was visible as it reduced to 46.6% compared to 52.3% in 2013.

The BJP made an inroad into the various communities in the state as its vote share increased among various communities compared to the 2013 election. For instance, among the general, the party could get a vote share of 49.7% in contrast to 2% in 2013. Among the SCs, the vote share jumped to 50.6% compared to 1.3% in 2013. The party also could wean away a vote share of 50.9% from earlier share of 1.9% in 2013.

Community wise Vote Share of Major Political Parties (in percentage)

Party	*General*		*SCs*		*STs*	
	2018	2013	2018	2013	2018	2013
BJP	49.7	2	50.6	1.3	50.9	1.9
CPIM	46.6	52.3	46.6	52.3	41.8	53.5
Congress (I)	2.2	45.6	1.3	44.1	1.4	43.4

To conclude, though the victory is astounding, it was the culmination of systematic campaign and mobilization by the BJP in Tripura. It has to be reminded that over the years, though the CPIM was the dominant force in the State, the BJP is making inroads in rural areas. For instance, the percentage of votes secured by the BJP in the CPIM ruled state was 7.82% (2004), 2.72% (2009) and 5.7% (2014). Though there is slight decline in the percentage of votes secured by the BJP in the 2014 general election in contrast to 2004 general election, the subsequent trends prove that the BJP has not abandon its electoral ambition in the red bastion of the region. In

May 3, 2015, in the Tribal Areas Autonomous District Council election the BJP got 7.87% of votes. In the by elections to two Assembly seats in June 2015, the BJP secured 23.33% votes, though CPM retained both the Scheduled Caste reserved states. Subsequently, in the 15th July, 2014-gram panchayat poll, the BJP won 141 of the 6, 111 seats and won a majority in five gram panchayats for the first time. Interestingly, the CPM often blamed the Congress, Trinamol Congress for the rise of BJP in Tripura. A postmortem analysis of electoral verdict in 2018 shows that the BJP's stupendous victory over the communists was due to multiple factors. Its mobilization and strategy often extend over mere political gain. The Hindu nationalist party was able to construct a counter narrative to the Marxist favouring the tribal communities and appropriation of their leaders and rousing the tribal sentiments against the dominant Bengali community. However, to catch the sentiment of the Bengali community, the party highlighted the developmental paralysis, growing unemployment problems and the inadequate salary conditions of the government employees. Added to this, the disarray of opposition parties such as the Trinamol Congress and Congress gave space for the BJP. Both these parties witnessed frequent political defection of it legislators and often fell under poaching strategy of the BJP.

Notes

1. Prime Minister Modi while addressing the election rally on 8 February, 2014 at Imphal.
2. "No Ban on Cow Slaughter in North East", *The Shillong Times*, 23rd April, 2015.
3. "BJP is not an anti-Christian Party: Meghalaya, Nalin S. Kohli", *The Economic Times*, 14th July, 2015.
4. "Letter bomb jolts state politics", *The Shillong Times*, 2nd June, 2016.
5. "Hoho hopes BJP will solve political issue", *The Assam Tribune 20th April, 2015.*
6. "Some Nagas are against memorial to Rani Gaidinliu in Kohima: Why?", *The Indian Express*, 28th September, 2015.
7. "Nagas Divided over Modi's Plan to Glorify Spiritual Leader", *The New Indian Express*, 30th August, 2015.
8. "BJP using Gaidinliu to polarize Nagaland", *The Times of India*, 25th August, 2015.

References

Bijukumar, V. (2017), "Politics of Counter-narratives and Appropriation", *Economic and Political Weekly*, Vol. LII, No. 18, May 6, pp. 12-13.

Dangmei, Soihiamlung (2013): "Cultural Positioning of Tribes in North-east India: Mapping the Evolving Heraka Identity," *Economic & Political Weekly*, Vol 48, No 1, pp. 27–30.

Debbarma, Sukhendu and Mousami Debbarma (2009), "Fifth Victory in a Row for CPI(M) in Tripura", *Economic and Political Weekly*, Vol. XLIV, No. 39, September 26, pp. 172-173.

Hausing, Kham Khan Suan (2017), " 'Equality as Tradition' and Women's Reservation in Nagaland", *Economic and Political Weekly*, Vol. LII, No. 45, November 11, pp. 36-43.

Index